INTRODUCTION
TO REPORTING

JUDITH L. BURKEN
Kellogg Community College

INTRODUCTION TO REPORTING

ucb

WM. C. BROWN COMPANY PUBLISHERS
Dubuque, Iowa

Copyright © 1976 by Wm. C. Brown Company Publishers

Library of Congress Catalog Card Number: 75-27985

ISBN 0-697-04307-X

Printed in the United States of America

For S. Joseph and my parents,
Cletus and Evelyn Burken

CONTENTS

PREFACE

This book is written for the journalism instructor and student who want a text that concisely states the principles of writing necessary in beginning reporting.

This is not a grammar book, nor a speller, dictionary or law book. While some aspects of all these areas are explored in the text, the true direction of it is in the area of beginning reporting writing techniques.

The topics covered in the book were suggested by more than 80 journalism instructors from across the country who answered a questionnaire and shared their thoughts on what topics they teach in their respective beginning reporting classes.

The book provides a practical application of what it preaches, giving newswriting techniques, principles, rules, problems, solutions and examples in simple language and logical sequence.

The basics of what is a news story, the spelling, style, vocabulary and a sampling of grammar and editing skills needed by the reporting student are presented first.

In preparation for the writing of the news story, a brief look at journalistic law is given. The student is also given some tips on how to locate and use news sources. Interviewing techniques and the use of dialogue in a news story are covered before the student is introduced to lead writing.

In the area of writing technique, extensive use is made of actual news stories as examples of how to and how not to write a story.

Much attention is given to discussion of straight news, obituaries and feature stories as these are three areas in which the news reporter will do much writing. Obituaries, touched upon in all texts, have a special chapter in this book. While generally presenting no challenge to the newswriter, the obituary can present unique problems for the reporter and the news medium.

While attempting to present an in-depth treatment of newswriting skills, I have not attempted this in-depth treatment in the areas of headline and cutline writing and of editing skills. All of these are subjects to be taught in advanced journalism courses. It is necessary, in my opinion, for beginning newswriting students to become familiar with these journalism skills. It is not necessary, at this time, to master them.

With the advent of electronic journalism, the sturdy newsroom manual typewriters are being replaced with electric typewriters. Electronic pencils and TV-like screens are becoming editors' tools. Initials like VDT (video display terminal) and OCR (optical character recognition) are becoming more commonplace, so a chapter on the role of electronic journalism is included in the book.

As a glance through the expanded Contents will show you, this book does not get into public affairs reporting or investigative reporting or a lengthy discussion of new journalism. In the course of one quarter or one semester, the instructor will barely find the time to drum the basic writing techniques into the student and view the final results in the form of news stories.

Within the covers of this book, it is not the quantity of the pages that I hope impress you but, rather, the quality of writing techniques printed upon them.

ACKNOWLEDGMENTS

An idea may begin with one person, but the realization of that idea most often takes the combined energies of the originator and many others. The writing of this book was no exception. Kay Lockridge of New York City read the draft and final manuscripts and made valuable content, style and grammatical contributions. Peggy Nelson of Detroit critiqued the original draft and provided me with a wealth of her excellent feature, dialogue and review stories from which I drew my best examples for this book. Steven Ames of Merced, Calif., Tom Kramer of Woodland Hills, Calif., and Lillian Lodge Koppenhaver of Miami, all offered lots of manuscript ideas, criticisms and just the right amount of praise to keep the whole project going. John Murray, Michigan State University journalism law professor, contributed sage advice and criticism for the chapter on law. And Connie Geisler of Battle Creek, Mich., typed the manuscript with all its corrections and additions. Then Joyce Oberhausen, production editor at Wm. C. Brown Company Publishers in Dubuque, Iowa, pulled it all together and was largely responsible for production of this book.

And special thanks go to Richard Crews, executive editor at Wm. C. Brown, who took a chance and held faith that this book would be written, and to the 82 journalism educators who sent me their content ideas for the book.

1

IS JOURNALISM FOR ME?

Stop the presses: What better place to start a discussion on news-writing than with the most familiar words in the fictional world of news reporting and the least heard expression in the real world of the newsroom.

In the complex newspaper operation, stopping the presses is unheard of for anything short of avoiding a libel suit or in the case of the death of a president—the only time this reporter ever witnessed the stopping of the presses, and then it was referred to as "making over the front page."

And, while killing the half-truths of news reporting, let's topple the myth of the drunken reporter who calls in a story about an event, the "facts" of which are made up as the reporter thinks of them.

Reporter Qualifications

If your idea of a journalistic job is of one having little supervision and calling for an ability to improvise a story when one hasn't time to get all the facts, steer clear of news reporting.

A job description for a news reporter might read:

> A reporter is able to gather information from various sources and write news stories and features in easy-to-read, factual accounts for the public to read or listen to. The reporter handles daily newsroom duties, such as obituaries, hospital and fire calls, and rewrites handout fact sheets. The reporter has the ability to take quick, accurate notes and organize his or her time, thoughts and self; is willing to work a flexible schedule; and works and writes well under pressure of deadlines. The reporter possesses an open mind and is able to meet all types of people.

Some qualifications the potential reporter might be expected to possess include the following:

> Physical characteristics: 18 years of age or older and in good health.
> Education: Minimum high school diploma or General Education Development certificate. College degree is an asset

and often is preferred by editors. Above–average intelligence.

Motivations: Very curious about world and people in it. Enjoys meeting, talking and working with all kinds of people. Self-starter. Displays flexibility in thinking and life style. Has a sense of humor.

Attitudes: A reporter wants to be the first to know what is happening and believes in the public's right to know. Also, he or she wants to be the one to tell it.

How do these criteria measure up to a professional's view of a prospective news reporter? Elwood M. Wardlow, managing editor of the *Buffalo* (N.Y.) *Evening News,* answered this question in a reply given to a college student who asked what are the most important qualities for which Wardlow looks when hiring a new reporter. His reply was:

We look for 10 things in adding editors and writers to our staff:

Intelligence. Smart people almost invariably do the best job, if they have a good mix of other desirable characteristics.

Effectiveness. The capacity to envision and effectuate easily and well. We need people who can get at things, and get them done.

Curiosity. People who do not have a questioning mind (or "a nose for news") need not apply. Most good newspeople read, listen, observe, argue and absorb during every waking moment. They know a lot, and want to know more.

Knowledge. A newsperson has to be able to deal with all facets of the human condition. And to do that well, he has to know a good deal about all of them.

Comprehension. When a person feeds bits of information into his mind all day, does he understand what it all means? Can he piece together the sense of what has been, and what might still be coming?

Judgment. In dealing with the world, and in producing stories, a newsperson must be very long on this quality. He approaches a story much as a professor might approach the writing of a book. First he does research and gathers information; then he sorts out information and evaluates it— deciding such things as what to keep and what to throw away, and how to organize the various themes or segments; and then he proceeds with the writing. The middle part, involving judgment, is the most subjective and difficult— and the most vulnerable to criticism.

Persistence. The people who read Brenda Starr probably think a newsperson has to be agressive—or even obnoxious.

He doesn't—but he does have to hang in there until he gets what he's after.

Literacy. A newsperson must be a craftsman with the language. He must know words, and love them, and have a feel for what they can do.

Motivation. The media offer a great opportunity for those who like to work with words, concepts and ideas . . . for those who like a close-up look at the world and its people . . . who like to have a usefulness and an impact in their community . . . and who enjoy working with others of that type. The primary product of the media is information; for those who would use it for other purposes—as a lever of power or persuasion, for example—journalism often falls short of fulfillment.

Personal stability. The general media serve all types, ages, occupations, sexes, classes, races and viewpoints. Media practitioners must be able to go anywhere, anytime, and deal with anybody under any conditions. That takes a very broad-gauge and stable person. He must, in his attitudes, at all times be a newsperson before he is anything else. Character, personality, appearance, bearing and manner are important.[1]

What Is News?

Probably no other profession defines its task as well in its name as does news reporting. A doctor may be asked for areas of specialization. A mechanic may be asked for kinds of automotive or engineering work done. But a news reporter does just what the name says: reports news.

News. What is it? The *American Heritage Dictionary* defines news as "recent events and happenings or a report about recent events."[2]

Report, according to the same dictionary, is "any account that is prepared or presented, usually in a formal or organized form."[3]

News is a fragile, fleeting commodity. What is news right now could be history in five minutes. If someone asks you what is new and your response is greeted with "Oh, I knew that," then you are an historian, not a news reporter.

However, that same item given to another person might bring the response "I didn't know that," and then you become a news reporter.

What is news is governed by as many conditions as there are people making, gathering, distributing and receiving it. Electronic media flash

1. Elwood M. Wardlow, *Some Specifics on Newspaper Careers,* brochure prepared by the Newspaper Fund, p. 2.
2. © 1969, 1970, 1971, 1973, 1975, 1976, Houghton Mifflin Company. Reprinted by permission from *The American Heritage Dictionary of the English Language.*
3. Ibid., p. 1103.

to people around the world events as they occur continents away. Yet, a newpaper several days, weeks or years old may be news to an astronaut returning from a space trip or a person lost when a plane crashed in a remote region. The question of news will be explored in depth in chapter 2.

Get the Latest Facts

In seeking news, the best rule is to look for the latest facts to the minute about any event or occurrence. A reporter does just this. Most reporters are on call 24 hours a day. If something happens, a reporter will be there to give out the first details to the world. News is not a respecter of time or elements. But when it occurs, a reporter—a real reporter, not just a technician who can build a decent story from a handout fact sheet—will want to be at the scene of the news event, regardless of the hour or the weather. This is part of the romance of being in news—it is also a part of the hard work, long hours, skipped meals and pressured writing.

In gathering the news, the reporter acts as a channel of communication. The reporter is rarely the maker of news. It is the reporter's job to find out as much as is available about an event and transmit this information via the print or broadcast media to the public.

In some cases, the information gathered is complicated or tied into other news events and it becomes necessary for the reporter to interpret what has been gathered to give the audience a framework in which to receive, understand and digest the news. (The reporter as a newsmaker and interpreter will be discussed throughout the chapters in this book.)

Reporter or Crusader

It is not uncommon for a person to seek a news reporting career because he or she wants to uncover all the wrongs of the world and set things right by using the power of the press. But the person who enters the profession for only this reason will soon become disillusioned. With rare exceptions, the news business is a profit-making one. It's a business entered by people for the purpose of earning a living while doing something that one enjoys. It is not a profession for persons who view themselves as world changers.

There may be times when the green of the advertising dollar will cause a blackout of an investigative story that displeases the advertiser and prompts the advertising person to tell the publisher or station owner so. At some time, advertiser pressure will be brought to bear on almost all media, although it is not always heeded. Accounts of such advertiser pressure are reported sometimes by the journalism reviews.[4]

And then there is the story that is in conflict with the golden idol of the publisher or station owner. Remember, there are at least two sides to every story and, when one belongs to the boss who pays the news staff's salaries, the boss will have the last word on what reaches the public. In electronic journalism, the Federal Communications Commission will check into such situations if the matter is brought to its attention. In the print media, such censorship often goes unchecked unless the journalism reviews or some other concerned citizen or group expose it.

If you have strong political leanings, check out the news medium you are considering working for before you join the payroll. If the publication or station shows a strong, consistent editorial policy for the opposition party, you may wish to think twice about joining the staff.

Journalism Reviews

To learn more about journalistic practices and ethics, a prospective reporter should read one or more of the journalism reviews. The journalism review was a product of the '60s. Published by working newspeople, the reviews' collective purpose is to tell the stories-behind-the-stories that never reach the public, discuss government restrictions put on news media, provide a forum on a variety of topics for disgruntled news staffers, look at competition techniques among news media and, in general, cover anything of interest to newspeople when there is no other medium of communication available.

Most large cities have a journalism review and there are two national reviews. The *Columbia Journalism Review* (*CJR*) was the first national journalism review and is the only review published by a college organization—the Graduate School of Journalism, Columbia University. *CJR* looks at media coverage of national and local events, sometimes comparing the coverage of the same event by two news media. The review regularly chides media that skirt an issue or slant coverage. On the other hand, *CJR* will present a laurel to media that practice truthful, noncompromising journalism.

After the 1968 Democratic convention in Chicago, that city's newspeople began the *Chicago Journalism Review.* Since then, journalism reviews have been springing up in major cities across the country. Founded to give a voice to a wronged working press, or to journalism ideals thought to be mislaid or lost by news media owners, some

4. For an example of advertiser pressure and news media response, see "*Daily News* Chickens Out on Hamburger Story," *Chicago Journalism Review,* December, 1973, pp. 3–4.

reviews are short-lived, dying when all that could be said about the issue that caused its birth has been said. Some other reviews, such as New York's (*More*), the other national journalism review, which was established in 1971, have a full-time staff.

Most reviews publish monthly and, with the exception of the *Columbia Journalism Review* and (*More*), are concerned for the most part with local journalistic issues. It is in the journals that the stories of alleged news suppression through advertiser pressure and media bosses are told.

The journalism trade journals provide another source for getting a peek into the profession. *Editor and Publisher* represents the newspaper field; *Advertising Age*, the advertising profession; and *Broadcasting*, the electronic media. *Quill*, a monthly publication of the Society of Professional Journalists, Sigma Delta Chi, and *Matrix*, the quarterly publication of Women in Communications, Inc., report critical analyses of the working press as well as stories on journalism careers, investigative reports and journalistic profiles.

One answer for an idealistic reporter who does not want to be fettered by the chains of corporate profit in his or her search for journalistic truth and freedom is to follow in the footsteps of I. F. (Isadore Feinstein) Stone. Stone was a onetime staff member of newspapers in Philadelphia and New York and of *The Nation* magazine. In 1953, on a shoestring budget of $6,500, Stone started his own paper called the *Weekly*, more popularly known as *I. F. Stone's Weekly*. With his professional background, Stone was able to draw 5,000 subscribers for his first issue. Stone answered to no one but himself and, as a result, he could write about what he wanted.

A meticulous researcher, his weekly became a legend in journalistic integrity. Stone ended publication of his *Weekly* in 1972, when it had reached a circulation of 70,000, to join the staff of *The New York Review of Books* as a political columnist.[5]

---

5. For more information about I. F. Stone and his journalistic enterprise, there is the *I. F. Stone's Weekly Reader,* edited by Neil Middleton, 321 pages, Random House, $7.95, or in paperback from Vintage Books, $2.45. It contains 100 articles taken from the *Weekly*. Also, there is a film by Jerry Bruck Jr., titled *I. F. Stone's Weekly*. Narrated by Tom Wicker, 62 minutes. I. F. Stone Project (P.O. Box 315, Franklin Lakes, N.J. 07417).

2

WHAT IS A NEWS STORY?

War is declared. A President is elected. A man is murdered. A baby is born. All these events are news if they are recent happenings, according to the dictionary definition of news given in chapter 1. Almost every event that occurs is news to someone. But, a question to be asked is: What makes some events of interest to many people, while other events may interest only those persons involved?

The elements which comprise the news event will determine the range of its interest. These news elements are consequence and human interest. Basically, the news audience is interested in an event if it has an effect on the individual's life or if it rouses the person's curiosity.

Consequence Stories

What effect will the event have on the lives of the persons who will learn of it through the news media? A flood is expected in a city a few miles away from the city in which the area newspaper is published. Is the story likely to be carried in the newspaper? Yes, because so many of the readers of the paper are going to be directly involved in the flood. Other readers will be indirectly involved because of friends and relatives living in the flood area. Another consideration is the proximity of the flood to other news areas. Metropolitan news media several hundred miles away but in the same state will probably carry the story because it has state interest. If the flood is severe, causing much damage, and the area is declared a disaster area by the governor, the interest in the flood will spread statewide. The national news media may pick up the story for the human-interest angle.

Other examples of stories with consequence news value would be any tax story that affects the individual taxpayer; a new business or industry moving into the area; a new housing development that will provide more homes for the community, business for the building industry, require additional city services such as fire and police protection and may provide a need for new elementary schools; city and school-board elections or an outbreak of dog poisonings. All of these events or happenings will have some effect on the news audience.

Human-Interest Stories

Probably the largest body of stories carried by the news media come under the heading of human interest. Here is the news element that will evoke the emotions of the news audience, sell newspapers and magazines and cause people to tune in a television or radio newscast to hear about a story that has no direct effect on their lives.

Under the heading of human interest are several categories that catch an individual's attention. *Children* are a natural human-interest hook in a story. A child dies under the wheels of a train at an unguarded crossing near a school and the citizenry takes action to put a guard at the crossing. True, the story also contains the element of consequence, with the parents of other children attending the school being concerned, but the unguarded railroad crossing was there long before the child died. It took the shock of a child's death to stir the people to action. Would the death of a hobo at that crossing cause the same action to be taken?

In almost any event, if a child is involved, mention of the fact will be made in the news story. People tend to identify with stories about children. They do this either through children of their own, children they know or their own childhood memories.

Sex is another human-interest angle that will catch people's attention. Often, ads will carry the word *sex* in large, bold letters at the top of the copy and beneath it say: "Now that I have your attention. . . ." Some magazines make a business out of sex, either filling their pages with stories about it or offering a cover that misleads the reader into thinking the entire issue is composed of material dealing with sex.

In the news pages, sex catches the reader's eye when the diary of a party in a divorce suit is to be read in court. Or, sex takes over the front page when a member of Parliament in England is caught in a blackmail plot because of involvement with a call girl. Less blatant sex stories make the news when a woman enters a predominantly male field, or vice versa. Examples of this are the little girl who joins a Cub Scout pack, but is then denied the merit badges she earned because she is a female, and the man who wins a cooking contest.

Oddities are another facet of the human-interest angle. A three-legged calf or a two-headed horse, sextuplets, Siamese twins, a new record for swallowing goldfish or cramming people into a telephone booth; all these events are news under the human-interest umbrella. The annual hunt for the abominable snowman always makes the news as an expedition takes off for the northern California mountains or the Himalayas. If the abominable one is ever captured, that will be page-one news.

Prominence is another human-interest news factor. Names make news. Two men are mugged in Central Park. One is a New York resident. The other is a visitor. The visitor makes the headlines. Why?

It is Howard Hughes. It was not the event, the mugging, that made the news. It was the person who was mugged.

People find many loopholes to avoid paying taxes. But when former President Richard M. Nixon's accountants apparently found a few new ones, it made the front pages.

People of local prominence are also newsmakers. Divorces are common, but if the mayor divorces his wife, that is news of local human interest. A policeman quits the force. In Chicago, the action would go unnoticed, but in a community of 2,500 people, the local news media would carry the story because the man would be a well-known member of the community.

Every story should contain an opening element of consequence or human interest. If it doesn't, there will be few readers for that story.

News Qualities

After the newswriter decides which element in a story to highlight in the opening sentences, a look should be taken at the whole story to see if it contains the qualities to make it an acceptable news story. These qualities are accuracy, objectivity, timeliness, a balanced view and a clear and concise presentation.

Accuracy in a news story is the first of the newswriter's commandments. Get the facts and check these facts to make sure they are true.

Newswriters should not guess at facts. If in doubt, check with a reliable source for clarification. If the funeral director says the deceased killed himself or herself, call the coroner to check out the cause of death. The funeral director is not an expert in causes of death. The coroner is. If a suicide was suspected, the coroner was called in to make the official ruling on the death cause. In all cases of death where the cause is not by natural means or is in doubt, the coroner will be called in to make the official ruling on the cause of death.

If the chief of police says there will be no school tomorrow, call and ask the school superintendent. In matters outside of police jurisdiction, the police chief is not the expert source of information. If the school superintendent says the police are going on strike, call the police chief or the head of the police union and check it out. In business matters, contact the appropriate source.

A traffic policeman estimates that 50,000 people witnessed the city's annual Easter parade. Use that figure and quote the police, either by naming the individual policeman or by saying "according to police estimates." It is the job of the traffic police to deal with traffic and, therefore, the policeman on the job is the source for the crowd estimate.

Never, never guess at any fact in writing a news story. If you can't find the expert source before the news deadline, omit that incomplete information until you can get the expert's answer. That missing information may give you the opening or lead for the follow-up story.

Objectivity is another reporting commandment. Give all the information that is available about the story to the reader. Keep reporter bias out of it. Opinion has no place in a news story unless it is a part of a direct quote of the newsmaker and is attributed to the person making the statement. Reporter opinion must never enter in a news story. The reporter is the carrier of news, not the maker of news.

If the reporter has feelings about the story being written, these feelings must not creep into the story to prejudice the reader. Of all the tenets of news writing, this is the hardest to enforce. Many reporters, David Brinkley of NBC News among them, have said there is no objectivity in newswriting. To a great extent, this is true. Reporter bias occurs when the person is seeking information for a news story and the initial selection of facts to be included is made.[1] A second bias occurs when the facts are assembled in a news story. Picking out the facts for the story lead will show favoritism to one story element or another. Another bias occurs when the editor makes a decision on how much of the story to run and where to run it, and, in the print media, when the editor writes a headline from the story information.

Usually, these are biases for the best presentation of the story and are not made to influence the reader in an undue manner for one side or the other represented in the news story. The real problem in objectivity arises when the newswriter deliberately seeks and writes the facts for only one side of the story.

Sometimes, errors of accuracy and objectivity are caused by a news reporter's eagerness to beat out or scoop the other news media. A prime example of this was the Jack Anderson story on Thomas Eagleton, Missouri senator and the first Democratic nominee for vice-president in 1972. Anderson, in a radio broadcast on July 27 of that year, reported that Senator Eagleton had a record of "half-a-dozen arrests for drunken and reckless driving" in Missouri. After a personal meeting with Eagleton, Anderson retracted the story and admitted that he ran the allegation for the sake of a news scoop without first thoroughly checking it out. Appearing on CBS' "Face The Nation," Anderson said that he should never have used the report.

Timeliness is a prime news factor. With news as fleeting as the second hand on a clock, getting the news out while it is news is a cardinal objective of the media. Broadcast media have the best crack at timeliness. A reporter with a hand mike and/or camera can instantaneously record the crack of rifle fire in a war, oceans and continents away, or in a civil disorder in a distant city or a block away.

1. Application of these reporter and editor decisions is called the gatekeeper function because the persons decide what material will be and will not be used in the story.

Competition is keen among reporters, print and broadcast, but generally each respects the news-reporting capabilities of the other. With the broadcast media, the public has the immediacy of an event. With the print media, the public has the written recording of an event, its background and causes and potential results.

The time limitations of the broadcast media—the fifteen-minute or half-hour news slot—allow only for a headline summary of major world and local stories and maybe nine or ten sentences of detail per story. Five or 10 minutes of broadcast news film or tape may be edited to a minute or two for on-air presentation. There is not much room for background material or result analysis. It is the print media that take up the slack and offer the public a permanent record of the event in a story many paragraphs long. Background material and analysis stories are also available through the print media. Broadcast news documentaries attempt to fill in this material on a special basis, but only the print media provide it on a daily basis.

Thus it is. The President dies today. By tomorrow there will be a new President. The first news media to get out the word of the death are the broadcast media. When Jack Ruby shot Lee Harvey Oswald in the Dallas police station in 1963, a nation of people watched as the fatal shot entered Oswald's body. Most were not able to distinctly describe what they had seen. But the vicarious thrill of being an eyewitness to so stunning a historical event was provided by photographer Robert H. Jackson of the *Dallas Times Herald,* who captured the scene. This picture, for which Jackson received a Pulitzer prize, was published in newspapers and magazines around the world and showed the television audience exactly what they had seen.

News Balance

Giving the public a balanced view of the news event is largely a matter of good judgment. An extension of objectivity—presenting all sides of a question—is the job of the news media. It is not always done. A news medium with a pronounced political leaning will likely stack its news columns with stories favorable to its political orientation. Reporter-initiated opposition stories may never find their way into print or on the air. This is a fact of journalistic life touched upon in chapter 1. Management of newspapers, magazines, television and radio may have biases; reporters should not. The general news media have the obligation to present a balanced view of any news story to the public. The management may not wish to present such a view, but the reporter must. This is true because, if the reporter ever hopes to get any more news cooperation from sources, every effort should be made to get that news before the public. If the story is suppressed, at least the news sources know the attempt was made by the reporter to tell the complete story.

Many times, reporter-initiated effort to get both sides of the story may result in a balanced view of an issue being presented. Whereas, had the reporter waited for the assignment to "get the other side of the story," it is possible that the order would not have been given.

In most assignments given to reporters, editors specifically include names of news sources representing both views of the issue for the reporter to question. Most editors were former reporters, not technicians, and they demand of their reporters the kind of stories they once wrote—complete, objective stories that give a balanced view of the issue or news event.

So, the reporter gets an assignment and, obeying the journalistic tenets of accuracy, objectivity, timeliness and obtaining a balanced view, returns to the office to write the story. What next? Next comes the hardest job of all: writing into a clear and concise account what the reporter has sandwiched in pages of scribbled notes.

To teach the student reporter how to write this clear and concise account of a news event is the main purpose of this book and of the beginning newswriting class. There is no easy formula for this.

To define a clear and concise story is simple. Such a story catches the reader's eye and the listener's ear with the opening words or lead. The body of the story unfolds, filling in details hinted at in the story lead. After the lead, the reader or listener should be able to exit at any paragraph and, without hearing or reading the end, still have the main gist of the story.

News Sense

How does a reporter recognize a news story? Reporters most often get news assignments from their editors, so it would be possible for a newswriter/technician to avoid initiating a news story until a story he or she should have written is missed and the editor demands to know why. A newswriter/reporter will always be on the lookout for possible stories about which the editor would have no way of knowing in advance to assign the reporter.

What is the difference between a news writer/technician and news writer/reporter? The basics of writing a news story can be learned by anyone with a decent English language background and an ability to learn and use a few simple writing and style rules. The ability to locate the facts of a potential story and compile them into an interesting, readable story takes more than can be learned in any textbook or in any classroom. It takes good judgment, curiosity and determination for digging up facts—the natural talents of a news reporter.

The technician will take a public-relations handout and rewrite it into a readable story that conforms to the style and spelling rules of the news medium. The reporter will take the same news release and look for one fact in the release that makes it unique from other similar releases and then get on the phone to get additional facts to build a story around it.

The technician will ride to work and see only the road. The reporter will ride to work and spot a United States flag flying at half-staff over a public building, or the sign pointing to a nonexistent container, inviting people to deposit their newspapers or bottles for recycling. Once at work, the technician begins the routine of the news day while the reporter checks out the reason for the lowered flag. Starting with the city editor and/or wire editor to find if any prominent national or state official died or, next, talking with the officials at the building where the flag is flying at half-mast to ask if a prominent city official died, the reporter will find the answer to the question. Next, a call is made to the parking-lot owner to ask when the containers for the bottles or papers will be in place. Probably amazed at the reporter's interest, the owner may assure the caller that the receptacles will be in place by the next day.

These may seem like small, almost insignificant, things for a reporter to trouble with but, if the reporter noticed them, so did other people and their questions will be answered in the evening newspaper or on the next newscast.

The reporter seldom takes anything at face value. This person knows there are always questions to be answered and stories to be told, and the reporter looks out for the clues that lead to these stories. When the technician arrives on a story scene, he or she will find the reporter already there.

Sorting Out What Is Not News

To the reporter, news is everywhere at all times. So the next problem is to decide what stories will be written. As stated earlier, most story assignments will be originated by the news editor. Covering an assigned beat, a reporter will also find story ideas. The criteria used by the reporter in determining story value are the same as discussed in the beginning of this chapter—consequence and human interest.

If in doubt about the merits of a story, the reporter should check with the news editor. If a reporter uncovers a story lead while on another assignment, the editor should be notified as soon as possible. Another tenet of journalism is to always tell your editor what you are working on and to report all news leads that you come across.

The reasons for constant communication with the editor are simple. One, the editor may want to assign another reporter to the story because the area or event involved may be part of that person's beat. Two, another reporter may already be working on the same or a similar story. Three, the news story lead may be so important that the editor will want the reporter to follow it up immediately. And, four, the editor may wish to assign a photographer to work with the reporter on the story.

Be Original

Avoid using clichés in writing news stories. A correspondence school for teaching writing sends out, as a part of its introductory material, a listing of familiar, but incomplete sentences. (Quiet as a _____.) The prospective student is told to complete all the sentences by coming up with a new word or words to fill in the blanks. Prospective news reporters would do well to take the hint and avoid sprinkling their stories with the old, tired and worn-out clichés that sparkled when first uttered decades ago but have tarnished with age and overuse.

Among the hackneyed news words and phrases are the following:

it was announced	caught in the crunch
victimized	violent explosion
feeling the squeeze	vast expanse
foreseeable future	thorough investigation
lion's share	generation gap
queried	tragic accident
snuffed out	brutal murder, slaying
nitty-gritty	protest against (redundant)
made off with	sweeping changes
highlighted	unveiled
freak accident	unique
low profile	violence erupted
uneasy calm	last-minute

But, remember, like every journalistic rule, there will be exceptions when the use of a word or phrase considered overworked will be exactly right for the sentence the reporter is writing. Or there will be times when the news source will use such words or phrases. It is sometimes better to insert a news cliché than to spend time struggling to come up with a different way of saying the same thing. This is especially true when the new idiom may be so unfamiliar to the reader or listener as to detract from the main message of the news report.

An example of this might be the statement: *As the first-place winner, she took the lion's share of the $150,000 prize.* Rewritten to avoid the cliché "lion's share," reader confusion might result from the statement: *As first-place winner, she took the elephantine portion of the $150,000 prize.*

Granted this is an extreme example, but the best way to avoid either the tired cliché or the contrived idiom is to be specific in telling the reader just what happened. *As first-place winner, she took $75,000 of the $150,000 prize.*

In newswriting, use of common sense will lead to good news sense.

3 SPELLING, STYLE AND A NEW VOCABULARY

The basic form of communications today is written. Whether it is a story for a newspaper or magazine or a script for a radio or television broadcast, the original message is written. To write clearly, one must be able to spell. An "A" in all spelling classes is helpful but not a prerequisite to becoming a news reporter.

Most English grammar books and newswriting workbooks include lists of frequently misspelled words. But for the individual newswriter, any word misspelled twice is a commonly misspelled word in his or her vocabulary. Special effort should be made to learn to spell the word correctly.

Spelling Rules

E. L. Callihan, author of *Grammar for Journalists,* lists nine hints for better spelling. He suggests they be used on words frequently misspelled.

The rules are:

1. Look up the word in the dictionary.
2. Study the spelling of the word and its meaning.
3. Fix in your mind the exact appearance of the word, paying particular attention to the sequence of letters and to the division of the word into syllables. (Many words are misspelled because the writer has failed to divide them into their correct syllables. Example: *in/ci/dent/ly* for *in/ci/den/tal/ly.*)

   You may find that you have been misspelling a word because you mispronounced it. You may have been inserting an unnecessary consonant in a word, as in saying "drownded" for *drowned.* On the other hand, you may have been adding an unnecessary vowel to the word in writing it, as in writing "athelete" for *athlete.* Do you make the mistake of using an unnecessary *i* in writing *similar*? It is not spelled "similiar." You may be omitting a necessary vowel in some words. The word *sophomore* is often misspelled "sophmore." Or you may be omitting a consonant, as in *gover(n)ment.*

Another fact you may have failed to learn is that many English words contain silent letters. You must learn to spell these words correctly. Note the following words. The letters in parentheses are not sounded, but they must be included when you write the words:

(p)neumonia   kil(n)   (w)rapped   tho(ugh)   thoro(ugh)

4. Pronounce the word aloud several times, syllable by syllable.
5. Type or write the word 10 times to fix it in your mind.
6. Now study the word again. Take a pencil and write the word divided into syllables with a slant line between each two syllables, like this: in/ci/den/tal/ly.
7. Underline the parts of the word that give you trouble, thus:

embarrass   fiery   separate   familiar   picnicking
disappoint   weird   believable   similar   questionnaire
judgment   arctic   recommend   marshal   cemetery

8. Devote as much time as you feel is necessary to reviewing the words that give you trouble.
9. Make sure that you can now spell the word correctly without using the dictionary.

However, whenever you are in doubt about the spelling or the syllabication of a word, *look it up in the dictionary.* [1]

Use of the Dictionary

One of a newswriter's most used reference books will be the dictionary. It is a good idea to have two dictionaries, a pocket-size one for quick reference and a full-size dictionary for checking spellings or definitions not given in the pocket edition.[2]

Learn to recognize a misspelled word. Sound silly? Some people are misspelling words because they have never learned to spell the word any other way. To them the incorrect way is the right way. How, then, does one learn the correct spelling of a word other than by digesting a dictionary? You read many books, magazine articles, newspaper stories, anything that is handy at any time. Recognition of the way a word is spelled is a prime way to learn to spell correctly. If the word looks wrong, check it out in the dictionary.

If you are tempted to use a word that you do not know how to spell and you decide you don't have time to look it up in the dictionary,

1. E. L. Callihan, *Grammar for Journalists* (Philadelphia: Chilton Book Company, 1969), pp. 311–312.
2. Another good reference book for a reporting student is the pocket-sized spelling book containing 20,000 or more words. There are several versions available.

discard the word. Use a word you can spell. The more familiar word that you can spell will probably be a better word for your story, anyway.

Writers of the world's masterpieces of prose do not force their readers to have a companion dictionary to look up the meanings for every other word—why should today's media readers? Remember, the newswriter's job is to communicate, not to *obfuscate.*

The Stylebook

Just as the reader should not be expected to look up every other word in a story to find its meaning, the reader should not be confused about style usage in a story. If a person is referred to as a 15-year-old at one place in a story, and in another story a child is identified as a two-year-old, the reader may wonder which usage is right, or is there a rule about writing out numbers nine and under and using figures for numbers 10 and above? Are the names of streets written out as in 1815 South Sixteenth Street or is 2321 N. 11th Ave. correct? Is Mr. John Smith or R. Bell or "Hup" Brown correct for a first reference in a story? The answers are found in a stylebook—a book giving rules for and examples of usage, punctuation and typography used in preparation of copy for publication.

Style in newswriting, whether for print or broadcast writing, is followed for the convenience of the reader or listener. A person wants to get the news in the quickest, clearest manner. It's enough to have to digest a constant flow of information without having to decide whether The Rt. Rev. Elder John Smith is a new religious title or a misprint.

The most commonly used stylebook in newswriting is the Associated Press-United Press International (AP-UPI) *Newswire Stylebook,* reprinted in the appendix of this book. Additional local style rules may be added to meet individual news employer preferences. On the campus, for example, a standardization of titles is desirable. Should Mrs., Miss and Ms. all be used? Should Mr. be used for faculty men and not for students? Is it all right to use Prof. or Dr. on first reference? These are all points of style that must be worked out locally.

Trouble arises where a conflict in style arises. In one story, a month is abbreviated according to the AP-UPI style, and in the following story the same month is spelled out. It's 8 a.m. once and 8:00 a.m. the next reference. Remember, the good reporter tries to get the news to the reader in the clearest, most concise manner while giving the important facts and sense of the story. Causing the reader to stumble over a mixture of style combinations in a story defeats this purpose. Consistency of style in a news story is vital no matter which stylebook is followed. The style used on the first page must be followed throughout the newspaper.

News Story Format

In a day filled with deadlines, the fewer directions that must be given the editor regarding a news story the better. Each news operation will have a certain way in which it will demand that copy be prepared prior to being read by the editors. Generally, this format will include placing the writer's name and slug line—one or two words identifying the story—at the top left of the page on which a story is to be written. Then the writer drops down about 10 or 12 spaces before the beginning of the story. This white space allows the editor to write in the headline or by-line and any other directions needed for setting the copy.

This format may be followed in the classroom. Other suggestions for typing copy to be handed in include setting margins at 10 and 75 for pica type or 10 and 85 for elite. Indent five spaces for paragraphs. Double space between lines. Do not hyphenate words at the end of a line. At the end of the first page, if the story needs to be continued on another page, write the word—*more*—and then continue on to the second page. It is not a good idea to split paragraphs at the end of a page.

On the second page of your copy, write your last name, slug line and add 1 at the top left section of the paper. This is protection against your copy being separated and the editor or typesetters not knowing where to find the rest of the story or how to correctly match the order. It will read: Name/slug/add 1. Add 1 indicates that this page is the first addition to your story. A second page will be marked with your name, slug line and add 2, and so on. Indicate the end of the story by typing -30- or #.

If you make mistakes in the story, do not erase and do not strike over the letters with other letters. Just xxxxxxx out the word you want to eliminate. Then with a pencil go over the xxxxxxx's and cover them and add a bridge ⌒ to indicate that no extra space should be left there. (A different method is used for computerized systems). Learn the copy-marking symbols (see chapter 4) and use them in correcting your copy.

Journalism as a Spoken Language

Learning the language of the journalism profession is an initial requirement for employment. When an editor yells: "Give me two grafs on this story and a take and a half on this one," the reporter had better know what is being demanded. The "graf" is a paragraph, and a "take" is one page of double-spaced, typewritten copy.

Some journalistic words and phrases are used by reporters, editors and printers alike, and some others are used almost exclusively within each department. A journalism dictionary or glossary of the more common words used by reporters is contained in the appendixes of this book.

In the newsroom, *beat* is an often used word. It means a series of news sources assigned to one reporter who calls or visits them on a regular basis. Examples would be the police department, the public library, the school board and the YMCA. *Beat* can also mean getting a story before other news media do. And getting *beaten* is the reverse. Since the word applies to the getting of the news, it has no use for proofreaders and printers.

Byline is a word used by the reporters, editors, proofreaders and printers. It is a line of type, set after the headline and before the news story, containing the name of the writer of the story. To the reporter, the word means visual recognition for a story written. It is usually the editor who affixes the name to a story. The proofreader reads it to see if it has been spelled correctly and the printer knows it as the setting of a name line that is usually in darker type (bold face) than the rest of the story.

For the reporter, the language used to read copy will be most important. After a story is written, errors must be corrected and any special directions for the printer must be made before the copy leaves the reporter's desk. While the editor may add or delete some of these directions, it is the reporter's responsibility to make the first corrections on his or her copy. It is a written language more than spoken. In chapter 4 a discussion of the copyreader's language and symbols is given.

4 CHECK THAT COPY

Writing the news story is only the second part of the job for the reporter. (Getting the story facts is the first part.) Now the reporter must read carefully through the story and catch any misspelled words. Taking a word out or putting two in, marking a paragraph or deleting a sentence is the next job of the reporter. To aid the printer in understanding all the directions pencilled in by the reporter and editor, a standard set of copyreading symbols has been devised.

Copyreading Symbols

The symbols are a shorthand for reporter and editor to give the printer directions on reading the marked copy. With the deadline ever hanging over the news staff, it is not possible for the reporter to retype copy. Most times, the first draft of a story is revised with the pencil, using copyreading symbols.

The AP-UPI copy-marking guide appears on page 22. It may be modified for the reporter's use. One paragraph designation should be chosen and used consistently. Designation of copy to be centered or printed in bold face (copy printed in blacker ink than the rest of story) is usually the job of the editor.

The use of the caret with quotation marks, apostrophes and commas in copy markings may be eliminated if the punctuation can be inserted in the copy so that it can be easily read by the printer. The period should always be circled to distinguish it from all other punctuation marks. The hyphen may be represented by only one line where it is convenient to insert it between words. Do not hyphenate words at the end of a sentence. Either finish the word by pushing the margin release on the typewriter and typing the rest of the word or go to the next line and retype the whole word, editing out the incomplete word. The dash may be inserted by using two broken lines - -.

The most misunderstood copyreading mark is the circle. The most used of all the copyreading marks, the circle has several meanings, depending on the word it encompasses and its location on the typewritten page.

Copy Markings

Marking	Copy text	Instruction
¶	ATLANTA—When organization of	paragraph
or	is over. Now it will be the first	paragraph
	the last attempts.	
	With this the conquering is to	no paragraph
or	according to ~~the~~ this compendi-	elisions
	the Jones Smith firm is not in the	transpose
	over a period of (sixty) or more in	use figures
	there were (9) in the party at the	spell
	Ada (Oklahoma,) is in the lead at	abbreviate
	the (Ga.) man is to be among the	spell
	prince edward said it is his to	capitals
	accordingly This will be done	lower case
	the acc user pointed to them	join
	in these times it is necessary to	separate
	the order for the ~~later~~ devices	retain
BF/c or BF]	By DONALD AMES [	bold (black) face centered
	J. R. Thomas]	flush right
	[A. B. Jones Co.	flush left
	president in a fine situation	caret
#	space (also 30 at end of item)	
	quotation marks, apostrophe	
	comma	
⊗ or ⊙	period	
=	hyphen	
⊢⊣	dash	
	a u n t (underline a u)	
	d o n e (overline n o)	

If contained in the body of the news copy, the circle will indicate to the printer to set the opposite of what appears in the copy. If the numeral *2* is circled, the printer knows that the *2* should appear *two* in the finished copy. If the word *sixteen* is circled in the copy, the printer knows the corrected version should read *16*.

There were 3 children among the twenty-six survivors. Corrected, the copy will read: There were three children among the 26 survivors.

Another meaning for the circle when used in the body copy of a story is to abbreviate that which is written out and to write out that which is abbreviated.

The hit and run took place in the thirteen hundred block of Rixen St. Corrected, it reads: The hit and run took place in the 1300 block of Rixen Street.

When the circle is used outside the body copy of the news story, the printer is being told to delete the written material from the copy to be set. This would include the writer's name, date and slug lines used to identify the copy. The word -more- to indicate additional pages of copy would be deleted by circling as would the -30- or # that signifies end-of-the-story.

Any directions to the printer written in the margin of the copy also would be circled. But, a circle in the body copy of the story will never mean to delete. There are other copyreading symbols to mark story copy for deletion. See the AP-UPI copy-marking guide for the complete listing of copy marks.

What Are Editors For?

If the reporter puts in all the copyreading marks for the printer, why pass the copy on to an editor? The editing job consists of much more than reading copy for spelling and punctuation errors. The editor does look for these errors, along with searching the copy for questions raised but not answered by the reporter, and for libelous statements.

The editor will catch run-on sentences that can be rewritten into two short sentences, giving the reader a better understanding of the point being made. The editor plucks out unnecessary words that clutter, not clarify, a story. Like a careful gardener, the editor prunes the copy of anything that detracts the reader from receiving a clear, concise, informative account of a news event.

A news story should have short sentences that contain movement and color, are free of inaccuracies and continue to hold reader interest to the last word. It's the editor's job to polish and shape a story that does not meet this criteria. It might mean giving the story back to the reporter and asking for a rewrite after pointing out the story's flaws.

The editor will usually write the headline for the story and then fit the story and headline into a page layout for the printer who makes up the page. (In chapter 16 we will look closer at writing headlines.)

It is the editor's job to make each page of the publication so interesting that the reader will want to read through the entire issue. If a

In the non-computerized news-room, editing tools include a pencil, dictionary, eraser and ruler.

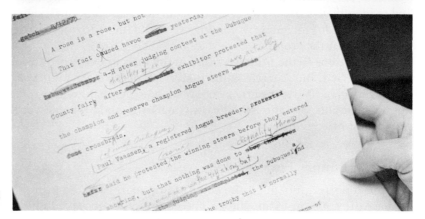

A close look at hand-edited copy.

When editing by computers, the editors call up the story on a video display terminal and type in corrections.

story is long, the editor may decide to have paragraphs of it set in bold face so that they will stand out from the rest of the story and catch the reader's eye. The editor may also choose to insert subheads in the story. These are one or two words, sometimes excerpts from the paragraph they head, that will attract the reader's attention and arouse the person's curiosity to read the whole story.

The selection and sizing of photos is also an editor's job. Editors often assign a photographer to accompany a reporter going on a news assignment. On smaller papers, the writer may be the photographer as well. The picture(s) are then run with the story to illustrate what the reporter is writing about. Some pictures tell a story by themselves.

Get an English Grammar

The English language is the basic tool with which the newswriter works. A thorough knowledge of it is a necessary prerequisite for the neophyte reporter. Being able to spell, or at least able to look up the word in the dictionary, as was previously discussed, is only a part of the English language usage that the reporter must work with.

The correct placement and use of punctuation marks is important.

Exclamation Marks

Exclamation points serve to give emphasis to a sentence. But may they be dropped into a story at the newswriter's discretion? *The answer is no. No!* The first sentence is a simple declarative sentence. The second is an exclamation. Some newswriters use the exclamation point every time the writer wants to make a point—not necessarily every time the newsmaker makes a point. Here lies the difference. If the speaker didn't utter an exclamation, don't dress up the remark to make it appear one by ending with the exclamation mark.

Apostrophe

The apostrophe is easily one of the most used and abused members of the punctuation family. And the word that most often carries the misplaced apostrophe is *it's. It's* means *it is. Its* represents a possessive neuter pronoun. Hardly an eyelash of similarity in the meaning of the two words, yet they are continually mixed in sentence construction by journalism students.

It's my new book. The book does not have its dust jacket.

Quotation Marks

The quotation mark is another member of the punctuation family that gives problems to newswriters. If a person is quoted verbatim, the entire passage must be placed in quotation marks.

"We will not leave the steps of this courthouse until the men are freed."

Duo Quotes

Another thorny quotation mark problem arises when a quote within a quote ends with the last word in the sentence.

Jack said: "Give me the book 'The Murder of Roger Ackroyd.' "

And, don't forget that quote marks close the quotation as well as open it. If a quotation runs several paragraphs, the first word of each paragraph opens with a quote mark; but only the final word of the final paragraph of the quotation will have the closing quote mark.

Fragmentary Quotes

Sometimes only a part of what a person has said lends itself to a quote. A portion of the sentence may have been rambling, repetitive, unclear or cut short. To quote a fragment of a sentence, the omitted part must be represented by ellipsis (a series of three dots), and the ellipsis must be inside the quotation marks.

". . . Money spent on the project is wasted," Hansen said. "I promise . . . to avenge her death."

To indicate a sudden break in the thought or the speech, use a dash that is placed inside the quotation marks.

"I had always wanted to visit the island but—." A ringing telephone caused him to break off the sentence.

Paraphrasing

If a statement is paraphrased, giving the gist of what was said but not using the exact words, no quotation marks are needed.

Standing on the steps of the courthouse, the spokesperson for the group said the members would not leave until the men were freed.

Other Marks

Placement of other punctuation marks in relation to the quotation marks can also be troublesome. Place the period and the comma within the final quotation mark. The colon and semicolon are placed outside the quotation marks. The exclamation and question marks are placed in or out of the quotation marks according to their use. If a part of the quoted matter, they go inside. If not a part, they go outside the quotation marks.

The book "Murder! Murder!" is on the table.
Has anyone seen the play "Ten Little Indians"?

Misused Words

Words that sound similar but have very different meanings may trip
would-be newswriters. *Then* and *than* is one example. *Affect* and *effect*
is another.

Then is an adverb used to denote time or the next in order. *Than*
is a conjunction used to denote the second element in a comparison.

Jack will leave first, then Harry.
Mary is taller than Ruth (is tall).

Affect, a verb, means to influence or change. *Effect,* a noun, is the
result of the influence or change.

How will the failing mark on this news story affect the overall grade point? The effect will be an "F" for the course.

Two other words frequently misused are *that* and *which. That* is an
easy word to use correctly in the spoken language. But, when the
transition to the written word is made, *which* gains in writer prestige
and will displace *that* many times when *that* is the correct word.

To determine whether to use *that* or *which* in a sentence, ask if the
phrase to be introduced is vital to the sentence meaning. If it is, then
introduce the phrase with the word *that.* If, however, the phrase provides additional, interesting but non-vital information to the story,
introduce the phrase with the word *which.*

The accident, which blocked the road, involved a police car.
The accident that involved the police car is under investigation.
"*That* is a defining, or restrictive pronoun. It can't be omitted without leaving the noun it modifies incomplete or even
altering the sense of a sentence.
Which is a nondefining, or nonrestrictive pronoun. The
phrase it introduces is normally separated from the rest of
a sentence by commas and can be omitted without affecting
meaning.
For example: The newspaper that is free of grammatical
errors, which can be even more annoying than typographical ones, will delight readers who respect correct usage."[1]

1. Gannett News Service Bulletin, *Wire Watch,* September 24, 1973.

5 NEWS AND THE LAW

For almost 200 years the press in the United States operated on the assumption that it had freedom to gather and report news from secret sources without being compelled to reveal those sources. This freedom was thought to be guaranteed by the broad language of the First Amendment. In part, the amendment states:

> Congress shall make no law respecting an establishment of religion, or prohibiting the free exercise thereof: or abridging the freedom of speech, or of the press . . .

Reporters and Subpoenas

During the decade of the seventies, however, the question of this right was taken to the Supreme Court with the case of Earl Caldwell.[1]

Caldwell, a black reporter for the *New York Times*, San Francisco bureau, was assigned to do an investigative story on the activities of the Black Panthers, a militant black organization. He wrote several

1. General background information for the discussion in this chapter on the First Amendment to the Constitution, although not directly quoted in most instances, was obtained from the following sources:

Annual Chief Justice Earl Warren Conference on Advocacy in the United States, sponsored by the Roscoe Pound-American Trial Lawyers Foundation, *First Amendment and The News Media.* Cambridge, Mass: Roscoe Pound-American Trial Lawyers Foundation, June 8–9, 1973.

Vince Blasi, "On The Question of Privilege: Newsmen May Have Little to Gain," *The Quill,* November 1971, pp. 9–11.

Fred W. Friendly, "Beyond 'Caldwell'—3: Justice White and Reporter Caldwell: Finding a Common Ground," *Columbia Journalism Review,* September/October 1972, pp. 31–37.

Fred P. Graham and Jack C. Landau, "The Federal Shield Law We Need," *Columbia Journalism Review,* March/April 1973, pp. 26–35.

Norman E. Isaacs, "Beyond 'Caldwell'—1: 'There May Be Worse To Come From this Court.' " *Columbia Journalism Review,* September/October 1972, pp. 18–24.

Peter Lisagon, "Three Cases for the High Court," *The Quill,* November 1971, p. 8.

Benno C. Schmidt, Jr., "Beyond 'Caldwell'—2: 'The Decision Is Tentative,' " *Columbia Journalism Review,* September/October 1972, pp. 25–30.

Twentieth Century Fund Task Force and Fred P. Graham, "Press Freedoms Under Pressure," *Report of the Twentieth Century Fund Task Force on the Government and the Press,* (New York, 1972).

stories in the *Times* about Panther activities and philosophies. A federal grand jury subpoenaed Caldwell to appear and testify concerning the aims, purposes and activities of the Panther organization. Caldwell refused to answer the subpoena, stating that even his entering a grand jury room would destroy his credibility with his sources. He argued that once behind the grand jury doors, he would never be able to prove to his Panther sources that he did not compromise identities. Caldwell claimed that mere association with the grand jury would destroy his credibility with future news sources.

In an historic ruling on the Caldwell case on June 29, 1972, the Supreme Court, in an opinion written by Justice Byron R. White, held that "the great weight of authority is that newsmen are not exempt from the normal duty of appearing before a grand jury and answering questions relevant to a criminal investigation."[2]

The broadcast media have not been spared investigation under the law, either. On Feb. 23, 1971, CBS News broadcast a program entitled: "The Selling of the Pentagon." The program's premise was that the U.S. military has spent millions of dollars of the taxpayer's money in an effort to win private and public support for its programs.

The program drew praise and criticism. The dismay of some members of Congress caused an investigation to be launched on May 26, 1971, and a subpoena was served on Dr. Frank Stanton, then CBS president. Under the subpoena, Dr. Stanton was directed to submit "all film, workprints, out-takes, and sound-tape recordings, written scripts and/or transcripts utilized in whole or in part by CBS" in connection with the program.

Dr. Stanton answered the subpoena by appearing before the House Committee on Interstate and Foreign Commerce, which has legislative jurisdiction over the Federal Communication Commission and the radio-television industry. But he refused to submit the materials called for. As a result of this refusal to comply to the letter of the subpoena, the congressional committee voted to recommend that CBS and Dr. Stanton be cited for contempt of Congress. The House, in the unusual action of not supporting one of its committees, voted down the contempt citation.

Shield Laws

As a result of these and other similar city, state and national reporter-government confrontations on the interpretation of the First Amendment to the Constitution, a public and congressional cry for a shield law sprang up. The law, as its name implies, would shield the

2. For a catalog of recent subpoena cases involving the First Amendment, see Fred P. Graham, Jack C. Landau, "The Federal Shield Law We Need," *Columbia Journalism Review,* March/April, 1973, pp. 26–35.

reporter from revealing his sources in answer to a court subpoena. There are 25 states[3] now carrying some form of a news reporter shield law on their books. For the most part, the common language of the current shield laws does no more than protect the news reporter from being forced to disclose identities of confidential news sources. Current demands on reporters from governmental agencies show that if an effective shield law is to be enacted, provisions for allowing privileged status for news material gathered but not used in a published or broadcast news program must be included.

Right of Reply

The government and press interpretation of the First Amendment goes beyond the reporter's involvement in the interpretation. The other two sides of the controversy belong to the print publishers and the broadcast station owners and to the government.

In 1974, the U.S. Supreme Court struck down a Florida Right To Reply statute. The case dealt with a series of editorials written by the *Miami Herald* in 1972. The editorials denounced the executive director of the Classroom Teachers Association of Miami, who was then a candidate for the state legislature. When the candidate brought his reply to the first editorial to the *Herald* office, the paper refused to print it and then ran another editorial blasting the man. A second reply, hand carried to the paper by the candidate, was also denied printing on the grounds that the letters did not come through the mails, the normal avenue of submission for such letters, according to the editors.

The candidate next moved to the courts and won a Florida Supreme Court decision upholding a 1913 state statute that provided that if a candidate for nomination or election was assailed regarding his personal character or official record by a newspaper, the candidate had a right to demand that the newspaper print, free of cost to the candidate, a reply that would appear in as conspicuous a place as the charges that prompted the reply, provided it did not take up more space than the charges.

The *Herald* appealed the Florida decision to the U.S. Supreme Court on the contention that the state statute was void because it purported to regulate the content of a newspaper in violation of the First Amendment.

The Supreme Court ruled unanimously on June 25, 1974, that Florida's Right Of Reply law was unconstitutional because it violated the First Amendment's guarantee of a free press.

3. States with shield laws in December 1974 were Alabama, Alaska, Arizona, Arkansas, California, Delaware, Illinois, Indiana, Kentucky, Louisana, Maryland, Michigan, Minnesota, Montana, New Jersey, Nebraska, New Mexico, New York, Nevada, North Dakota, Ohio, Oregon, Pennsylvania, Tennessee and Rhode Island.

In giving his opinion on the case, Supreme Court Chief Justice Warren E. Burger said:

> A responsible press is an undoubtedly desirable goal, but press responsibility is not mandated by the Constitution and like many other virtues it cannot be legislated.[4]

Paid Reply Denied

Offering to buy an ad in print or broadcast media to gain a communications avenue to the public can also be thwarted by the publisher or station owner under interpretations of the First Amendment as upheld by the courts.

Ben H. Bagdikian, news media critic and national correspondent for the *Columbia Journalism Review*,[5] writing in the May/June, 1974, issue of the magazine, explored the advertising access issue.

> ... The Chicago Joint Board of the Amalgamated Clothing Workers of America wanted to buy ads in the four Chicago papers to tell their reasons for striking; all four papers refused the ad, and the U.S. Court of Appeals upheld the papers. When the Business Executives Move for Peace in Vietnam tried to buy commercial time on WTOP, the CBS affiliate in Washington, they were refused and this, as well as a later refusal of CBS to the Democratic National Committee, was upheld in the courts.

Bagdikian, in a critical commentary, states that:

> ... the media in their ad exclusion policies—apart from libel or obscenity—are telling the public that if the public dislikes editorial decisions on news and editorial space, there is absolutely no recourse, even in advertising, to the party who wishes to address the community at his own expense.

> Yet newspaper groups have had no hesitation to ask for special governmental factors for corporate convenience— in child labor, postal rates, and exemption from certain antitrust laws—all in the sacred name of the First Amendment, the public's right to know and the need to preserve a free flow of information. When publishers crowded the corridors of Capitol Hill to lobby for the Newspaper Preservation Act (exempting papers from standard antitrust and monopoly laws) they were plainly asking governmental in-

4. "High Court Rules on Access and Accountability Cases," *Editor and Publisher*, June 29, 1974. p. 37.
5. Ben H. Bagdikian, "First Amendment Revisionism," *Columbia Journalism Review*, May/June, 1974, pp. 39–46. Copyright © 1974 by Ben Bagdikian. Reprinted by permission of the Sterling Lord Agency, Inc.

tervention to, as the act says, maintain a press "independent and competitive in all parts of the United States." That it applied to only 22 of the 1,530 newspaper cities in the country is not the point. There has generally been little restraint in begging the government to intervene in such instances and apparently not much thought that a logical extension would be government intervention in press performance.

Bagdikian accuses most papers of showing

> . . . no comparable basic interest in illuminating and reforming problems affecting the mass of readers—the poor, the lower, middle class, the consumer. . . . It has taken Ralph Nader to do for the consumer what newspapers should have been doing for the last 30 years.

The *Columbia Journalism Review* correspondent further accused "publishers as a whole (to) have been quicker to protect their corporate interests under the First Amendment than their journalistic ones . . ."

For those who would swing to the side of government in seeking controls on the press as a remedy for all its ills, Bagdikian admonishes that to think "that judges and legislatures will remedy the present lack of access among the powerless is to misread the dynamics of politics." To prove his point, he quotes the words of the late Zechariah Chafee, the leading legal scholar of press freedom for many decades:

> Whenever anybody is inclined to look to the government for help in making the mass media do what we desire of them, he had better ask himself one antiseptic question: "Am I envisioning myself as the official who is going to administer the policy which seems to me so good? You and I are not going to be on the committee which is charged with making newspapers or radio scripts better written and more accurate and impartial . . . We must be prepared to take our chances with the kind of politicians we particularly dislike, because that is what we may get.

The Devil's Advocate

Off and on during U.S. history, the government has been the news media's adversary while the press was the devil's advocate. These roles were probably never more clearly defined and acted out than under the second administration of Richard M. Nixon. Former President Nixon, smarting from old scars inflicted by the press corps in his unsuccessful bid for the 1960 presidency and then humiliated at his defeat for the governorship of California, came to the office of president in 1968 with no love of the media in his heart.

Using his first vice-president, Spiro Agnew, as the carrier of the word to the press, Nixon launched bitter tirades against the media. One of the most famous of the tirades was delivered by Agnew in Des Moines, Iowa, on Nov. 13, 1969, in which Agnew launched an attack on how the public got its news, singling out the television news reporters for hardest criticism. A week later in Montgomery, Ala., Agnew expanded his media criticism to include the print media in the form of the *New York Times* and *Washington Post.*

But then came the second Nixon administration, which was inaugurated with a break-in of the Democratic headquarters in the Watergate Building in Washington. Two news reporters from the *Washington Post,* Carl Bernstein and Bob Woodward, covered the break-in like hundreds of newspeople on that June 17, 1972, Saturday morning. But, in a few weeks, as the rest of the reporters were letting the break-in and subsequent capture of five suspects fade in their collective memory, Bernstein and Woodward were digging away at the story behind the break-in. After months of work and many stories, the two reporters were to be credited with keeping the spotlight on the biggest political scandal since the Teapot Dome scandal of 1923 and possibly the biggest political scandal in the U.S. government's history.

These two men, who were awarded the 1973 Pulitzer Prize for their reporting, suddenly brought respectability and credibility back to the ranks of news reporting. With Agnew's resignation due to the uncovering of some legal improprieties while the governor of Maryland that he carried over into his first term as vice-president, a strong, critical administration voice was silenced. In the wake of the Watergate discoveries, no one rose to take his place.

For now, the First Amendment, as it stands, appears to have retrenched itself in the broad interpretation given it by the founding fathers. The talk of national and state shield laws, while still present, is not as loud as before. The free press appears to be enjoying a period of freedom from legal questions.

Writing Right

While the foregoing discussion of law and the press has sweeping impact on news reporting, the majority of the reporting profession is not directly touched by the events. It is the everyday journalistic law problems that the average reporter tangles with while writing a story.

In the media, the legal pitfall is libel. Textbooks have been written about libel laws, and it is well for the journalism student to familiarize himself or herself with the outlines of the libel law—if not actually taking a journalistic law course—before accepting that first reporting job. For the beginning reporting student, an introduction to the libel law—how to recognize libel, how to avoid libel and what to do in defense of libel—should suffice at this time.

Libel, according to the Black's Law Dictionary, is "a method of defamation expressed by print, writing, pictures or signs . . . injurious to the reputation of another."[6]

Recognizing Libel

The rule is to avoid libel in writing news stories. One way to do this is to not use words that have shown up in United States court cases in the last 75 years that may be in themselves libelous.

Some of these words include: Communist, Nazi, atheist, Ku Klux Klan, shyster, plagiarist, bankrupt, crook, blackmailer, influence peddler, swindler, drunk, drug addict, charlatan, quack, prostitute, adulterer, bigamist, deadbeat, mistress, liar, con man, scab, and rogue. Do not label a place as a brothel, disorderly house, gambling den or vice den. Do not charge people as guilty of malpractice, fee gouging, strike-breaking or moral turpitude.

The key to remember in dealing with libel is intent. You, as a writer, cannot use these words to describe a person or place, unless it already has been proven to be true or unless an expert source—police or professional in the area under investigation—has used the labels in the story facts.

In some cases, use of the words might be not only permissible but necessary for story clarity. If the Communist party held a convention and a person from the local news area was a delegate, use of the word *Communist* with the person could be used in the story. If, in a story on drug addicts, a self-confessed drug addict is interviewed, the use of words such as addict, junkie, dope peddler as applied to himself or herself might be used without fear of libel.

The following example, submitted by an editor who claims it actually saw print, illustrates how misphrasing can present a potentially libelous situation.

To Err Is Human

It all started with the following classified ad: FOR SALE: A. R. Pike has one washing machine for sale. Phone 643 after 7 p.m. and ask for Miss Dirk who lives with him cheap.

On Tuesday—NOTICE: We regret having erred in A. R. Pike's ad yesterday. It should have read: One washing machine for sale. Cheap. Phone 643 and ask for Miss Dirk who lives with him after 7 p.m.

6. Henry C. Black, *Black's Law Dictionary*, 4th ed. rev., (St. Paul, Minn.: West Publishing Co., 1968) p. 1060.

On Wednesday—A. R. Pike has informed us that he has received several annoying telephone calls because of the error we made in his classified ad yesterday. His ad stands corrected as follows: FOR SALE: A. R. Pike has one washing machine for sale. Cheap. Phone 643 after 7 p.m. and ask for Miss Dirk who lives with him.

Finally on Thursday—I, A. R. Pike, have no washing machine for sale. I smashed it. Don't call 643 as the telephone has been taken out. I have not been carrying on with Miss Dirk. Until yesterday she was my housekeeper, but she quit.

Avoiding Libel

The quickest way to become involved in a libel lawsuit is to deliberately print a lie. In assuring that the facts carried in a story are true, the sources of the facts must be accepted experts in the field about which they are giving information for publication. For example, only a coroner or medical examiner can rule conclusively on the cause of death when such is in doubt.

However, some news media do publish reports from secondary experts in some stories. Police reports listing the cause of an unnatural death have appeared in print as the official word on the death cause. In most of the stories of this kind, the police are correct. But the one time the police report is in error, a lawsuit could result because the sole authority for the publication of the death information was not accurate. Make sure that the facts used in a story are true and that the justification for using them would stand up in a court of law during a libel trial.

Correct Identification

Threats of libel action can result when a news medium has incorrectly identified a person in a story. All persons have two types of identification, primary and secondary.

The primary identification is the one that the most people will recognize the person by. This includes the full name, including first name, middle initial, last name, age and address, if the person is over sixteen. Under sixteen (the age in most states at which the person may hold a job), parents' names and address will be a primary identification factor. Various news media may affix a different age for the dropping off of parents' names in identifying the youth. Secondary identification includes school or occupation, church affiliation and civic and professional affiliations.

One's name is a most important possession. Therefore, the news reporter should make every effort to see that every name in a news story is correct. On a student's newswriting assignment, a misspelled or incorrect name should qualify for an "F" on the assignment.

Again, an example makes the point.

> Imagine, if you can, the southern Indiana daily's discomfort (if not terror) when it discovered (after the press run) that a young reporter had confused the name of the judge and the defendant in the story of a criminal trial on "assault and battery with intent to satisfy sexual desires on a 14-year-old girl.
>
> The story read all right for the first few paragraphs, but the writer then had a mental lapse and he repeatedly used the judge's name for the defendant. The last paragraph gave the judge's name again and said he was pleading an alibi defense.
>
> Despite staff prayer, the article came to the attention of the judge, who thereupon wrote as follows:
>
> "I enclose a Xerox copy from your paper which has just been handed to me. I appreciate the fact that, because of bad circulation, your paper is understaffed and your writers are poorly trained. The subject matter of this article was highly technical and, therefore, the writer of this article could not be expected to get it right the very first time. I, therefore, am going to point out some of the idiom used in court and identify the cast of characters.
>
> "First, the judge (that's me) sits up front of the courtroom on a raised dais with a robe on and scowls at people. Secondly, the defendant is the fellow sitting at counsel table representing truth and justice. The press are those people sitting over at the side of the courtroom with long hair, whiskers, and barefooted.
>
> "Now in criminal proceedings, the judge is not charged with crime. The defendant is charged with crime. The judge does not claim alibi. The defendant claims alibi. The judge does not have to have an alibi. He is the head honcho.
>
> "I AM SURE THAT IF YOUR WRITER carefully reviews the above information he may eventually be able to get his article correct.
>
> "I wish you to know, in passing, that I am a great admirer of the Fourth Estate, and sometimes get very emotional when I observe their crusade for truth and justice. Therefore you have my permission to pass these instructions on to other newspapers who are in like situations so that they may benefit from these simple instructions."[7]

7. Larry Incollingo, "When Judge Becomes 'Defendant' Watch Out," *Daily Herald-Telegram,* Bloomington, Ind., May 29, 1974.

Primary Identification

Most name mistakes are the result of carelessness.

A national crime magazine once carried a story about a murder suspect in a grisly sex murder. A picture with three men accompanied the story. The man on the left was identified as the murder suspect. The man in the middle as a sheriff and the man on the right as a deputy sheriff. In fact, the man on the left was the sheriff and the man in the middle was the murder suspect.

A newspaper carried a story about a local citizen who was involved in a bank hearing. However, the reporter must have taken the story over the phone and didn't double check the name spelling and pronunciation because the man, whose first name was Ellis, was identified as Alice in the news story.

Such careless attention to identification detail results in publication of correction notices.

"John D. Smith of 2121 Nowhere was incorrectly identified as a bank robbery suspect in Tuesday's story. The suspect should have been identified as John F. Smith of 1916 Somewhere."

Name Spellings

Phoned information can easily be confused, especially with names. *F* sounds like *S*, *T* sounds like *V* and *P* sounds like *B*. Spelling a name by saying *S* as in Sam, *F* as in Frank, *V* as in victory is common reporting practice.

Names with different spelling variations need to be carefully checked. Steven may be Stephen. Smith may be Smythe. John may be Jon. Judy may be Judi, Judie or even Judee. Marian may be a male Marion. Leslie, Shirley, Evelyn, Joyce and Beverly may be either female or male names.

Nicknames may be full names. Don is not always short for Donald. Jack, Bobby, Mike, Rick and Hank may be first names. W. B. or J. B. may be the initials for a person without a first name. Check out any name or initials and the correct spelling of all names in a news story, but be especially alert and careful when taking the names over the telephone.

Middle Initial

With a name like Zachery Isaac Biblebelt, use of a middle initial is not as vital as with the name John David Smith. A quick check of the telephone directory might tell a reporter that there is one Zachery Biblebelt in the news area, but there are many John Smiths. Therefore, use of the middle initial should be used in Smith's name, while it could be omitted in Biblebelt's name.

If the middle initial is not readily available for the news source, then additional primary identification must be used to pinpoint the identity.

Addresses

With all names, addresses must be used in news stories. Getting the correct address is not usually a difficult task. A telephone book or city directory should yield the information. In handling an address, be careful of area designations. It has happened that two persons, not related but having the identical first name, middle initial and last name, have lived at identical street addresses, only in different sections of the town. One may be at 555 North Wisconsin and the other at 555 South Wisconsin. One may be the bank president and the other a local bad-check writer. A misidentification in a situation like this might bring a libel suit against the offending news medium.

In newswriting, the lead should usually carry primary identification. The body of the story can handle secondary sources. The exception would be when the person is a newsmaker because of a secondary identification, such as a professional glassblower or a coin collector.

Of course there are always exceptions to the general rule. A celebrity would be one. An actor or an athlete will have as primary identification his or her name and profession. Because of the profession, the person's name gained prominence and both should be used together as primary identification.

Libel Defense

Truth is a complete libel defense, except in a few states that require truth plus good motives and justifiable ends. If this is kept in mind when researching every story, whether potentially libelous or not, the reporter will come up with a better story.

Fair comment may be used by a reporter in reporting in an area of public interest. For example, a theater critic may review a play and say that the performance of a certain actor was poor. It is the personal opinion of a reporter assigned by a news medium to give such in a certain area. This same right of reporting is given sports announcers, book reviewers, political columnists and editorial writers.

Qualified privilege allows news reporters to cover proceedings or events where the need for the public to be informed of the action taking place is more important than for the individual(s) involved to have legal recourse. The use of qualified privilege occurs most frequently in judicial or legislative proceeding reports or in stories concerning government administration. A fair and balanced account of what took place within the privileged arena is necessary for the reporter to plead qualified privilege as a libel defense.

New York Times Rule

In 1964, the United States Supreme Court greatly changed the rules of libel where public officials are concerned, and in later cases extended the ruling to "public figures." In a case involving the *New York Times,* the Court ruled that public officials in order to sustain a libel action would have to prove "actual malice," which the Court defined as "knowing falsehood" or "reckless disregard of the truth." This means that the news story or editorial comment can be in error but still not be libelous unless the reporter knew what he was writing to be false or recklessly disregarded whether it was true or not. The burden of proof is on the public official. He must prove that the newspaper acted under the "actual malice" definition above.

This enlarged freedom from libel, however, ought not to be used by the press as an excuse for sloppy or inadequate reporting. Devotion to accuracy and truth is still the best defense against libel actions.

Retraction and Correction

After a libel threat has been made, and many times to head off the possibility of such a threat, the news media will print or air a retraction of the offending story. Though not a legal libel defense, a retraction sometimes cools the temper and satisfies the plaintiff who is not sure of having a strong case to prove libel in court. The correction column in a newspaper, sometimes labeled *Setting It Straight, Pardon Us* or a similar designation, serves this purpose.

Tell an Editor

If a reporter is in doubt about a story getting into libel trouble, the story should be brought to the attention of the news editor immediately. In almost all situations, the editor or the medium's management will take control. Most news media employ lawyers to handle any libel questions. Wait and clear the story with the editor, rather than rush into print or air the story and face a libel suit.

NEWS SOURCES AND HOW TO USE THEM

Working Illustration

One of the best ways to illustrate the use of news sources is with a working illustration.

It's community fund-raising time again and the city editor asks for several stories about the campaign leaders, financial goal, agencies involved and campaign dates, including the kickoff dinner and first report meeting. The editor's request is relayed to the reporter via a note tucked in the typewriter. The name of the campaign chairperson is given. Nothing else. How does the reporter get all the information necessary to write the story?

Immediately, several avenues of research click in the reporter's mind. If the person had this assignment last year, a personal clip file on the campaign is probably in a desk drawer. In this file, or the one kept in the newspaper or broadcast media's library, will be background information on last year's goal, agencies involved and campaign officials.

The name of this year's chairperson is the next research clue. If the reporter is not familiar with the person, a quick check of the city directory kept in the newsroom will tell the home address and phone number of the person as well as a place of employment. Now the reporter is ready to call the chairperson and get the pertinent information about the campaign.

Community fund raising extends into community fund collecting and this is usually a year-round job. Therefore, a permanent community fund campaign office is maintained, with a full-time executive secretary or director. A call to the office will bring information about this year's campaign. A check of the telephone directory will yield the campaign office number.

Another source of information will be last year's campaign chairperson. If the reporter is unable to reach this year's chairperson, a call to last year's campaign head should put the reporter on the trail of other campaign officials. Last

Most newspapers have full-time librarians . . .

. . . and resource materials that rival many school libraries.

(*far right*)
Newspaper stories are filed according to topic, and reporters have easy access to them.

(*far right*)
Files of complete copies of each day's papers are kept for quick reference. Sometimes a second set is kept for reporters to cut up if a story is needed for their own personal file.

year's leader will no doubt be an active participant in this year's campaign.

While the clips from the previous fund-raising year will list the organizations composing the community fund group, a quick check of the list with the fund secretary or director will spot any deletions or additions to the list for the current year.

After the names of the officers of this year's campaign are learned, the reporter checks the news library for biographical information on the persons. Civically prominent persons have individual folders that include a head and shoulders' picture (called a mug shot or a 1 X 3, indicating the number of columns wide and picture depth in inches). From the news clippings and interviews with the campaign leaders, the reporter should have enough material to write several stories.

Let's look again at the various news sources the reporter used.

The *editor* in giving the reporter the story assignment also gave the reporter a name. Had the reporter been unable to find any other sources, the city editor would have been the first person to ask for help.

Next, the reporter checked his or her *personal news story files* and the *news morgue* for back stories on the campaign. The *city directory* and the *telephone directory* aided the reporter in getting phone numbers and places of employment where news sources might be reached.

Contact with campaign leaders, either personally or via the telephone, provided another avenue of story research.

The Beat

Other sources of news research include the reporter's beat and news releases. Beat, as you will remember from an earlier chapter's definition, is a series of news sources assigned to one reporter who calls or visits them on a regular basis. These news sources may be city officials, such as a municipal court judge, mayor, police chief, health department head, recreation director and the clerks and secretaries in all these and other city offices.

In visiting these offices, as well as attending regular meetings, such as those of the city council, library board and zoning commission, a reporter mingles with many different people. These people represent varied backgrounds and interests, both professionally and socially, and the reporter will pick up story leads and ideas from many of these people.

Also, these people will form a pool of information sources that the reporter may tap as the news need occurs. For example, a city councilperson may be a college dean. When information about a story

Checking out the police blotter is a daily job for the police reporter. Details and leads for many more stories than the reporter can write or follow up are found in this log. The reporter, working against a news deadline, must be able to sort out the important information from the trivial.

City council meetings are a part of the government reporter's beat. Reporters are usually assigned seats near or at the council's table where they have access to all material discussed by or given to the council members. The reporter here is seated on the bench at the left of the picture.

dealing with the college appears, the reporter can call the dean and, if he can not get the story details from this person, he can learn who is the college administrator to contact.

A personal contact in a news story will often reap a reporter more news facts than going through the "official" channels. For this reason, a vital part of the reporter's job consists of cultivating contacts, through being friendly and proving reliability and consistent fairness on all stories.

The News Release

News releases come from a variety of sources. Large businesses and corporations, such as automobile manufacturers, cereal companies, chemical corporations and utilities, to barely scratch the surface of consumer-oriented groups, have two departments—public relations and advertising departments—whose main jobs are to get publicity about the product or service before the public via the news media. There are also private advertising agencies and public relations groups whose sole business is to work with corporations in turning out news releases and advertising materials and come up with publicity-oriented events to catch the media's attention and recognition.

Thus, the average news reporter is besieged with press releases daily from such diverse sources as a movie company sending pictures, movie plot synopses, actors' biographies and prepared interviews for current movies, to documented reports from an independent testing laboratory regarding the new safety features of a tire.

Every civic and social organization with four or more members will have a publicity chairperson whose main function is to get the organization's name in the news and provide a clipping for the club's scrapbook. The PTA, duplicate bridge groups, church circles, flower clubs, Little League associations, camera groups and men's and women's social groups all have publicity officers. And eventually, many with alarming regularity, all these groups will have news items for the reporter.

Some releases will be neatly typed on four pieces of regular typing paper, and after reading the whole thing, the reporter will still not know where the event is or was held, the time, and the person to contact for additional information. Or the news article may come in on a torn grocery bag, looking as though it had been written by a chicken walking across the page through spilled ink. A course in hieroglyphics is not a bad elective for the journalism student.

Rarely will the reporter receive a typed, half-page release with the simple news questions of who, what, when, where, why and how answered. Yet this is the format and information needed for every story. Even the professionals in the large corporations and businesses may omit vital story details at the expense of long-winded puffery about the project at hand. Four pages of words extolling a product's wonders isn't going to get the story into print if the news-release writer didn't bother to include information on the product's availability in the news medium's area, including store names where the enterprising reporter can go or call for information to localize the story.

As a reporter builds a list of personal news sources, these names and phone numbers should be kept in a desk file. This will save the reporter time when a quick piece of information is needed and only the personal phone directory need be consulted.

Reporters specializing in certain areas, such as city government, education or entertainment, should also keep reference material that is germane to each area. Examples would include a listing of all city officials, schedules of city meetings, a listing of all city schools and administrators and a movie encyclopedia.

Specialized areas of a news medium, such as the sports department, women's or family sections and book reviews, will also have special libraries of information including record and rules books, cookbooks and etiquette books and current best sellers.

But remember, resource centers are only as good as the reporter who uses them. A city directory will tell the name of a person, the address, phone number, place of employment and name of spouse, and whether the person rents or owns a home, yet if the reporter doesn't know this information is only a few steps or an arm's length away, what good is it? A new reporter should take a tour of the newsroom and the news library to become familiar with the resources of the news operation the first day on the job.

7 INTERVIEWING—THE ART OF ASKING QUESTIONS

A reporter's job is to get the facts of a news story and present these facts to the public in clear and concise form. The job of getting the facts may be done in several ways. One way is through the press release sent to the reporter. Another is by researching the story through the news medium's morgue, a public library, public records and other resources.

But, probably the most common method by which the reporter gets the facts is by interviewing a participant or an eyewitness to the news event.

There are two kinds of interviews: the prepared-in-advance interview and the on-the-spot interview. A reporter must be able to conduct both.

Prepared-in-Advance Interview

For most reporters, the prepared-in-advance interview is used frequently. This interview takes place when the reporter is either given the assignment to get a story from a specific source or the story on which the reporter is working requires it.

The reporter has time to prepare for the interview, as does the person who is going to be interviewed. Arrangements the reporter should make before arriving for the interview begin with setting an appointment with the person concerned. This can be done most often by telephone. The appointment for the interview should be made at least 24 hours in advance and several days ahead when possible. Story deadline may dictate the lead time for the interview.

Setting Up the Interview

When setting it up, tell the person the reason for the interview. This gives the subject time to prepare for questions to be asked and it will result in a better meeting for both persons. If there is specific information the reporter is seeking, (for example, the foreign exchange program that a local student took part in or a look at the building plans for the new city civic center), tell the person so that at the time of the interview the person will be prepared to give the information sought. If photographs are to be taken, tell the interviewee so that any props (books or a diploma from the exchange student or the maps or a model center from the city official) will be available for the photographer.

Sometimes, reporters prefer to conduct the interview first and then make arrangements for photographs. This allows the reporter to make the decision on what sources available will make the best picture.

In conducting interviews, especially with persons not used to being the subject of press attention, putting the person at ease is most important. The place of the interview will help do this. If possible, the reporter will generally go to the home or office of the person to be interviewed. The interviewee will feel more comfortable in familiar surroundings. If such an arrangement is not possible, then a quiet neutral place such as a conference room should be suggested. The reporter's newsroom usually is not suitable because of the general noise and, to a non-news person, the general confusion that appears to prevail.

After the interview is set up, the reporter should do some homework about the person to be interviewed and the subject of the interview. For the exchange student interview, the reporter should know in advance how and why the student was selected; when the student left and returned; the country where the student studied; the year of school in which the student is; and the student's parents' names and address. Some information on parents' occupations is also easy to obtain in advance. Remember from chapter 6, most, if not all of this information will be found in the news morgue. Stories written about the student when the person was first selected to take part in the exchange program will be on file. A city directory will identify the parents' occupations, if this information is not in the original stories.

When seeking complex information from the person being interviewed, the reporter should compile as many facts as possible before the interview. If such complex information does not come up until the interview, then the reporter should ask for any explanatory documents that clarify it.

Gathering Background Information

In any interview, background information on the person and his or her area of expertise should be gotten by the reporter. This information obtained beforehand will serve several purposes. First, it will allow the reporter to save time getting into the interview because he will not have to ask these questions, and it will tell the interviewee that the reporter has thought enough of the importance of the interview to spend some time preparing for it. Before arriving for the interview, the reporter should quickly review the news clips. If possible, photocopies of the clips should be made for easy reference.

If the interviewee has to spend time explaining basic details, the interview may be switched around, with the interviewee becoming the questioner to learn how much the reporter knows about the subject at hand. As a result, the reporter loses control of the interview at the outset as well as the professional respect of the person to be interviewed. The reporter will also find that after the initial briefing, there is little time left in the interview to ask any questions.

While the exchange student may have all afternoon to spend with a reporter, the city official, who is going to explain the civic center building plans, most likely will not.

The element of time brings up two questions. How much time should be allowed for an interview, and at what time in the interview should the first question be asked?

Allotting time for the interview will be the concern of the person being interviewed. The reporter should ask for a minimum of an hour. A two-hour interview is preferred, but it will take at least an hour to conduct any thorough questioning.

Unless the person to be interviewed is quite at home with the press, a warming-up or a time for establishing rapport with the interviewee will be necessary. This will give the person a chance to draw some impressions about the reporter and should set the tone of the interview. Upon arriving at the interview, the reporter should take a cue from the interviewee on the timing of the first question.

If the person is nervous or apprehensive about being questioned by a reporter, a time must be allowed for the person to get used to having the reporter present. Some remarks about general subjects— yes, even the old saw about the weather—can be used. Some general remarks about the topic to be discussed may serve the purpose of putting the person at ease and at the same time let the person know that the reporter has the necessary background information and interest to handle the interview.

For example, the exchange student might feel an instant rapport if the reporter relates some information about the city in which the student had stayed. A common bond of knowledge between reporter and subject can get the interview off on a positive note. It may help put the interviewee at ease if several easy non-controversial questions come first, such as name spelling, address and professional title. And, the reporter should make certain that the information is correct, by reading or spelling it back.

For the city official with the civic center plans, a few words about the site selection, architect chosen, fund raising or bond proposal will show that homework was done and tell the official that the questions to be asked will come from research on the part of the reporter. But don't try to impress the interviewee with how smart you are. Let the person read your story to find out.

Preparing Questions

The questions to be asked are the most important part of the interview. It is the rare reporter who goes to an interview without questions prepared in advance. Certainly no beginning reporter should arrive at the appointed time and place with an empty notebook and head to match.

Professional reporters intimately familiar with the subject of the interview may wing the questions as the interview progresses, but few reporters will have the time or inclination to become this specialized. So about 10 questions prepared in advance are a must for the reporter on an interview.

Preparing the questions is not difficult. The first question is one the reporter must answer. What is the purpose of the interview? If it is to get the exchange student's impressions of academic life at a foreign school, then the reporter should ask in what courses the student was enrolled. Did the teaching methods vary between the teachers there and here? What were the cultural and social differences between the students there and here? Will credit for the courses taken be transferred to the local school? Questions can also be asked about extracurricular activities, research facilities, punishment for rule infractions and student dress codes.

For the story of the civic center plans, the reporter should seek information about facilities to be included in the center, ground-breaking date, estimated cost, contractors to whom various stages of the building will be assigned (i.e., electrical, plumbing, foundation, carpenter), date the building will be ready for occupancy and penalties, if any, to be assessed if completion date is not met.

As a general rule, prepare specific questions. These will get specific replies. Present the questions in an organized manner. Keep questions on similar areas together. It will aid the continuity of the interview by helping the interviewee organize his or her thoughts on the subject.

The Interview

With an appointment made, background obtained on the person and the subject and a list of questions to be asked, the reporter is ready for the interview. The reporter should arrive at the place of the interview on time—or even a few minutes early—and immediately set about putting the person at ease.

Getting the Interviewee Alone

In some home interviews, other persons may be present with the person to be interviewed. If another person attempts to dominate the scene, the reporter is not going to accomplish the purpose of the interview. The distracting person must be dismissed. The reporter should take the lead and ask the person to be interviewed if there might be some place where the interview could be held so as not to interrupt the normal routine of the other people in the home. If this doesn't work, the reporter may just have to say that for him or her to get the story, more private surroundings are necessary.

Sometimes an additional person or persons with the interviewee can be helpful. But, judgment on the part of the reporter must be exercised. If the person appears distressed at having to face the questions alone, then don't press for privacy or most likely the entire interview will be lost. However, the reporter should not lose control of the interview. This is where those prepared questions come in handy. If the subject or someone else attempts to stray away from the subject, a reference to the question at hand should bring the interview back in line.

Being Flexible

A good interviewer not only asks questions and records the answers, but also listens for comments that will lead to a question not among the ones written down. If the exchange student should mention meeting another person from the reporter's news area while in the foreign country, the reporter should not ignore the information and blithely move on to the next question on the pad. The reporter should follow up and get the name and occasion for the meeting. This will add more human interest to the story. If the subject then strays too far afield, bring the person back with a prepared question. Saying something like: "I find this most interesting, but I realize our time is limited and I have a few other questions I would like to ask you," should bring the interview back to its original course.

Getting Around an Evasive Answer

While looking over the submitted bids for the civic center, the reporter notes that the lowest bid on the electrical work was not the bid accepted. The question "why" draws an inconclusive reply. What does the reporter do now? Re-ask the question. Make sure that the city official understands exactly what is being asked. If the official is still evasive, point out that fact. If the reason still cannot be pinned down, drop the matter and make a mental note to get in touch with another city official who worked on the contract letting and ask him or her. If no satisfactory explanation can be gotten, note the bidding discrepancy in the story and note that no clear explanation for the matter could be obtained from the officials involved. Sometimes just telling the officials involved that this is what will be printed if no explanation can be given will quickly bring out that explanation.

Handling a Lie

What happens if, during the interview, the subject tells a lie and the reporter catches it? The reporter's action will depend on the nature of the lie. If it's a lie about a personal fact, such as age, let it pass. You can document the correct information from other sources. If it is a lie about a major fact in the interview, the reporter must ask introspectively what is to be gained by calling attention to the lie. Will calling attention to it terminate the interview or put the subject in a highly hostile, defensive position, thus negating further attempts to go on? Does recognition of the lie cast doubts on the veracity of the entire interview? Probably the best action is to take no action. Close out the interview as though the subject had not lied and, once back at the office, review the interview and see how the lie affects the overall information gained. If in doubt about what action to take, ask the city editor. *Whenever in doubt about a story, ask the city editor.*

Reading Body Language

Books have been written on the meaning of various body positions. The arms crossed across the chest, the legs crossed at the ankles, the clenched fists—all have special meanings when coupled with words and other actions. Thus, the reporter should be aware of body language as spoken by the person being interviewed. But, a word of warning, don't get so involved in reading the meanings in the movements of the subject's hands, head, mouth, arms and legs that the impact of the words being spoken is lost.

If the candidate who has just lost the election gives the concession speech in a clear, unshaking voice while the hands that grasp the podium are visibly shaking, this paradox of human emotions should be called to reader's/or listener's attention.

The description of body gestures, facial mannerisms and clothing or articles carried by a person should be used to give the reader or listener a visual picture of that person when such an image will add the dimension of reality to the story.

For example, in conveying to his audience a sense of gentleness in a woman celebrating her 100th birthday, the reporter opened his story by describing the woman, as she greeted persons coming to her birthday party, as possessing "a soft voice and easy manner." Later he described her as "slight, bright and gentle." In another description, the reporter wrote: "Her love was manifest in the gleam in her eyes and smiling face as she greeted her many friends . . ."

In a story about a pregnant teen-age runaway, the reporter showed the girl's distress when he wrote: "Sitting uncomfortably on a floor cushion, twisting her hair into tangles, occasionally glancing at a soap opera on TV, the girl says it all with despair."

As the girl tells her story, she cries. The reporter conveys this to the reader with a quote and description. ". . .'And I guess I cry a lot.' Indeed, she does cry a lot. In great sobs, while repeating her story. In small, quiet whimpers, when pausing for breath . . . The girl wipes her eyes with her hair. She looks at the television set."

In using body language descriptions, be careful not to allow these to dominate the copy and become more important than the story of the person being interviewed. Such descriptions should help move the story along and not detour a reader or listener.

Off-the-Record

If, during the course of the interview, the person asks that the following remarks be "off-the-record" or at the outset of the interview says that all information provided in the interview is off-the-record, the reporter should stop the person immediately. The first thing that is necessary is to clarify what both parties, reporter and interviewee, mean by off-the-record. To the reporter, such a request can mean that if agreed to, the reporter is bound by journalistic ethics not to use the information in the story. The interviewee, on the other hand, may just mean that information provided needs to be checked further before using or that it can be used, but not as quoted by the person giving the information. Informed sources is the tag line used in many news stories where attribution of a fact cannot be tied to a specific person.

If the person is asking that the information to be given is not to be used in the story, the reporter may agree, and hear what the person has to say. But once away from the interview, the reporter has every right to attempt to get the same information from another source and use it in the story attributed to the second source.

Two things need to be considered by the reporter before making a decision about honoring the off-the-record request. One, how important a news source is the person asking for the confidentiality? Is it a person with whom a continuing news relationship is likely? Is the reason for the off-the-record request valid? If the person has a valid reason in the reporter's judgment and this person is likely to be a news source again, the reporter, if agreeing to the request, must honor it. If, on the other hand, the person is not likely to be a regular news source and the reasoning for the request is faulty in the reporter's judgment, then the reporter must decide whether to learn what the information is. If the reporter decides that it has valid news value, the reporter may want to use it in the story. However, should the reporter decide to use this information the interviewee should be informed and an explanation given as to why it is not possible to keep it off-the-record.

Right of Review

After the reporter has exhausted the list of questions, the interviewee often asks the toughest question of the interview: "May I read the story before it is printed?"

If caught unaware, the reporter, in stumbling to answer the question, may give the impression of having something to hide in not immediately granting the request. Basically, the answer to the question of the right of review can be handled by explaining that the pressure of deadlines makes the right of review impossible in most cases. Publication is usually the next day or maybe for the same evening's news for the broadcast reporter.

The reporter should ask why the person is seeking the right of review. A quick review of points discussed and the notes taken will probably clarify any questions the interviewee has. It will also give the person confidence in the reporter's professional ability. If, however, the person still insists on reading the story before publication, the reporter should say that the request must be made of the city editor.

Also, the reporter should always ask for the right of calling the person to clarify any notes that might become undecipherable over the next few hours, or for any additional information that might be required once the reporter begins writing the interview story. This prepares the interviewee for the possibility of a call back and also gives him or her confidence in the reporter's concern about accuracy.

In interviewing situations, some reporters prefer to use a tape recorder to make sure that all quotes used are correct. But unless you want to spend an hour or two back at the office listening to the entire interview again, take notes as the person talks. These will provide you with a quick guide to the approximate location in the interview of the material you want.

Pencil Vs. the Tape Recorder

One way to avoid having undecipherable notes is to tape record the interview. With the arrival of the compact reel-to-reel tape recorder and the even more convenient cassette tape recorder, many reporters are now using them as frequently as they once used the pencil and pad.

But, before the novice reporter runs out and buys a recorder or dashes to the college audiovisual center to borrow one for future assignments, there are some considerations to be mentioned. The biggest advantages of taping an interview include having everything said as a permanent record and a safeguard against the accusation by the subject of being misquoted.

But, with exclusive use of the tape recorder comes a problem. If the interview lasted one hour and during that time only the tape recorder was used, the reporter on returning to the newsroom faces relistening to the one-hour taped interview to write the story from it. This is a luxury few news reporters can afford. And few reporters have a secretary to transcribe it.

At the actual interview, another problem can arise. The appearance of the tape recorder in front of the interviewee can bring on a nervous condition accompanied by a tied tongue. The subject immediately realizes that everything said is going to be captured on that machine. Poor grammar, a misused phrase, all those mental lapses filled in with "ahs" and "hmms" are going to be available for the reporter to play back at will. Persons who are frequently interviewed by reporters with pencils and pads are often taken aback and become hesitant to talk freely when a microphone is suddenly thrust before their mouths. And, just as the freedom from misquoting is a plus in the reporter's use of the tape recorder, the same condition becomes a minus for some interviewees who previously were able to cling to that one phrase, "I was misquoted," whenever their words in print caused questions or criticism.

Another disadvantage of the tape recorder is its ability to not function correctly when the record button is not depressed before the interview begins, or the microphone connection looks complete but a blank tape reveals that the plug was not all the way into the recorder sockets.

Unlike the pencil that breaks and the interview stops for a minute while a new one is picked up by the reporter, the malfunctioning tape recorder may not be discovered until the reporter is seated at the typewriter in the newsroom, ready to start writing the story.

Cassette tapes have been known to jam. This is a problem that sometimes occurs on cassettes having 60 minutes of recording tape on one side. Also, extreme cold affects tapes. A recording made on a tape under freezing temperature conditions will have to be played at the same temperature for a true reproduction of the subject's voice. The reason for this is that the tape will contract from the cold exposure when the recording is made. Later, when played back at inside room temperatures, the tape will appear to be running at a slower speed because the tape will have expanded, thus "stretching" the speaker's voice, forcing loss of clarity in the speech pattern.

Now let's look at the old pencil-and-pad method of conducting an interview. Writing down everything said in longhand is an impossible task. As a result, most reporters develop their own brand of shorthand. Few actually use shorthand as used by secretaries. The reason is simple. A shorthand note taker is trained to catch every word spoken. Just the words, not necessarily the meaning. For the reporter, the result could be the same as relying solely on the tape recorder. Once back in the office, the reporter would have to go through the entire interview to pick out the important story facts.

The compromise is usually a mixture of some shorthand symbols and a dash of speed writing, salted with the reporter's own way of shortening words. The result is that the reporter writes and listens at the same time, getting the sense as well as the words on paper. The most frequent problem the pencil-pad user will incur is the breaking of the lead and/or running out of paper. Both problems can be eliminated by carrying several pencils and a note pad.

Of course, the problem with the pencil-pad method is the chance of not getting a quote exactly as it was spoken. The handling of this problem will be discussed in chapter 8, "Dialogue in a News Story."

Perhaps the best interview recording is done by the reporter who combines both the tape recorder and the pencil-pad methods. When the appointment is made for the interview, the reporter should tell the person if a tape recorder is going to be used. This prepares the person for the sight of the microphone and also offers the opportunity for any objections to be made in advance of the interview.

The reporter should check the recorder out before leaving the office. Tape a few minutes of conversation to make sure the operation of the recorder is understood and that it is in proper working order. Take along enough tape, and then add another cassette or reel—just to be sure. Two or three pencils and a full pad of note paper should be added to the interview kit. The pad should already have about ten questions to be asked at the interview written on it.

Once at the interview, the reporter should attempt to establish a rapport with the subject before whipping out the recorder and microphone. It might be a good idea to explain how the machine works to the interviewee if the person appears nervous or curious about the tape recorder. Place the microphone so that it will pick up both voices, but not so conspicuously as to be distracting to the person during the interview. As the interview progresses, the person may tend to ignore the microphone's presence.

Note taking during the interview will facilitate using the tape recorder while writing the story. The notes should parallel the conversation as recorded so that if a certain quote is needed in its entirety, a quick look at the notes will give the reporter an approximation of where on the tape (how far into the interview) the quote will be.

While constant note taking is good during the interview, the person will not want to see just the top of the reporter's head the whole time. Eye contact is important also. It tells the person that the reporter is interested in what is being said. It makes the reporter appear as more than an automated note taker. Put yourself in the place of the interviewee for a minute and you'll quickly realize this.

Points to Remember

To be a successful interviewer, the reporter should do several things. First, make an appointment for the interview, seeking at least an hour of the person's time. Research on the person to be interviewed and the subject matter of the interview should be done in advance and a list of about ten questions prepared.

Before leaving the office, check out any tape-recording equipment to see that it is working properly. Arrive at the appointment on time and set about putting the subject at ease before the interview begins. Start the interview with a prepared question, but during the course of the interview be able to slip in any questions that might come up. Be able to handle an evasive answer or a lie. Note the subject's physical reactions to the questions as well as the verbal ones. And be prepared to answer any off-the-record requests or the question of the right of review.

Having covered these points in the course of the interview, both the reporter and the subject should be happy with the published or broadcast results.

On-the-Spot Interview

The other interview takes place on the spot. This means the reporter conducts an interview without advance preparation. It might happen when the reporter is sent out to cover a disaster, such as a fire, accident or murder. It also can occur when the reporter is sitting comfortably in the newsroom and a legislator comes in unexpectedly with a statement.

The talent most necessary for a reporter in the on-the-spot interview is an ability to think fast. Rarely will the reporter conduct an on-the-spot interview in a totally foreign subject area. These interviews most often occur while the reporter is covering a beat or has been sent out by an editor to cover something in the reporter's beat

On-the-spot interviews can happen anywhere. Here, golfer Bobby Nichols is interviewed in a press tent on the golf course after winning an Iowa tournament.

area. Therefore, the reporter should have some background information on the interviewee or the subject to be discussed.

However, if the reporter is caught in a situation where the news to be obtained is completely foreign to his or her assigned news areas, the reporter with a good liberal arts background and general curiosity about the world will be best able to respond. An ability to lead the subject into conversation is vital. No matter how little information the reporter has about the subject, use of this knowledge may be just enough to open up the subject. Questions can then be formed from what the subject says.

Be Prepared

The worst fate to befall a reporter faced with an on-the-spot interview is to be caught without the tools to record it. Reporters should always carry a pencil or pen and some paper.

Sometimes a reporter will have a chance for some rapport-setting conversation before conducting the interview, but most on-the-spot interviews occur spontaneously and are off and running from the start. A reporter must be able to adjust to the situation. Be flexible. The reporter who needs the rapport-setting introduction will be left standing alone by the time he or she has established enough rapport to ask a first question.

News is a competitive business. Those who succeed are the reporters who can adjust to any news situation; ask pointed, tough questions under pressure; get answers;—then, return to the newsroom and write a clear, concise account and meet their news deadline.

8 DIALOGUE IN A NEWS STORY

Newsmakers always have something to say. Their comments, reported in a story, can sometimes put an aspect or a point in perspective or provide the exact mood or feeling that could be gotten across in no other way.

Job of Direct Quotations

A first-person narrative by an eyewitness to a disaster will bring home to the reader or listener the horror of the event faster than any secondhand attempt by a reporter. Sometimes the reporter is also the eyewitness. Such was the case on May 6, 1937, in Lakehurst, N.J., as radio reporter Herbert Morrison stood in a field awaiting the arrival of the German dirigible *Hindenburg.* As the huge airship came into its mooring area, Morrison reported matter of factly:

It is practically standing still now.

Then he shouted:

It burst into flames! It's falling on the mooring mast! It's one of the worst catastrophes in the world!

At that point Morrison became hysterical and the rest of his comments were incoherent.

Morrison's report was recorded. Today, those words, delivered by a calm voice that became hysterical as the Hindenburg burst into flames, have been heard by most journalism students who have ever listened to records of the great moments in radio.

Show Emotion

Emotional impact can be truly recorded only by the broadcast media. Nothing can replace the actual voices of people making news. However, the print reporter can do the next best thing. Using direct quotations in stories can give as much as possible of the flavor of the moment being recorded as possible.

For example, turn to chapter 14 on feature writing and read the section on the murder of Gerald Franklin (page 144). Through direct quotes from the eulogy given by the rabbi who conducted Franklin's funeral service, the first insight into Franklin's life is given the reader. It showed a man who had few friends, had a temper, was a generous tipper and loved his four children. Then move on to the interviews with Franklin's friends, business associates and contacts. Note how the reporters build a humanistic picture of the murdered man. The reader is made to know the man as the persons who dealt with him on a daily basis knew him.

It's a reporting technique that quickly draws readers into a story and involves them. Who can better tell a story than the person who has lived it? Again, in chapter 14, (page 149) there is the story of the mother who wrote to an Action Line column to seek help for her son who was in the Marines. The Action Line writer contacted a state senator and soon the young man was home with an honorable discharge from the Marine Corps.

A reporter talked with the youth and brought the readers up-to-date on the story after the paper's Action Line had entered the picture. The reporter used the technique of direct quotes and let the ex-Marine tell the story, after setting the scene:

> After his release from the medical platoon, Snyder was reassigned to a new training unit. As soon as he reported, he said, he was called into an orderly room.
>
> "Five or six drill instructors then proceeded to beat me for half an hour," Snyder said. "One held me by the throat, nearly choking me, while the others worked me over with their fists.
>
> "They called me a 'slime' for 'squealing' to the Senator. They told me that I couldn't call home any more, and when I sent letters I would write only what they wanted me to write."

The story then relates that Snyder's mail was opened, he was ordered to perform 100 "bends and thrusts," a type of exercise, to climb a rope and to run two miles. Unable to complete these requirements, the drill instructors threatened him with imprisonment for "disobedience of a direct order."

> "By this time," Snyder said, "I couldn't take it any more."

He readily accepted the discharge offered by his regimental commander, Col. Edmund G. Derning. Derning was asked about the brutality charges. Again the reporter let direct quotes by Derning tell the story.

> "You have to remember that our drill instructors are dedicated men who want to turn out fine Marines," he said. "But there's always the possibility of someone going overboard.

We're going to investigate Pvt. Snyder's allegations completely."

Snyder again, summing up his attitude and the story, said:

"I feel very badly about all of this," Snyder said. "I really wanted to be a Marine. My father was one, and proud of it. I joined up to play in the Marine Corps band, and I wish it had been possible for me to finish training. But it was impossible under those conditions."

Snyder's mother had the last words.

"This isn't something you expect to see in America . . . That Marine base makes me think of a concentration camp."

Add Credibility

The use of direct quotes in a story adds credibility as well as human interest to the story. In another example—the story's headline reads: "Parked Car Is Couple's Home." The reporter sets the scene and then acts as narrator, moving the story along between the direct quotes of the persons involved.

A New York couple, the Konarskys, were living in their car "parked beside a sludgy river in a backwater section of the Bronx." They had been there for about eight months. Their landlord raised their apartment rent, and the Konarskys (he was 59, with an arthritic arm that forced him to quit his work; she was 55 and in poor health, unable to climb stairs—a point that made apartment renting difficult), moved onto the boat of a friend.

"It was comical, really," Konarsky says. "I had a lot of time so I fixed up the boat. Then somebody saw it and bought it, so we were out of a place to stay. That was the first time we went to the car."

The couple refused, at first, to go on welfare.

"I kept thinking: well, I just banged my arm, it will heal up," he says. "I was just monkeying around, thinking we could get away without it."

After a short stay in a room in back of a store—that was soon rented —the couple sold some of their furniture, stored in a friend's garage, to pay for motel lodging.

"It was $16.80 for the cheapest room," Konarsky says. "One night was all we could take."

The couple went back to their car. Winter came. Huddling under blankets for warmth, salvaging copper wire from abandoned cars to sell, digging steamer clams in Long Island Sound to eat, the Konarskys finally faced a day when they were down to their last can of beets. They decided to abandon their pride. They went to the welfare office, where they were turned away.

> "They told me I couldn't get any because we didn't have a permanent address," he says.
>
> A welfare spokesman said they refused to answer questions about their backgrounds. He also noted that their clothes seemed so neat and the car so well kept.
>
> "We got some water from the hydrant and got fixed up to go down there," Konarsky explains. As for the car, "I don't have much else to do but keep it nice."
>
> Now the Welfare Department says it is looking into the couple's case again. Meanwhile the Konarskys continue to live in the car, sitting in it by day, sleeping in it by night and driving to Mamaroneck for clams when they have enough gas.

Place Emphasis

Direct quotes will also place emphasis on a point the reporter is trying to make. In two stories on the murder of Catherine (Kitty) Genovese, in chapter 11 (page 95) the point of the *New York Times* follow-up story was to emphasize that a woman was killed while 38 witnesses did nothing—not even place an anonymous call to the police until it was too late.

The *New York Daily News* story played the murder for its sensationalism. Both newspaper stories carried her final words in direct quotations. Yet let's see how each newspaper played the same quote to make its own point.

The *New York Times:*

> Miss Genovese screamed: "Oh, my God, he stabbed me! Please help me! Please help me!"

The *New York Daily News:*

> "I've been stabbed! I've been stabbed!" the brunette gasped.

The *Times* by carrying the pleas for help, reinforced the impact of the neighbors ignoring the plea. Use of the verb *scream* implies that the words were said loud enough to be heard. The *News,* ignoring the story angle of the neighbors' refusal to aid the dying woman, used the verb *gasped*—a word that hardly implies force enough to carry the message beyond a few feet of the speaker. The omission by the *News* of the repeated cries for help also puts full emphasis of the story with the victim.

Establish Rapport

The use of dialogue in a personality story quickly gives the reader a feeling of rapport with the subject. As the person reads the story, a feeling of having the subject talking directly to the reader is developed. Direct dialogue brings the subject alive, with opinions, thoughts and reactions to the questions asked.

Adds Life to Story

A good dialogue writer will bring any scene to life and have the characters act out the drama so that the reader hears what's going on as well as sees it. Part of making dialogue come alive lies in having the speaker become as real as possible to the reader. One way to accomplish this is by interjecting into the dialogue the person's speech patterns. The result is that people who already know the subject will recognize the person by *the way he or she speaks.* Readers not acquainted with the subject may identify the speech pattern as like their own or someone they know.

For example—Angelo Mango is an actor. During the summer, he stars in a summer stock theater in Michigan. According to the reporter who wrote the working story, Mango talks with dashes. He interrupts himself to interject another thought, dash—dash, and then he is back on the track of the original subject. Sometimes, his thoughts tumble forth so fast that not all the words in the translation get out before Mango is on to another thought. When the reporter interviewed him for a personality profile, she incorporated his speech pattern into the story. Some excerpts follow:

> Angelo Mango has been the sweetheart of the Barn Theatre for the last nine summers, but what makes him such a favorite?
>
> It is true he is a fine actor but that magical quality that captivates audiences is more than just talent; it is love and respect.
>
> All conversation with Angie gets back to those two things. He has an unqualified love and respect for his coworkers, the audiences and himself.
>
> "My mother—a sweet lady—always told us, 'If you can't make people happy, don't make them unhappy.' She taught us to respect life," he said.
>
> To Angie, this is an important part of acting.
>
> "You've got to be in love with theater and the audience wants to feel some of that love. It's a two-way thing. You've got to have a happy company," he emphasized. "And you cannot con the audience. It's beautiful to be a part of this."
>
> How successful he is at this is demonstrated by the fan mail

and other personal responses he receives from audiences (and it is not just the ladies that think Angelo is terrific).

The last time he came to Battle Creek (which he said he digs) to shop, it took two hours because of people stopping him in stores and on the street who recognized him and wanted to talk.

He has no false humility when it comes to fans. He loves it.

"Hey, don't kid yourself, for me part of (being an actor) is an ego trip," he admitted. "People don't come to (theater) to be depressed, uh-uh baby, they come, maybe to learn, but mostly to be entertained."

"I know it cost them for those tickets, maybe a babysitter and dinner—I'm going to give them the best I can for their enjoyment," he said, in his habitual way of leaving a gap between what he says and what he is trying to say. (The actor in him is always apparent as his hands, face and body accent everything he says).

Ego-satisfaction may be part of the reward for acting, but Angelo works hard for it.

"Theater is work—it's my job—it's my life. I take it very seriously—it's not fun and games," he asserted.

Note, however, that speech patterns do not mean speech accents. If a person ends every sentence with *you know,* or interjects into most sentences the word *man,* this is a speech pattern. But, if a person speaks a broken English—that is, placing native tongue pronunciations on English words, *dat* for that, *dose* for those, avoid attempting to work this language aberration into the story unless it's necessary for meaning or interest. While the ear may pick up the English meaning of the words, the eye will only stumble over the words. It will confuse and slow the reader down, detracting from the story's main message. Few fiction writers are capable of writing plausible, smooth-reading accent dialogue. The average news reporter should avoid it altogether. The way around using direct quotes is to paraphrase the person. This technique will be discussed later in this chapter.

Let Subject Tell Story

What's the best way to describe what an artist, a musician, a conductor does? Let the person do it in his or her own words. A midwestern symphony conductor was interviewed and asked about his work. The reporter, using direct quotations, lets him explain.

First, on working with the musical score:

"I focus on every notation—every note, symbol and description. I organize it in my mind and see what it sounds like. I have to hear with my eyes; and that's not easy," he explained.

On conducting:

> "A conductor must command authority as a human being
> and on his knowledge of the score," Bill said. "A conductor
> also must use subtlety, diplomacy, cajoling and humor to
> convince 70 people to do what the conductor wants."
>
> "My prime responsibility is to my own conscience but the
> age of the dictatorial conductor is long gone," he said.

On his music:

> "I do it for the contact with the music literature. I don't get
> an ego trip out of it—I'm much too shy. I don't approach
> the orchestra with a sense of expressing my ego.
>
> "We're in it together. We make music together. I have a
> responsibility and so do they. I respect their ability on their
> instruments and their sensitivity as human beings.
>
> "What it boils down to," he said, "is that the music is the
> pleasure."

To paint the best word picture of a person, combine the colorful
dialogue with a colorful description. Read the following and see if your
impression doesn't match the headline writer's.

Merry Grandmother Finds
Joy, Humor in World of Art

Art is many things to many people, but surely few get the
rollicking enjoyment from it that Peg Clagett does . . .

She stands about 5-foot-1, wears a large Mickey Mouse
watch and carries a little wire purse which is shaped like a
chicken. Her light brown hair is pulled tightly back into a
stubby ponytail near the top of the back of her head.

She wears short, straight bangs and her distinctive face is
highlighted by almost-invisible eyebrows (very blonde), a
sagging chin and engraved smile-lines at the corners of her
eyes and mouth.

She jumped into art about 20 years ago and hasn't come up
for air since . . .

Although she is the wife of a prominent attorney . . . and she
sells much of her art, she remains an earthy merry person
who finds humor in almost everything—including her own
art work.

"When you're painting you sit awfully close to the canvas
—because your arm is not that long," she chuckled as she
began one of her stories. "I did a painting once of a girl,
barefooted, with a guitar. I took it home and hung it on the
wall to look at it.

"I kept looking at it and then I said to my son, 'Do you know
what's wrong with this?'

"He said, 'Ya, she's got two right feet!' "

"Oh, I laughed," she said, roaring hilariously at the memory. "That just killed me it was the funniest thing . . ."

"My family has gotten used to me," she said. "One time my children had some friends over and the friends kept watching me. I felt I was on exhibit." Her children later explained to her: "Other people don't have mothers like you!"

One pitfall she warns beginning artists of is becoming "too happy with themselves. . . . . ."

To remind herself of this pitfall, she has an early creation sitting outside her door, which she calls her humble pot.

"It's the worst looking thing I ever saw," she said.

Short Quotes Are Effective

Sometimes long excerpts of dialogue are not necessary to paint a word picture of a person. A simple, four-word quotation from a world-famous figure probably provoked more commentary and sparked more writers and editorialists to take pen in hand in response than any other quote made by the man. The quotation:

"I'm not a crook!"

The speaker: Former President Richard M. Nixon

Quotes Serve Dual Purpose

In straight news stories involving a controversial topic, the use of direct quotes serves a dual purpose. They explain the problem and allow the reader to draw an independent conclusion about the persons involved.

The following example story concerns a book burning ordered by the school board in Drake, N.D., a community of 600 persons. Kurt Vonnegut's novel, *Slaughterhouse Five,* was the first book to be burned. Others on the list to be burned included 60 copies of *Deliverance* by James Dickey, and *Short Story Masterpieces,* an anthology of stories by Hemingway, Faulkner, Steinbeck and others.

The following are quoted excerpts from The Associated Press story.

. . . "They got the books out of the classrooms and that's all we asked," said Mrs. Lester Berger. "Now I wish we could just let it die . . ."

. . . "The newspapers and radio and television make it sound like we burned some hard-cover classics," said one school board member who asked not to be named. "You know what we burned? We burned some cheap paperbacks."

... "If you read this book (*Slaughterhouse Five*) you know it can be taken only one way," she said. "A man with any gift would not write such filth ... It's nobody's business in New York, Chicago or Bismarck."

... "The school board decided the books were obscene and they were backed by some of the local clergy," said Mrs. Bruce Severy, whose husband was teaching from the books.

... "Severy said he chose *Slaughterhouse Five* for its modern style, brevity and because it deals with current problems "in an honest and straightforward manner."

... "Severy said he had not received threats he would be fired or forced to resign. "But the school board has made it clear to me that I wouldn't be rehired next year," he said.

... Dellis Schrock, president of the State Council of English Teachers, said, "We know that any book to which no one objects is probably valueless."

Feature Story Dialogue

Feature stories are best told with a generous use of direct quotations. Rarely will the reporter be called on to translate straight facts into dialogue—but it can happen, as with the story of the reporter who interviewed a turtle.

By PIEPY KIBLER
As Told To
KATHY RICKETTS
Herald Staff Writer

"I'll never forget the day I crossed the Mexican border for the last time ... it was in the trunk of a car with 300 pals and was it HOT," said Piepy ...

Opening a feature with a quote is an attention-getting device, as well as an interest-provoking one. Piepy was impounded at the border by officials and later given to an Iowa family, the Kiblers. What might have been just a bright feature, two or three paragraphs long, was turned into an interesting, 19-paragraph story with four pictures. The trick was to interview the Kiblers and then put their answers into direct quotes from Piepy—allowing the turtle to tell the story. Some results follow:

It took Piepy several months to become used to the Kiblers. "It wasn't that I didn't like the folks, it was just that I wasn't used to humans and missed the old gang down south of the border.

... "One nice thing about residing with the Kiblers is that I have really learned a lot about football and they even have it on a moving screen called TV. That's where I first learned about it. We have a lot of good times on Monday night sitting around the set (munching lettuce leaves) and watching the pigskin fly past.

"Those Kiblers kids sure keep me busy too, they take me to school all the time and even entered me in a race with a frog. Well, of course I won. I even took top honors in a pet parade with the boys one year," said Piepy.

. . . "Boy I remember one time I got out. I really scared the carpet layer that day. The Kiblers had shut me up in the back room so this guy could put the carpeting down. Well, he got the job done and went and fetched the Mrs. for her inspection and I snuck out. The guy about fell over from shock. He thought I was a big roach. Now do I look like a bug??

. . . "Yup, things are pretty comfortable here . . . with the Kiblers, except for those basement stairs. I just can't seem to make it up them without landing on my back. And that rocking on my shell can sure shake a fella up."

To accurately record and use direct quotations in a news story is a natural talent of a few reporters and an acquired technique for most. It is acquired through hard work. Developing a good shorthand and good ear for the quotable statement is a must.

The Art of Paraphrasing

To paraphrase is to restate a direct quote by putting it in third person context. For example: "I am not a crook," can be paraphrased to—former President Nixon said he was not a crook.

Paraphrasing serves the reporter in several ways. Sometimes in giving a statement, a person wanders from the topic and then wanders back. To give the direct quote, the reporter would have to use ellipsis marks (three dots . . .) several times in the quotation to show that not all of what was said is recorded. If the quotation is long and involved, it serves the reader better to have the remarks paraphrased.

Moves Story Quickly

Also, in many news stories, paraphrasing moves the story along more quickly. For example, in the following story two escapees from a county jail are caught in a field. The only direct quote in the 11-paragraph story is their response as a patrolman surprised them in the field. The two men "surrendered with cries of 'don't shoot!' " Note that the story loses no impact through the use of the paraphrasing.

The men surrendered meekly to Brady. Their biggest concern upon capture was when they would be allowed to eat.

They said hunger was the worst thing they had to face after their escape . . .

The men admitted stealing a car on the south edge of Tipton shortly after their escape and later abandoning it. They told of staying in a cornfield Friday afternoon and watching an airplane as it circled overhead looking for them.

Gives Story Perspective

In interviews, the combining of direct quotes and paraphrasing is done often. If an explanation is long or is given in bits and pieces, paraphrasing helps put the statement in proper perspective to the problem. Again, an example will illustrate.

The story concerned a fellow who does motorcycle jumps. He wanted to stage a jump over a fountain in a community park during a summer celebration. Ramps would have to be built on both sides of the fountain. The goal of the jump was to be 130 feet at 100 miles an hour.

> "It would draw thousands," says Truckenmiller.
>
> Agreed, says Jim Marshall, who is a member of the board of directors of Riverboat Days, but such a crowd would present problems of space and probably would mean changing the location of various other attractions at the affair.
>
> That was one reason the board vetoed the plan, says Marshall. Another major reason was that the board did not have the $5,000 fee Truckenmiller requested for the stunt.

Note that paraphrasing can read like a direct quote, *but it is not.* The above paraphrase is a summation of all the thoughts that Marshall verbalized to the reporter. Most likely they rambled, perhaps going into detail on what attractions would have to be moved and naming places that these attractions could and could not go. Marshall may have talked about the expenses involved in staging the whole celebration and showed how the total budget could not be stretched to meet the $5,000 jump fee.

The reporter simply cut out all the unnecessary fat from the statement and put the meat of the refusal to allow the motorcycle jump in three sentences. Because space limitations are severe in most newspapers, this is an important device.

Aids Reporter

Paraphrasing is a most helpful tool for a reporter who is not a fast note taker. Getting the gist of the remarks and then paraphrasing the statements may lose some impact, but not the sense of what was said. Also, if the direct quote is in a sensitive area, an accusation, a defense, a detailed statement of purpose or something similar, the reporter will want to be very careful in using a direct quote to make sure that every word is correct and in the exact order in which the person said it. If the interview was not tape recorded and the reporter doubts the word-for-word accuracy of his or her notes, the best solution is to paraphrase what was said with proper attribution.

Most persons reading something they said a day or two earlier will not remember the exact positioning of the words they spoke. They will remember the gist of what they said.

In most straight news stories, reporters can say something more clearly and concisely than most speakers. It is necessary to use direct quotes when the material may be libelous, suspect, or technical, or just because the speaker said it better than anyone else could (after all, who could rewrite the late General Douglas MacArthur's statement, "I shall return," into anything more concise or clear?), but, otherwise, paraphrasing gets to the point of a story—and that's the reporter's main job.

Avoid Dialect Quotes

Remember what was said earlier about speech patterns? A person reading a direct quote of what he or she has said that contains awkward sentence construction and/or poor English grammar will become furious at being made to look foolish in the public eye. Even if the person was quoted precisely, there will be a cry of misquote. If such revelations of a person's poor command of spoken English serve no legitimate news purpose, why use them? This is one reason for the use of paraphrasing.

On the other hand, never clean up the poor grammar of a person and then use his or her statement in a direct quotation.

Certainly one of the most difficult persons to quote must have been Casey Stengel, former baseball manager of the New York Yankees and later of the Mets. His murder of the English language merited him the distinction of having his own language, "Stengelese," according to sports writers. To clean up his imaginative malapropisms for a direct quotation would bring cries of "he doesn't talk that way" from anyone who ever listened to the man interviewed on a sports program.

The same might be true of any person with a definite speech pattern. Change it in a direct quotation and the reporter may invite a cry of misquote.

It is also true of working with paraphrasing. While a person might not remember exactly what he or she said, how it was said will be remembered. If the interview was informal and the conversation the same, don't use big words in paraphrasing. The speech pattern of the speaker should be remembered. Make the paraphrase sound like what the person said. If the person reads the story and says, "That doesn't sound like me," he or she might just be convinced that indeed that was not what was said and claim a misquote. Certainly, further encounters with the same reporter will be treated with reserved suspicion as to what is said being changed in print. The result could be a limited statement, if a statement at all.

In sum, then, direct quotes can make a feature come alive by establishing a rapport between the reader and the person being interviewed. Dialogue moves a story along and builds credibility when a situation, problem or conclusion is given in the subject's own words. But, with the use of direct quotes, comes the reporter's responsibility to take quick, accurate notes—or use a tape recorder—and to reproduce the quotes, as the person said them, in the story.

When such is not possible, a reporter should paraphrase what has been said. In paraphrasing, the reporter puts the gist of what was said in simple, clear sentences attributing them to the person who made them.

When to use direct quotes and when to use paraphrase is left to the judgment of the reporter.

TIME TO WRITE— THE LEAD

The hardest part of the story to write is the lead. It also is the most important part of the story. After the headline, the lead must catch the listener's/reader's attention and hold the person for the rest of the story. Once written, the other story facts or body of the story will fall into place.

What are the important facts of the story contained in the lead? First, a reporter must be familiar with all the facts of the story before deciding on which are more important. The old journalistic rule of who, what, when, where, why and how still holds value today. But, perhaps the most important one, or at least the one that will separate the reporters from the technicians, is one referred to by the late Walter A. Steigleman in his journalism classes at the University of Iowa as the WHAMMY.

The Whammy

The whammy, Dr. Steigleman would explain, is that fact that makes the story unique. The one item that makes a particular bike theft in New York's Central Park different from any other bike theft that occurred there: the bike belonged to John F. Kennedy Jr.

Certainly, the person involved also qualifies under the "W," who. And so it is that the whammy of the story is found sometimes in the presence of another "w" or even the "h." But, sometimes, the whammy is not that evident.

For example, there was the woman who committed suicide in London. She was elderly, not well known, and she hanged herself. There are probably several such self-inflicted deaths by elderly women over the course of a year in London. Why did this one make the American newspapers? Because of the reason for the suicide as written in a note left by the woman. She wrote that she was worried about her garden, a boiler in her house "and now this decimal calculator. It's worrying me that I cannot understand it."

The woman was referring to England's changing to the new decimal currency. A sharp-eyed reporter bothered to read the suicide note and the "why" became the "whammy."

Here's one where all the "w's" and "h" can be answered without uncovering the whammy.

A circus python drops dead in Milan, Italy, of a heart attack.

Everything is accounted for. Who/What—phython. What—dies. Where—Milan, Italy. When—Nov. 5 (dateline of story). Why and how —heart attack. The whammy? The snake dropped dead after biting its trainer, who said ill pythons often bite. The trainer was not seriously hurt from the nonpoisonous bite.

For the nonbeliever, one more. This one with a double whammy.

A Maine woman is arrested for driving a car without an inspection sticker. She appears in court. Pleads guilty and is fined $15.

Who—woman. What—is arrested, appears in court, pleads guilty, fined $15. Why—driving car without inspection sticker. When—June 5. Where—Presque Isle, Maine. Where is the double whammy?

First, the woman appeared in her own son's court. The son, the judge, fined her $15. And the second whammy? The courtroom, on the third floor of a former hospital, was a converted hospital delivery room, the same one in which the last time the woman appeared she gave birth to a son—the judge.

Well, sometimes truth is stranger than fiction. And it is the alert reporter who proves it by digging out such stories from the routine of the beat.

How did the reporters in each of these stories convert the whammy into a lead? Here are the leads for the stories:

One of the reasons an elderly woman committed suicide was because she could not understand Britain's new decimal currency, a coroner determined recently.

* * *

A circus python bit its trainer's hand and dropped dead yesterday.

* * *

Judge Julian W. Turner fined his mother, Mrs. Marjorie Turner, $15 Thursday in the room in which he was born.

Simple? Of course, for the reporter with an eye for the best facts of the story. These leads have several technical points in common. Note the length of the sentences and the fact that each lead consists of only one sentence. The suicide story opens with 23 words. The python story lead contains 11. And the judge fines his mother in the room of his birth is only 20 words.

All the leads clearly and concisely get the gist of the story in 23 or less words. This is a feat quite common to most reporters and one to be cultivated by the neophytes.

Kinds of Leads

The Inverted Pyramid Lead

The ability to fill the lead with the main story facts is called writing an inverted pyramid lead. The main facts of the story are presented first, with the rest or supplemental facts laid in place in descending order of their importance. This kind of story building has several advantages.

First, it lets the reader have the gist of the story in a few words at the opening, as already illustrated. Earlier, in defining a lead, the idea of having the reader quickly learn the story facts allowed exiting at various points in the story. It also facilitates the editor who must cut the story to have it fit into a predetermined number of inches on the newspaper page. The editor starts with the bottom paragraph, containing the least important story facts, and works upward, cutting out paragraphs until reaching the point at which the story slips into the news hole.

The inverted pyramid is the traditional method of writing news stories. But, it is not the only way. The suspended interest lead is one used frequently with short, human interest stories.

Suspended Interest Lead

The suspended interest lead gets its name from the fact that the most important element of the story—that which normally would be in the first sentence—is kept from the reader, or suspended, until the end of the story. Some sample stories will illustrate this:

> Being very closely followed by a strange car was most disturbing for a woman driver in Globe, Ariz.
>
> After three blocks, she could stand it no longer and pulled over to the curb. But the car behind trailed right along and stopped at the curb too.
>
> Determined to find out what was up, the woman driver jumped out to investigate.
>
> To her surprise and horror, she discovered that she had been towing another automobile, whose bumper had caught her own car in a parking lot.

*　*　*

> The bride and groom got a particularly big batch of valuable wedding presents. Among them was a pair of theater

tickets with a note written in lipstick: "Guess who sent them?" Shrug. Didn't matter, they used said tickets that weekend, enjoyed the play immensely, and returned after midnight to find their apartment cleaned out completely, all the gifts gone. Scrawled on the bathroom mirror in lipstick was the message: "Now you know."

Summary Lead

Another type of lead that can be used to open a story is called the summary lead. This lead is used frequently by a reporter writing a story about a meeting covered. Sometimes, several important items appear on the agenda and the reporter is hard put to pick one over the other for the lead. So, the reporter uses two or three items in the lead. A hypothetical example:

> The city commission Tuesday accepted the resignation of city manager John Doakes and approved the promotion of John Doe to police chief.

Summary leads are also popular among police reporters who must handle numerous police reports in compiling their story. Here are two examples:

> Money, whiskey, guitars, cases of nails and gasoline were stolen in a series of 12 break-ins reported today and Wednesday in the city and Pennfield Township.

Using a humorous introduction, a reporter uses two paragraphs to sum up a busy weekend for police.

> The Easter Bunny wasn't the only one busy over the week-end. Police were kept on the hop, chalking up 16 arrests including five juveniles.
>
> The charges ranged from possession of stolen property, resisting arrest, carrying a concealed weapon, possession of beer as a minor and illegal possession of marijuana.

Feature story writers often use summary leads. Here is an example:

> In its first 10 years, the Peace Corps has sent volunteers to improve the Philippine rice harvest, restore the Grand Mosque in Tunis, repair city buses in Guinea and dig innumerable latrines.
>
> They have also picketed Vice-President Spiro T. Agnew in Afghanistan, been officially kicked out of 10 countries, "liberated" two floors of the agency's Washington headquarters during a sit-in, and drunk great quantities of native beer. One volunteer was eaten by a crocodile.

Teaser Lead

Another lead, most frequently used in feature stories, is the teaser lead. This is a lead resembling the suspended interest lead, in that the most important facts are omitted. In the teaser lead, however, these facts may be revealed in the second or later paragraph. They are not left until the story's end.

The teaser lead's job is just what the name says—to tease the reader with a few hints into wanting to read more of the story and find out what happened.

Here are some teaser leads:

Mrs. Georgia Lange is probably one of the few people in the country to feel police brutality by a meter maid.

(The story tells of a woman motorist blocked from backing out of a parking space by a meter maid and then handed an overtime parking ticket. The ticket cost the woman 25 cents.)

* * *

Five feet six inches tall, and 175 pounds of muscle and scar tissue. Fast as a cat, strong as a bear. And mean. Very mean. Yessir, she's quite a girl.

(Story deals with the woman skaters in the roller derby.)

* * *

Tommy Bennett, 22 months, had been unlocking the back door at his home all summer, but when it really counted the other day, he clutched.

(It was 49 degrees out when Tommy's mother, coatless, went out to hang up laundry and Tommy locked the door behind her. After 35 minutes, Mom finally persuaded Tommy—using a loud, angry shout—to open the door.)

Teaser leads should never be used with stories dealing in tragedy.

John Probasco doesn't have to search for his daughter any longer.

(Daughter, Brenda, 4, was found dead in a creek.)

What Is a Good Lead?

There is no one answer to the question, "What is a good lead?" The purpose of the lead, remember, is to state briefly the most important facts of the story and to make the reader want to finish the story. Thus, any lead that makes the reader do this must be judged a good lead, at least by that particular reader. Here are some leads that caught this reader's eye:

Police arrested Newton Foster of Sedalia Friday and booked him for "disorderly conduct by biting Mrs. Scroggins' dog." He was released on $100 bond pending appearance in city court.

* * *

Police say the woman whose body was found in a home freezer apparently had been shot in the head last Aug. 4, her birthday.

* * *

A kitchen fire about 2:15 p.m. Wednesday caused about $2,500 damage to the home of N. J. Jenks, 504 Woodhaven, Delta Township firemen reported.

* * *

Bernice Gera broke professional baseball's umpiring sex barrier Saturday night, then abruptly quit after officiating at her first game.

The next time a news story catches your eye, stop and ask yourself what was it about the story that made you want to read it. What piques your curiosity will probably catch other readers, too. Don't be afraid to try it in your news writing. One of the best textbooks for news writing is the daily newspaper. The newswriting student should read several papers each day, the hometown and state papers and a metropolitan paper, as well as watch television news, local and national, and catch a radio newscast. News magazines should also be on the student's reading list. All of these sources provide the student with hundreds of newswriting examples every day—good and bad.

Start a collection of news stories considered good and bad. It will make you aware in your own writing of the reader's criteria for a good lead. If you won't read the lead, why would anyone else?

What Is a Bad Lead?

The antithesis of the summary lead is the news-cram lead in which the reporter cannot decide which fact to lead off with so every available "w" and "h" is included. An example:

Mary J. Doe, 18, daughter of Mr. and Mrs. John Doe of 2121 Nowhere St. and sponsored by Technical High School, was named Miss Opinion Poll Wednesday in ceremonies held at Wilson Auditorium.

It's all there in 33 words. Who—Mary Doe. What (named)—Miss Opinion Poll. When—Wednesday. Where—Wilson Auditorium. How —sponsored by Technical High School. But need it be?

> Mary J. Doe, 18, of 2121 Nowhere St., was named Miss Opinion Poll Wednesday.

In 14 words, isn't that what happened? The rest of the information is important, but it can be used in the body of the story just as effectively as in the lead.

In weeding out facts from the news-cram lead, let's look at the judgment used. In a story, all persons must be clearly identified. There are two types of identification, primary and secondary, as stated in chapter 5.

In the example lead, both primary and secondary identification information is given. To shorten the lead, removal of the secondary identification, parents' name and the school affiliation, was all that was necessary. Location of the proceedings was dropped because it was past history. No one would be rushing over to the Wilson Auditorium now to see the ceremonies, so its importance lies only in recording the fact of where the event took place. This is a fact belonging in the body of the story.

Misplaced Modifier

> Sister Anna Mary is a Mount St. Clare nun with a face that beams of gentleness and an invitation to a hanging among her worldly souvenirs.

A misplaced modifier in this lead would have the reader believing that Sister Anna Mary's face beams of an invitation to a hanging as well as of gentleness. Actually the writer was attempting to present a contrast between a gentle-looking nun and the fact that one of her prized journalistic trophies was an engraved invitation to the hanging of a woman in Arizona.

It might have been rewritten:

> Sister Anna Mary, a Mount St. Clare nun with a face that beams of gentleness, counts among her worldly souvenirs an invitation to a hanging.

Sometimes a reporter reaches too far to wring emotion from a reader with a story that, in itself, does the job.

> A futile and agonizing 100-mile ride across the scorching desert to save the life of little Jimmy Carlos was made in vain, possibly because of a flat tire.

"Little" Jimmy was 14. Would the omission of the word "little" have lessened the impact of the tragedy upon the reader? In the story, a service station attendant tells a deputy sheriff, whose car had the flat, that the tire had been slashed. Would not this information in the lead have heightened the emotion?

> A futile and agonizing 100-mile ride across the scorching desert to save the life of Jimmy Carlos was made in vain, possibly because of a slashed tire.

Avoid sexist descriptions in news stories where such do nothing but add alleged cuteness to the story. Be especially careful of writing leads, such as:

> The tallest jockey at Aqueduct this season is also the prettiest.

*   *   *

> Lansing's 22-year-old Linda Clayton is acclaimed by the Michigan Association of Home Builders as the youngest and prettiest licensed girl builder in the nation.

*   *   *

> The Republican party's new cochairman is a pretty blonde who fits the image of the All-American girl.

Well, you get the idea.

Be careful of searching so hard for the lead that the reference is never explained. The writer of the following lead even misled the headline writer in compounding the unexplained reference by playing it in the head, which read:

> WFL Drafts Priest, Ex-NBA Star

And the lead:

> Monday's World Football League professional player draft had a little bit of everything: one team selected a priest, another took a former pro basketball player, and a third chose the sport's greatest active rusher—in the 39th round.

The basketball player and the rusher are accounted for in the story. But the only reference to the "priest" comes in sixth paragraph and reads:

> The back led the Canadian Football League in rushing in 1972, but sat out last year after entering the ministry.

The final six paragraphs carry no further mention of the "priest."

Backing Into a Story

A newswriting pitfall that catches many student newswriters arises when the student is so anxious to get proper attribution into the lead that the story opens with the reader immediately bogged down in a long title, name and affiliation introduction before ever reaching what it was the person said or did.

> Tom Smith, vice president of the First National Bank and chairperson of the United Givers Fund, said today. . . .

> * * *

> Investigating officer, Harold Doe of the Fifth Street Police Station, and first officer on the accident scene, reported. . . .

If the speaker is the news focus point, then open the lead with the name.

> Pope Paul said today. . . .

But, if what was said or done is more important than the person making the announcement, put the event up front and the attribution to the source at the end.

> The United Givers Fund goal of $150,000 was reached at today's report luncheon. Tom Smith, fund chairperson, reported that 36 organizations went over goal.

Smith's professional identification—vice president of the First National Bank—was not prime identification for this story and therefore was eliminated.

> Two persons were taken to Mercy Hospital at noon today as the result of a one-car accident at Country Road and Main Street.
> The accident occurred on wet pavement when the driver, Bill Brown, apparently lost control of the car and struck a utility pole, according to the investigating police officer, Harold Doe.

Attribution does not always have to appear in the story lead. The first sentence of the body of the story may carry the attribution without loss of story continuity. But in assigning blame for the accident, attribution must be used or a libel suit may be initiated.

Localizing the Story

All reporters eventually draw a story assignment that calls for localizing a wire story or a press release. Localizing simply means finding the news peg or angle that ties the story to your circulation area.

> Former Laugh-In star Dick Martin, who lived in Battle Creek and attended Fremont School from 1926 to 1932, has been divorced from actress Dolly Read, 30.

Sometimes, a story in itself cannot be localized, but a story dealing with like subject matter can be initiated and run as a sidebar (accompanying story) to the wire story.

The headline read *World's Big Airports Employ Own Nurses.* The wire story told of nursing services at Chicago's O'Hare International Airport and of similar facilities at London, Paris, Tokyo, New York and Washington.

The *Lansing* (Michigan) *State Journal* ran a sidebar story on the Lansing Capital City Airport. The story explained that the airport does not have an infirmary, but all the field's security officers have completed a first-aid course and the airport has a "hot line" to the city fire department ambulance dispatcher.

Another wire story carried the headline: *VA hospital waiting list 6,300, doubles in year.* A sidebar story appearing in the Battle Creek, Michigan, *Enquirer and News* localized the hospital crisis with a story that carried the headline: *64 on waiting list here.*

Second-Day and Follow Leads

First-day news stories—story appears the day it occurs—often have a second-day story or a follow-up story. The second-day story involves a continuing news event. A follow-up may appear days, weeks or months later. Writing the first story, the reporter simply selects the best story facts for the lead. The second-day or follow lead may be easier or harder to write, depending on the information available.

The key to writing a second-day (or third-day or two-week later) story lead is this: *Get the latest fact that has occurred in the story into the lead.*

For some news media, it is necessary to write a second first-day lead because of the publishing or broadcasting deadline. Other news media have already broken the story and, to appear as current as possible, the media that publish or air later must come up with a fresh lead.

Common second-day stories are concerned with trial coverage or a similar situation that continues to make news. A usual follow-up story is the meeting that follows a story announcing the agenda. This follow-up story lead relies on what happened at the meeting. Covering meetings will be covered in chapter 16.

Let's examine a hypothetical fact sheet from which a newswriting student might be asked to write a story.

> Gregory Jewell was injured Sunday when he ran across a street. The boy darted out from behind a parked car. Another car, driven by Dennis Z. Smythe, 21, of Newville, struck the Jewell youngster. Gregory is the son of Mr. and Mrs. Carlton Jewell of 225 Wilson Drive, Newville. He is seven years old. The accident occurred in the 200 block of Emmet Street in Newville. Gregory was taken to Community General Hospital. His condition is listed today (Mon-

day) as satisfactory by hospital officials. Smythe pleaded guilty to speeding when arraigned today in municipal court. He was fined $100 and costs, which he paid.

The city ambulance took the Jewell boy to the hospital, after the accident occurred at 7 p.m.

Now to dig out the lead. First, note that "today" in the story is Monday and that the accident occurred at 7 p.m. on Sunday. There were late night news programs on both radio and television and the morning newspaper is on the street. Therefore, the reporter assigned to write this story knows that several other media had first crack at the initial accident reports. This, then, becomes a second-day story for the reporter. (But it's still the first time the readers have seen it, so all the background information is necessary.)

Now, what does the reporter look for? It should be the latest fact that has occurred in the story. There are two. One, the driver of the car has appeared in court, pleaded guilty to a speeding charge and paid a fine. The second is the latest hospital condition report on the boy injured in the accident.

These two current events must be weighed by the reporter, considering how old these facts will be by the time they reach the news audience.

For the broadcast reporter with a noon news program, both events might be carried in the lead.

> Twenty-one-year-old, Dennis Z. Smythe of Newville, pleaded guilty today in municipal court to charges of speeding. The charge was made after a car Smythe was driving struck and injured Gregory Jewell, who was listed in satisfactory condition at noon by Community General Hospital officials.

The story would continue and give the details of the accident, including the identification of Gregory's parents, their address, Greg's age and Smythe's fine.

For the newspaper reporter with a noon deadline for a paper that will not reach the streets until 3:45 p.m., the lead decision is different. A satisfactory condition report at noon might change by 3:45 p.m. This eliminates the condition report for the lead and leaves Smythe's court appearance.

> Dennis Z. Smythe, 21, of Newville, was fined $100 and costs in Municipal Court today after pleading guilty to speeding. Smythe was ticketed Sunday after the car he was driving struck and injured Gregory Jewell, 7.

The body of the story will contain the rest of the story details, including the report that at noon today the boy was listed in satisfactory condition by the hospital.

A most important point to remember in writing second-day stories is to include a paragraph giving the background of the original story. Every edition of a newspaper and every news broadcast will have some audience members who did not read or hear the original story. If some background is not given for these readers, they will not have any idea what the story is about.

An example will illustrate the point. In a murder investigation, there may be several follow-up stories. In this case the murder took place on a Sunday evening. The local newspaper would not be out until about 2 p.m. Monday. Thus, the first story the paper carried was literally a second-day story, as well as being a follow-up to the broadcast media and an area morning newspaper. The story lead and opening paragraphs:

> Many questions and puzzles confront Clinton police today as an around-the-clock investigation continues into the weekend murder of Edwin F. Jacobs, 55, 214½ 4th Ave. S.
> Det. Capt. Donald Flood said that scores of persons, including relatives, friends, acquaintances and shopkeepers, have been interrogated and more questioning is being carried on.

Two follow-up stories were written in the succeeding days. Their leads and background paragraphs follow.

> Where was Edwin H. Jacobs—what was he doing—who was with him during the last four hours of his life?
> Those are a few of the answers police are trying to find in an intensified investigation into Jacobs' murder.
> Police are seeking to fill in the time gap from 10 p.m. when his brother, Richard, reportedly let Jacobs out in front of his apartment building at 214 4th Ave. S., Saturday until his body was found near Ike's Peak clubhouse at 2:37 a.m. Sunday.

By the third story, the reporter wrapped the new element and the background information all together in the lead paragraph.

> Clinton police are enlisting the aid of the general public in tracking down the slayer of Edwin J. Jacobs, whose body with three bullet wounds was found near Ike's Peak at 2:37 a.m. Sunday . . .

The murder still remains unsolved.

Media deadlines and delayed police reports can give editors fits. They can also force a reporter to write a second-day story when none exists. Such was the case of a reporter writing for an afternoon newspaper. The body of a woman, who died during the night, was found on a Saturday morning. The story of the death and subsequent discovery of the body made the Saturday edition of the paper. An autopsy report was to be available by Monday. However, by the newspaper's Monday noon deadline, the reports were not back. The problem—write a story for the Monday edition.

Since there was nothing new for the lead, the reporter had to rehash the facts from the original story. The fact that nothing new had been learned was the story lead.

> The exact cause and time of death of Mrs. Herman (Bonnie) Otten Jr., 43, 1215 8th Ave. N., has not yet been determined by authorities, Chief of Police H. J. Fries said today . . .

The next two paragraphs state that an autopsy was held, but results were not known by the county medical examiner. The fourth paragraph backgrounds the death.

> The frozen body of Mrs. Otten was found at 7 a.m. Saturday near a driveway at 1215 4th Ave. N., just four blocks from her home. Her purse, lying nearby, provided identification of the dead woman.

The remaining four paragraphs of the story contain information that the police are continuing an investigation of the death and are questioning friends who said the woman's car wouldn't start when she attempted to leave work and that she refused an offer of a ride with them in the minus-17 degree cold, preferring to walk. The story on the death cause appears in chapter 12 in the discussion of autopsy follow-up stories.

10 STORY BEHIND THE LEAD – THE BODY

The body of a story is the payoff hinted at in the lead. It takes its cue from the lead and flows in logical sequence, giving the reader or listener all the facts behind the lead.

Keep Related Facts Together

The main point to remember in writing the body of a story is to keep all the related facts together. In one paragraph, don't talk about the hardships the person endured in learning to do something and then go on to what the person is doing today and next relate another item about the person's background.

Let's use an example to illustrate the point. In chapter 8, a lead taken from a story about a meter maid and police brutality was used. Here is the whole story. Note how the story follows, chronologically, what happened, continues with the driver's reaction and ends with the outcome of the whole incident. The story carried a Clinton, Iowa, dateline and appeared in the *Des Moines Register.*

Meter Maid Blocks Exit, Shocks Motorist With Fine

Mrs. Georgia Lange is probably one of the few people in the country to feel police brutality by a meter maid.

It happened, Mrs. Lange says, when she got into her car and attempted to drive away from a downtown parking space.

"A meter maid drove up beside me so that I couldn't pull out, and she wrote me a ticket for overtime parking," Mrs. Lange said.

"She handed me the ticket and I told her that I was just leaving. She said that she'd already written the ticket so I had to take it.

"I was shocked, too. It shook my day up and made me lose a little faith and trust."

Although she believes the ticket shouldn't have been issued, Mrs. Lange paid her fine rather than fight it. The fine was 25 cents.

The body of the news or feature story should be so constructed as to carry the reader to the end. Note how effective the use of telling a story chronologically carries out this purpose. Once the reader is hooked by the lead, the person will usually stay with the story to its end.

In a summary lead story, such as the police report stories' leads discussed in chapter 9, an effective method for getting the reader past the lead is the use of names starting the various paragraphs.

Opening with a name of a burglary victim or an establishment that was robbed lets the reader know at a glance all the persons and places involved. Recognition of a name will interest the person in the story.

Use Transitions

As a reader moves through a story, there must be smooth transition from paragraph to paragraph. There must be a logical reason for the next paragraph being where it is. In English composition class, transitional devices were listed as words and phrases; repetition of a word, phrase or idea; by synonym or restatement of an idea and by pronoun reference.

Words and phrases used for transition include *also, moreover, however, therefore, in fact, on the other hand, indeed, later* and *at last.*

Transition by repetition of word, phrase or idea is the use of one of these in a new sentence when it has just been used in the previous sentence. For example: "Put the *book* on the table." "Which *book* do you mean?"

Transition by synonym means the use of a word that means the same as a word already used in a previous sentence. For example: "Get out of this house." "Yes, we must leave this place at once."

Place is the synonym for *house.*

Repetition can be a distraction for the reader or listener if a long statement is repeated word for word, so restatement of an idea gets around this transition problem.

"The slums are marked for removal . . ." "With the removal of the blighted area . . ." Same idea expressed in different words.

Pronoun reference as a transitional device simply means the replacing of a noun in a later sentence with its pronoun.

"The girl fell from the swing. She was unhurt."
She is the pronoun for the *girl.*

While transitions may be used several times within a paragraph, there are several places where they should appear in a news story. If a summary, teaser or suspended interest lead is used, a transition must carry the reader to the first paragraph of the body of the story. Transitions are needed for the reader to move from paragraph to paragraph.

Also, if the story has an introduction or a summary ending, transitions will be needed to move the reader into the story lead and/or from the last paragraph to the story close.

The best text to illustrate use of transitions is the newspaper. Every story in it will use transitions. Start looking for them. Along with the good transitional sentences, you will occasionally find a classic horror, such as the roundup story on opening day of the deer-hunting season that appeared in a Michigan newspaper. An area man shot to death while hunting provided the lead and the next three paragraphs. Then came a listing, in successive paragraphs, of three state hunters who had died of heart attacks on opening day. Next, the reporter dropped in the ghoulish transition. Moving from the human death toll, the reporter carried the reader into a wrap-up of the local deer kill with the following sentence:

Several more local hunters have reported opening-day kills.

The Sidebar Hunt

The reporter, in writing the story body, should be careful not to overcrowd it with details that would better make a sidebar story. This is a secondary story to the main one that supports or expands the major story. For example, let's go back to the hypothetical United Giver's story in chapter 9. In gathering information for the story, a complete list of organizations affiliated with the fund is obtained. Certainly, that list is something that should be mentioned in the story. Yet, after giving all the names of the campaign leaders, the goal and details of the initial kickoff meeting, the reporter already has a story 14 inches long. The listing of United Giver's organizations will add at least six more inches. What to do? Write a sidebar story. The lead simply states that the following are the 15 organizations that make up the United Giver's Fund. Break the listing into two or three paragraphs.

In writing the body of a story, if the eye catches an item that might lend itself to a separate news story, the reporter should tell the city editor of it and offer to follow up. Again, an example.

Remember the football draft lead used in chapter 9? The heading was *WFL Drafts Priest, Ex-NBA Star.* And the lead was cited as faulty because there was no explanation about the priest. This, then, could be an idea for a sidebar story. The main story was the World Football League's player draft. The sidebar could tell about the priest-player. It might answer questions such as: Is the player combining the two professions? Why did the player enter the ministry and then decide to return to football? What is the church's view? What is the priest-player's view of being a part-time participant in both professions?

You can probably think of other questions that could be asked. But, this gives the idea of pulling out a possible sidebar from a main story.

Attribution

Attribution has been briefly touched upon before, but some tips on the subject might well be mentioned here. Attribution means identifying the person who made the statement. It has several purposes, including clarity. The most important is the avoidance of a libel suit. This would be especially true in the covering of public meetings where the results are considered privileged and may be used, if properly attributed, without fear of a libel suit. As an example, if, during a city council meeting, the mayor accuses a council representative of misappropriating funds, the quote may be used if attributed. If the accusation is later proved false, the news medium is protected because of the libel privilege that allows reporting public meeting results, properly attributed, without fear of a libel suit.

In many cases, what is being said is more newsworthy than who said it. Therefore, the attribution should be there for libel protection and to tell the reader that the reporter is not the source of the statement, but the attribution should not become as prominent as what was said.

The reader or listener should be able to read or hear who made the statement, but the mention should not detract from the audience's smooth movement through the story.

That is why the word *said* is used so frequently in news stories. In print-media copy, it usually appears at the end of the sentence ("the senator said,") and, because of its frequent use, the reader or listener recognizes it and glides on by to the next sentence.

Said is a bland word. It tells you nothing about the tone of voice in which the statement was made. It gives no indication of the gestures made by the speaker. It will rarely provoke a reader to give a second thought to it or to register an emotional feeling upon seeing it. Therefore, it serves the quiet purpose of telling the audience who the speaker was—nothing more. For most quotes in a news story, *said* is the workhorse word.

However, it should not become the sole attribution word in the reporter's vocabulary. Judgment must be used by the reporter in covering a story and in writing it. If a violent exchange takes place at a public meeting—fists are shaken, voices shout, words slurred, faces contorted—then the reporter should not end every sentence describing the incidents with "he said." This is not accurate reporting. It does not give the reader or the listener a proper interpretation of what happened. It is not honest reporting.

Instead, the reporter should write:

> Suddenly the meeting turned into a shouting match. Smith was on his feet. Face contorted, jaw set, neck muscles bulging, he slammed his fist on the table and shouted: "You're a damned liar."

Now, the audience can visualize this scene. Could they if it was written:

> Suddenly the meeting turned into a shouting match. Smith was on his feet. Face contorted, jaw set, neck muscles bulging, he slammed his fist on the table and said, "You're a damned liar."

Yes, right up to that word *said.* Then, the audience would stop short and ask—what? No person so outraged would simply say something. It would be *shouted.* And, so, the reporter should tell it the way it is. Hopefully, no reporter given the same scene would write:

> Smith said his opponent was a liar.

Not every statement a person utters will be delivered with force or special emphasis but when it is, the reporter should record it as such. On the other hand, the reporter should not attempt to create an impression that isn't true. In chapter 3, making a sentence an exclamation was discussed. The same principle applies here. Don't become a fiction writer just to put some pizzazz in the story. Adding emotion to a story that by nature should be bland will easily be spotted by the reader. Another example:

> The Giver's fund reached half of its goal today, chairman Tom Smith gleefully announced.

The following are some words that with discretion might be substituted for said.

according to	denied	opined
affirmed	disavowed	parroted
allowed	disclaimed	pronounced
announced	echoed	questioned
asserted	enunciated	repeated
averred	granted	repudiated
avowed	harped	stated
commented	iterated	stressed
contradicted	mentioned	suggested
conceded	noted	urged
declared	offered	vouched

Before rushing to use one, stop and see if *said* won't do the job in a less obtrusive fashion. If it will, and the statement made deserves such treatment, use *said.*

11 STRAIGHT NEWS ON A CROOKED PATH

Straight news means what it says. A clear, concise recitation of facts, without an in-depth attempt to interpret, explain or background them in the news story. It is also called hard news.

One of the purest forms of a straight news story is an obituary. Laid out in three or four paragraphs is a person's entire life without editorial comment or reporter interpretation.

A straight news story simply tells what has happened. It does not require many, if any, direct quotes for credibility as do personality sketches, other feature stories and speech coverage. An example will illustrate this. In chapter 9, the following was listed as a good lead. A second paragraph completes this straight news story.

Oven Starts
Kitchen Fire

A kitchen fire about 2:15 p.m. Wednesday caused about $2,500 damage to the home of N. J. Jenks, 504 Woodhaven, Delta Township firemen reported.

Firemen said heat from the kitchen oven ignited paper materials stored beneath the appliance and fire damaged the oven and cupboards.

All the facts are accounted for—even the "how."

The average reporter's working day may be made up of researching and writing straight news stories. For most reporters the welcome break from the straight story writing is a feature assignment. A look at feature writing will be taken in chapter 14.

The title of this chapter is derived from the journalistic fact of life that objectivity is a scarce commodity. The straight news story is the essence of objectivity. The slanted news story is its nemesis.

Slanted News

To slant a news story is to favor one side of the elements or factions involved. For example, the news editor receives a press release about a meeting of a group favoring abortion. A reporter is assigned to cover the meeting. In the course of the meeting, a speaker attacks the anti-abortionist group in the city. The person accuses the anti-abortionists of falsifying reports and doctoring photographs for use as emotional gimmicks to influence public opinion.

A representative from the anti-abortion group, present at the meeting, gets up and denies the accusations in a fiery, 15-minute oration.

Once back at the office, the reporter writes the story. The detailed accusations of the pro-abortionists are included in the story. But, the reporter, who favors the abortionists' view, summarizes the defense presented in two sentences.

> Present at the meeting was a member of the anti-abortion forces. She denied the accusations.

The condensation of the anti-abortionist's rebuttal, after the full play of the accusations, slants the news story. The usual purpose is to influence the reader or listener to form an opinion already held by the reporter and/or the news medium.

Slanted reporting is a charge hurled at the media most often when a criminal trial is pending. News stories about the crime and profiles or investigative stories on the circumstances of the crime often lead the defense attorneys to ask for a mistrial or change of the trial site. These lawyers charge that the pre-trial publicity has prejudiced the potential jurors' minds and a fair trial would be impossible for their client.

The slanting of a story can take place in several ways. One is for the reporter to tell only one side of a story. An example would be a story concerning a political campaign in which one politician accuses the other of wrongdoing and slurs the other's character and reputation. A recitation of what the one person said and no rebuttal or statement from the accused politician would be slanting the story, unless the latter could not be reached for comment or refused to comment—which should be so stated.

Another method in slanting a story is for the reporter to make a selective presentation of facts and to color the story with details that support the picture the reporter wishes to present. Like an artist who paints an entire canvas in various shades of blue, an effect is created. The same picture painted in various shades of red will elicit a different feeling or mood. So it is with the words with which the reporter chooses to write the story.

The following two news stories should prove this point. The subject of both stories is a young woman, Catherine "Kitty" Genovese. She was stabbed to death in New York as 38 neighbors watched, and not one called the police. The stories were written as follow-up stories to the slaying as attempts to explain what happened on the night of March 14, 1964.

38 Who Saw Murder
Didn't Call Police
By Martin Gansberg

For more than half an hour 38 respectable, lawabiding citizens in Queens watched a killer stalk and stab a woman in three separate attacks in Kew Gardens.

Twice their chatter and the sudden glow of their bedroom lights interrupted him and frightened him off. Each time he returned, sought her out, and stabbed her again. Not one person telephoned the police during the assault; one witness called after the woman was dead.

That was two weeks ago today.

Still shocked is Assistant Chief Inspector Frederick M. Lussen, in charge of the borough's detectives and a veteran of 25 years of homicide investigations. He can give a matter-of-fact recitation on many murders. But the Kew Gardens slaying baffles him—not because it is a murder, but because the "good people" failed to call the police.

"As we have reconstructed the crime," he said, "the assailant had three chances to kill this woman during a 35-minute period. He returned twice to complete the job. If we had been called when he first attacked, the woman might not be dead now."

This is what the police say happened beginning at 3:20 A.M. in the staid, middle-class, tree-lined Austin Street area:

Twenty-eight-year-old Catherine Genovese, who was called Kitty by almost everyone in the neighborhood, was returning home from her job as manager of a bar in Hollis. She parked her red Fiat in a lot adjacent to the Kew Gardens Long Island Rail Road Station, facing Mowbray Place. Like many residents of the neighborhood, she had parked there day after day since her arrival from Connecticut a year ago, although the railroad frowns on the practice.

She turned off the lights of her car, locked the door, and started to walk the 100 feet to the entrance of her apartment at 82-70 Austin Street, which is in a Tudor building, with stores on the first floor and apartments on the second.

The entrance to the apartment is in the rear of the building because the front is rented to retail stores. At night the quiet neighborhood is shrouded in the slumbering darkness that marks most residential areas.

Miss Genovese noticed a man at the far end of the lot, near a seven-story apartment house at 82-40 Austin Street. She halted. Then, nervously, she headed up Austin Street toward Lefferts Boulevard, where there is a call box to the 102nd Police Precinct in nearby Richmond Hill.

She got as far as a street light in front of a bookstore before the man grabbed her. She screamed. Lights went on in the 10-story apartment house at 82-67 Austin Street, which faces the bookstore. Windows slid open and voices punctuated the early-morning stillness.

Miss Genovese screamed: "Oh, my God, he stabbed me! Please help me! Please help me!"

From one of the upper windows in the apartment house, a man called down: "Let that girl alone!"

The assailant looked up at him, shrugged, and walked down Austin Street toward a white sedan parked a short distance away. Miss Genovese struggled to her feet.

Lights went out. The killer returned to Miss Genovese, now trying to make her way around the side of the building by the parking lot to get to her apartment. The assailant stabbed her again.

"I'm dying!" she shrieked, "I'm dying!"

Windows were opened again, and lights went on in many apartments. The assailant got into his car and drove away. Miss Genovese staggered to her feet. A city bus, Q-10, the Lefferts Boulevard line to Kennedy International Airport, passed. It was 3:35 A.M.

The assailant returned. By then, Miss Genovese had crawled to the back of the building, where the freshly painted brown doors to the apartment house held out hope for safety. The killer tried the first door; she wasn't there. At the second door, 82-62 Austin Street, he saw her slumped on the floor at the foot of the stairs. He stabbed her a third time—fatally.

It was 3:50 by the time the police received their first call, from a man who was a neighbor of Miss Genovese. In two minutes they were at the scene. The neighbor, a 70-year-old woman, and another woman were the only persons on the street. Nobody else came forward.

The man explained that he had called the police after much deliberation. He had phoned a friend in Nassau County for advice and then he had crossed the roof of the building to the apartment of the elderly woman to get her to make the call.

"I didn't want to get involved," he sheepishly told the police.

Six days later, the police arrested Winston Moseley, a 29-year-old business-machine operator, and charged him with the homicide. Moseley had no previous record. He is married, has two children and owns a home at 133-19 Sutter Avenue, South Ozone Park, Queens. On Wednesday, a court committed him to Kings County Hospital for psychiatric observation.

When questioned by the police, Moseley also said that he had slain Mrs. Annie May Johnson, 24, of 146-12 133d Avenue, Jamaica, on Feb. 29 and Barbara Kralik, 15, of 174-17 140th Avenue, Springfield Gardens, last July. In the Kralik case, the police are holding Alvin L. Mitchell, who is said to have confessed that slaying.

The police stressed how simple it would have been to have gotten in touch with them. "A phone call," said one of the detectives, "would have done it." The police may be reached by dialing "O" for operator or SPring 7-3100.

Today witnesses from the neighborhood, which is made up of one-family homes in the $35,000 to $60,000 range with the exception of the two apartment houses near the railroad station, find it difficult to explain why they didn't call the police.

A housewife, knowingly if quite casual, said, "We thought it was a lover's quarrel." A husband and wife both said, "Frankly, we were afraid." They seemed aware of the fact that events might have been different. A distraught woman, wiping her hands in her apron, said, "I didn't want my husband to get involved."

One couple, now willing to talk about that night, said they heard the first screams. The husband looked thoughtfully at the bookstore where the killer first grabbed Miss Genovese. "We went to the window to see what was happening," he said, "but the light from our bedroom made it difficult to see the street." The wife, still apprehensive, added: "I put out the light and we were able to see better."

Asked why they hadn't called the police, she shrugged and replied: "I don't know."

A man peeked out from a slight opening in the doorway to his apartment and rattled off an account of the killer's second attack. Why hadn't he called the police at the time? "I was tired," he said without emotion, "I went back to bed."

It was 4:25 A.M. when the ambulance arrived to take the body of Miss Genovese. It drove off. "Then," a solemn police detective said, "the people came out."[1]

* *

Queens Barmaid
Stabbed, Dies
By Thomas Pugh and Richard Henry

An attractive 28-year-old brunette who had given up a more prosaic life for a career as a barmaid and residence in a tiny Bohemian section of Queens was stabbed to death early yesterday.

1. © 1964 by The New York Times Company. Reprinted by permission.

Catherine (Kitty) Genovese, 5 feet 1 and 105 pounds, was stabbed eight times in the chest and four times in the back and she had three cuts on her hands—probably inflicted as she tried to fight off her attacker near her apartment in an alley-way, at 82-70 Austin St., at Lefferts Blvd., Kew Gardens.

Late yesterday, police said the 30 detectives assigned to the case had not come up with any clues or a possible motive for the savage murder.

HAD TEEN NUPTIAL ANNULLED

Police of the Richmond Hill precinct said Kitty had had her teen-age marriage annulled two months after her wedding and, when her large family moved to Connecticut, she stayed in New York on her own.

She worked for an insurance firm, but gave that up for a barmaid's career. In August, 1961, her travels with a "fast crowd" contributed to her arrest on a bookmaking rap.

Police pieced together this account of her last hours: at 6 P.M. Thursday, she left Ev's Eleventh Hour Tavern, 193-14 Jamacia Ave., Hollis, where she had been a barmaid and co-manager for 1½ years.

She and a male patron went on a dinner date to Brooklyn, and returned to Ev's at midnight. Her escort left (he was questioned by cops yesterday and his alibi freed him of suspicion in the crime).

3 GIRLS SHARED APARTMENT

Kitty left the bar at 3 A.M. and drove her Fiat sports car seven miles to her home. She parked in the Long Island Rail Road's parking lot next to the group of buildings where she and 2 other girls shared an apartment.

She walked along Austin St., instead of going more directly to her apartment via a walkway at the rear of the building. Police said she apparently walked out front to have the protection of the street lights.

GASPS "I'VE BEEN STABBED"

Neighbors suddenly heard screams and the roar of an auto driving off. Leaving a trail of blood, Kitty staggered back toward the parking lot, around the rear of the structures, and collapsed in the doorway of 86-60 Austin St., next to her home.

"I've been stabbed! I've been stabbed!" the brunette gasped.

Kitty died in an ambulance en route to Queens General Hospital, Jamaica.[2]

2. Richard Henry and Thomas Pugh, "Queens Barmaid Stabbed, Dies," *New York Daily News*, March 14, 1964.

Both stories were written about the same girl, but by different reporters, almost two weeks apart. Two entirely different pictures of the girl emerge. Basically, the reporters used the same techniques in getting the story. They interviewed the police who investigated the murder. They used the police records in reconstructing the events leading up to the stabbing, the stabbing itself and the lack of neighbor reaction to the stabbing. Why, then, are the stories so different in their presentation? Because the *New York Times* reporter, who wrote the first story, was painting his word picture with a blue palate. The reporter recounts the events of the night in a detached, factual manner. The woman, whose full name is given, is referred to on second references as "Miss Genovese." She is described as "manager of a bar." Her actions as she comes home from work are described in chronological order. The *Times* reporter makes no effort to pass judgment on the victim or the neighbors. He simply states the facts as received from police records and interviews.

The *New York Daily News* reporters, authors of the second story, strike a personal, almost intimate image of the victim with the opening words of the story. They are using a red palate to paint their picture. Words used to stir emotional visions in the reader's mind are employed—"attractive brunette," "prosaic life," "stabbed to death," "savage murder," "teen-age marriage," "fast crowd," "barmaid," her "arrest," "bookmaking rap" and the personal reference to her as "Kitty."

The *News* account pulls the reader into the scene. One sees the cuts on the girl's body, the trail of blood leading to the doorway where she died, the attractive, young brunette, who ran with a fast crowd, drove a red sports car and is now very dead.

The slanted news story will influence the reader or listener. If it didn't, the slanted story would have failed in its purpose. A variation of slanted news writing is called *new journalism.*

New Journalism

The antithesis of the straight news story is represented by the new journalism. While the straight newswriter keeps all hint of personal involvement and bias out—usually such stories do not carry a byline —the new journalism reporter works hard at immersing him or herself into the story.

The term *new journalism* stems from the concept that the reporter is not only a channel of news, but also a maker or participant in it. The new journalist not only reports the news but participates in it and, when things aren't fitting together, may invent a composite character to help carry the story along.

New journalism was a product of the sixties. In 1962, Gay Talese published a story about boxer Joe Louis in *Esquire.* This is credited generally as being the first appearance of new journalism writing. It read like a short story and opened with a scene of Louis and his wife at the airport, complete with dialogue between the two. Talese was there and simply recorded what he heard and used it in his story. Reporters often become eavesdroppers in conversations concerning persons about whom they are writing. However, most dialogue is discarded if it is not germane to what the reporter is after. The new journalist discards nothing. It all becomes part of the story.

Books on new journalism flourish, as do the books by the new journalists. Certainly, one of the most famous of the latter is Truman Capote's *In Cold Blood.* It took Capote six years to compile and write the story about the murder of a Kansas farm family—which he calls a non-fiction novel. That's a bit longer than the average news reporter has to prepare a story.

The time put into a story is another hallmark of the new journalist. Books and short stories, not articles, are produced by the new journalist. Total immersion in the subject at hand is another. Take Gay Talese's *Honor Thy Father.* It is the account of a New York Mafia family, the Bonannos, as seen through the eyes of a son, Bill. To get this insight, Talese lived with the family, traveled with them and was an ex officio family member for six years. The book was the result.

Among the new journalists, besides Talese and Capote, are Jimmy Breslin, Tom Wolfe, Lillian Ross, Hunter S. Thompson, Norman Mailer, George Plimpton, Rex Reed, Terry Southern, Gail Sheehy, Joe McGinniss, Barbara Goldsmith, Tom Gallagher, Carl Bernstein and Robert Woodward.

Certainly, the Bernstein-Woodward book, *All The President's Men,* will become a classic in new journalism. For one thing, the book was compiled while the two reporters were writing straight, hard news stories every day for their paper, the *Washington Post.* The book puts all those straight news stories in perspective with the efforts that the reporters went to, to get them.

Bernstein and Woodward and all the other new journalists have one journalistic point in common. All mastered the art of the straight news story before they tackled the new journalistic form.

Writing the Straight News Story

As a beginning newswriting student, simple, straight news stories become a regular writing diet. These stories are to the reporting student as the musical scales are to a music student—the basics of the field. And, like all basics, the student must master them before moving on. The straight news story is the skeleton for any other news story— feature or investigative. Almost any story could be expanded from a straight news story into a feature or investigative story, if the reporter had sufficient time to work up a story angle.

Straight News Examples

Listed among straight news stories are obituaries, court cases, police and fire reports, weddings and engagements, club notices, weather stories, scouting news, PTA news, service notes and most press releases from businesses, utilities, clubs and organizations. City meetings, such as council, zoning, park and library, are also straight reporting assignments, as are news stories of county commissions, state legislature, elections and school board meetings.

The following are a few examples of how reporters put some punch into routine straight news stories.

Police Stories

Traffic offense stories seldom have readership outside of the area in which the offense took place. But, sometimes the punishments meted out for the traffic offense can have wide reader appeal. It just takes a good reporter to build the local story into one of national interest. One Associated Press reporter did that. In San Francisco, some traffic violators could escape a stiff fine by spending a night in jail. The AP reporter filed the following story:

Nite in Jug Way to Beat Fine

Traffic violators with warrants pending against them have found a way to beat the fine: Spend a night in jail. It has reached the point where there is a waiting line on Sundays.

The fines could run $25 to $150. So the violator turns himself in, spends a night in jail, has breakfast on the city, appears briefly in court and then usually goes free without having to pay.

Police Capt. J. William Conroy said Sunday is the best time for a traffic violator to turn himself in. That way he's in custody when the Monday warrant deadline rolls around.

As a custody case, said Conroy, the person is given credit for time served and, in most cases, the fine is dismissed completely.

"It's the fastest hundred and fifty bucks a guy ever made," said Conroy.

In putting the story together, the reporter first picked out the story whammy—the way to escape paying a traffic fine. Then, the writer opened with a lead featuring the whammy, followed with details on the fine costs and what happened when the traffic violator went to jail.

Getting a quote from a police officer nicely tied the story together and gave the reporter a good punchline for the story end.

Weather Stories

Straight news fact sheets are the fleshless bones of a story. Put a little meat on the bones and even a weather story can become readable. The weather fact sheet:

> No rain, cloudy, little change in temperature. Lows tonight in low '60s, Wednesday highs in mid '80s. Scattered showers and thunderstorms Thursday.

The story:

Weather Prophet
Predicts No Rain

> No rain, some clouds, and high temperatures, that's what the weather prophet has in store for the Clinton area. Lows tonight will be in the low '60s with highs Wednesday in the mid '80s.
>
> For Thursday, the weather outlook is for some moisture in the form of scattered showers and thunderstorms.

Details Make a Story

Every city has ordinances that were needed 50 to 100 years ago but which became outdated and outlandish. And, sooner or later, almost every city council will get around to taking a look at the old ordinance book and will undertake a revision of the city laws. The story can be given reader interest if some of the ordinances are explained in the story.

Camanche Acts on Old Ordinances

> A poll tax and a nude swimming law are two of the statutes still found in the Camanche City Ordinance book. Many of them will be thrown out in a sweeping revision of ordinances authorized by the City Council . . .

The story went on to explain that the poll tax was "levied on every able-bodied male citizen, between 21 and 45 inclusive, in the amount of $2.50 or four eight-hour days' labor."

Other outmoded ordinances included the 1878 swimming law that made it illegal for any person 10 years of age or older to swim nude. Then, there was the law that made it illegal to ride or lead any horse or mule along or across a sidewalk, or tie a horse or mule to a shade tree, or let swine run loose within the city limits or bury any animal in an alley, city street or highway. A $100 fine and 30 days in jail awaited baseball players in 1904 who were caught playing on Sunday.

These and other ordinances were carried in the story, each with an explanation of the nature of the offense and the punishment it incurred.

Using a Summary Lead

Summer boredom quickly takes over the waking hours of youngsters and one escape is to have a neighborhood circus. The results are often called in to a reporter if the money raised is to go to a charitable cause. Sometimes a summary leads gets the story moving.

Youngsters Stage Circus,
Charity Benefits by $86

A miniature circus, lots of games, an auction, and the combined efforts of five youngsters and some willing adults netted $86.50 for the Clinton chapter of Iowa Crippled Children's Society.

Feature Lead—Straight Body

Scout camps, national roundups and jamborees in which local young people take part also cross the reporter's desk each year. A press release from the local scouting organization with the name of the scout from the area who is attending the event and the full details on what is going to take place, can be expected. It's up to the reporter to come up with the story that ties it all together. One reporter solved the problem with the following opening paragraphs and teaser lead.

Local Scout To
Attend Roundup

Build a tent city, in one day, on ground of granite.
That's the assignment that awaits Joyce Swanson, 606 16th Ave. N., and 8,500 other Girl Scouts at Button Bay, Vt. The scouts, from 50 states and many foreign countries, will attend the National Girl Scout Roundup July 15 through July 31 . . .
The roundup, held every three years, requires the scouts to build their own living facilities. Button Bay offers a foundation of solid granite for their tents . . .

The other eight paragraphs of the 11-inch story tell of the purpose of the roundup and of the preparations the Scouts made in advance of their arrival in Vermont. With the teaser lead, it is necessary for the reader to read the first three paragraphs of the story but, after that point, an exit may be made, with the reader having the full flavor of the whole story.

When Usual Becomes Unusual

The average wedding story will receive readership from persons involved in the wedding, friends and relatives of the participants, but few others. But, the wedding with a whammy will receive far more readership. The following is an example. The headline is an eye stopper and catches the reader's curiosity.

Nothing Stops
This Wedding

Although the bridegroom wore a hospital gown instead of a tux and the bride was on crutches, a Clinton and Elwood couple was married Saturday afternoon in his room at the Maquoketa Hospital . . .

The next two paragraphs tell of the two separate traffic accidents—the first of which caused an initial delay in the wedding—involving the bride and then the groom. The exchange of wedding vows was summarized with a description from the bride.

The bride said her husband pronounced the vows "mostly with his eyes," because he hardly could talk because of the serious mouth injury. In traction, he lay flat on his back during the brief ceremony. He had insisted that he be taken to the Clinton church on a stretcher, but the doctor would not release him . . .

Making Dull Interesting

A local student wins first place in the state mathematics competition. The reporter's assignment—write the story. Sound easy? It is, if the technician reporter whips out the lead:

A local youth took first place in the state mathematics competition.

The youth's name might be included in the first sentence, along with the location of the competition. The body of the story might tell how many other students took part and the prize money that the boy won. And, after three or four paragraphs at the most, the story would end. Readership might reach slightly beyond the youth and his family.

Fortunately, the reporter at the *Lansing* (Mich.) *State Journal* was a journalist and wrote the following story:

Southfield Senior
Winner in State
Math Contest

Suppose that P sub 1 equals P sub 2 squared plus P sub 3 squared plus P sub 4 squared, where P sub 1, etc. are primes.

Prove that at least one of P sub 2, P sub 3 or P sub 4 is equal to 3.

Coming up with the correct answer took David Garlock, a Southfield High School senior, about five minutes—and earned him the $500 first prize Saturday in the 14th annual Michigan Mathematics Prize Competition at Michigan State University.

Garlock correctly worked all five problems in the 100-minute runoff exam among 41 finalists, aged 13 to 18 years, who competed for $200 second place prizes and $50 third place awards. More than 25,000 Michigan high school mathematicians entered the competition. The problem of finding a P equal to 3 involves number theory and a contradictory answer, says Ronald Hamelink, the MSU professor who administered this year's competition.

It can be proved "but in a variety of ways," he said.

Here's the answer Hamelink gave:

Assume that P2, P3 and P4 are not equal to 3. Then each is congruent to plus or minus 1 modulo 3. Then P2 square plus P3 square plus P4 square is congruent to zero modulo 3.

This implies that P1 equals 3, but P1 is greater than 3. Contradiction.

Therefore, one of P2, P3 or P4 must have been equal to three.

"It really goes quite quickly if you see what to do," said Hamelink.

A flaw in the story lies in the reporter's change of verb tense from past to present back to past. In the fourth paragraph, Professor Hamelink *says*, while in other references the professor *said.* The rest of the story is set in the past tense.

Look for the Whammy

There is no secret to turning a dull, straight news story into a bright, interesting one. It simply takes a good look at all the facts available, a decision on the most interesting aspect to the story and some imagination to turn that aspect into an eye-catching lead. Keep in mind the *whammy.* Once found, it can provide the story angle that will lift the story from the ordinary, run-of-the-mill category to one that the headline writer can put a eye-stopper headline on, and the newspaper reader will want to stop and read.

12 OBITUARIES

Obituary writing is one of the most important writing assignments for the news medium. The reason is simple. The obituary is the last tangible bit of evidence that a person lived. It is cut out of newspapers, put in family Bibles or in other places where family keepsakes are kept and sent to relatives and friends. If there is a mistake in an obituary, the mistake will never be forgotten, nor will the newspaper that made it. Every time the clipping is taken out, the person doing so will remark about the paper that never could get anything right.

A reporting student who is careless about getting names correct now will plunge his or her newspaper into an eternity of being labeled never right, inept, stupid and many other names. For this reason, there are some papers that do not assign new reporters to obituary writing.

Classifying Obituaries

There are several kinds of obituaries: average person, prominent person, suicide, extraordinary death and family feud. The death of a person who lived a life mostly within one community, who reared a family, went to church and was moderately active in civic and social organizations represents the average obituary the reporter will write day after day.

If a prominent civic, social or professional person dies, the beginning reporter may not even be given the assignment to write the obituary. The suicide and extraordinary death present social problems, as does the family feud. These will be discussed later in the chapter.

Formula Writing

The initial task a new reporter should undertake the first day on the job is to dig out some back issues of the paper or back newscasts and read them from cover to cover. Read twice all the local stories and read the obituaries three times. Find out how the paper or broadcast station writes them. For the most part, obituary writing is formula writing. Each news medium may have a different formula, so learn it and use it. Never, never tell an editor how you wrote an obituary—or any news story—in college or at another news medium.

Obituary Writing Rules

A few rules for writing obituaries observed by some news media follow. Check them out with the editor before writing that first obituary.

1. Always include the cause of death when such information is available. In case of suicide or an extraordinary death, the coroner or medical examiner will be the only expert source of this information.

2. Avoid the word *unexpectedly* in saying the person died. Deaths are all unexpected. It's human nature to expect to live a little longer and die a little later. A person may die suddenly. But, even this is a word to avoid, if possible. Just report the person's death, include the day—and time, if the news medium uses these details. If the person wasn't ill and died of a heart attack, say so. In this case, there would be a coroner's investigation. Quote the coroner.

3. In writing the funeral services, priests celebrate or say Masses, ministers and rabbis officiate at or conduct services. If the news medium uses the name of the clergyman, be sure to get the name. Always identify the clergyman with his church. Most times the priest will be affiliated with the church where the Mass is celebrated. However, if a family member is a priest and is in charge, mention of this should be made in the obituary. Most Protestant and Jewish services will be held at the funeral home. Use the minister's and rabbi's church or temple affiliation with his name. See section 8 on religion in the wire services stylebook for additional writing rules.

4. Do not use euphemisms in writing obituaries. A person dies. He or she does not pass away or go to an eternal reward. The body is buried. It is not interred. There is a burial, not an interment. However, a body may be cremated. And, a cremation will take place at a crematorium. Broadcast reporters should be especially careful not to mispronounce or misread the word and have a body taken to a creamery, as one announcer said.

5. Sometimes a person chooses not to use a given name. When the person dies, the funeral director may identify the person as Hap Wilson or Bud Johnson. The full, given name must be used in the obituary. It should be written:

   Isaac "Hap" Wilson
   Marvin "Bud" Johnson

Place the nickname in quotation marks and use it between the given name and last name. Do not use the nickname again in the obituary.

6. In writing the person's affiliations for the obituary, do not use initials for organizations. The OES might be given as an organization to which a woman belonged. Ask the funeral director for the name, which is the Order of Eastern Star. The FOE is the Fraternal Order of Eagles. The KC's is the Knights of Columbus. The BPW is Business and Professional Women. An exception is the PEO. This philanthropic educational organization is commonly identified by its initials only.

Paid Obituary

All broadcast media and most newspapers publish obituary notices without charge. The exceptions are large city newspapers where news space is in short supply and news is not. In these papers, such as the *New York Times, Washington Post, Detroit News, Los Angeles Times,* the only free obituaries are written for nationally prominent civic, social or professional persons, or in some cases, for newspaper employees or their immediate relatives.

In large, metropolitan papers, paid funeral notices are placed by the funeral director as a part of the service. A typical paid notice might read:

> Smith—John Edward. On Nov. 16. Beloved husband of Irene (nee Shay). Devoted father of Irene Hatch and Donna. Loving son of Henry. Dear grandfather of Denise and James. Reposing, Howard Funeral Home, 6311 N. Winston, Brooklyn. Funeral Friday, 10 a.m. Interment Calvary Cemetery.

Instructions for flowers and memorials often also are included.

Average-Person Obituary

Most funeral directors have obituary forms that they fill out with information obtained from the family. Sometimes the forms are provided by the local news media. This is to assure that all the necessary information for the obituary is obtained by the funeral director. Usually the funeral director has more experience in gathering the information than the reporter.

A typical obituary fact sheet that has been filled out is shown on page 110. From this information the obituary is written. Normally, the funeral director will call the news media with the information but, as the deadline nears, if the calls have not come, the reporter should call the funeral directors—all of them in the news medium's area.

On newspapers, the reporters assigned to the state desk (all news not local, social or sports) will contact the area funeral directors. In broadcast stations, smaller staff requirements may see one reporter making all the calls.

Sample Obituary

Some media will use longer obituaries, with more information than others. So, in this chapter, attention will be given to the most complete obituary that can be written. It is always easier to drop off details than to add them.

SAMPLE OBITUARY

NAME: Elizabeth B. Faith , AGE: 63

ADDRESS: 2731 Jolley Road

CITY: East Lansing , STATE: Michigan

DIED WHEN: Wednesday Hospital WHERE: Sparrow Hospital

FUNERAL SERVICES: Friday, 11 a.m. at Baker Funeral Home, where friends may call after 7 p.m. today. Burial will be in Oakland Cemetery. Pallbearers will be Kurt Smythe, Henry Zoll, Michael Brown, Richard Frett, John Allen and William Green.

CLERGYMAN OFFICIATING: Rev. John Michaels, pastor of Zion Lutheran Church

BIRTH DATE: August 6, 1913 , WHERE: Eddyville, Wisconsin

PARENTS: Henry and Sarah Wilson Dunn

MARRIAGE DATA: SPOUSE'S NAME: William J. Faith

DATE: April 21, 1933

WHERE: Eddyville, Wisconsin

SCHOOLS ATTENDED: Eddyville schools, graduate of Michigan State University

CHURCH AND CIVIC AFFILIATIONS: Zion Lutheran Church; PEO; East Lansing Civic Women's Club; Martha Church Circle

OCCUPATION: Director of Library Services for Lansing Public Library

SURVIVORS: Husband, William J.; two daughters, Mrs. Frank (Joan) Brown of Seattle, Washington, and Mary of Lansing; two sons, James of Miami, Florida, and Richard of East Lansing; six grandchildren; one brother, Alex Dunn of West Covina, California; several nieces and nephews.

PRECEDED IN DEATH: parents, one son, in infancy; four brothers and one sister.

From the sample obituary information given, the following obituary could be written. Remember, this is using all the information that could be given.

Mrs. William (Elizabeth) B. Faith, 63, of 2731 Jolley Road, died Wednesday in Sparrow Hospital. Funeral services will be held at 11 a.m. Friday at the Baker Funeral Home, where friends may call after 7 p.m. today. The Rev. John Michaels, pastor of Zion Lutheran Church, will officiate. Burial will be in Oakland Cemetery. Pallbearers will be Kurt Smythe, Richard Frett, Henry Zoll, Michael Brown, John Allen and William Green.

Elizabeth Dunn Faith was born Aug. 6, 1913, in Eddyville, Wis., the daughter of Henry and Sarah Wilson Dunn. She attended Eddyville schools and graduated from Michigan State University. She married William J. Faith on April 21, 1933, in Eddyville.

She was director of library services at Lansing Public Library, and a member of Zion Lutheran Church, PEO, East Lansing Civic Women's Club and Martha Church Circle.

She is survived by her husband, William; two daughters, Mrs. Frank (Joan) Brown of Seattle, Wash. and Mary of Lansing; two sons, James of Miami, Fla. and Richard of East Lansing; six grandchildren, one brother, Alex Dunn of West Covina, Calif.; several nieces and nephews.

She was preceded in death by her parents, one son in infancy, four brothers and one sister.

Obituary Editing

Let's review the Faith obituary. If the person who died did so within the city where the newspaper is published or the broadcast originates, the location of death—Sparrow Hospital—may be used without mentioning the city's name. The same is true for all other local addresses. All cities mentioned within the state of the media's publication or broadcast will be listed by city name only. Cities outside the state will be listed with the city and state on first reference and by city only on succeeding references, i.e., Eddyville, Wis.

Now for the elimination process. The listing of pallbearers will not be carried by many publications and rarely, if ever, by the broadcast media. The officiating clergyman may be named in the paper, but most likely not on the broadcast stations.

The birth, education, marriage and work, church and club affiliation data may be condensed, but some form of this information will be carried by all media. Survivors will be carried through brothers and sisters by both media. Nieces and nephews most likely will be dropped by all media. Grandchildren's names will not be listed by any media.

It will be a local news medium option as to the listing of family who preceded the person in death.

In newspapers listing survivors, the first names of daughters and sisters will be mentioned in brackets if the women are married. This is for primary identification purposes. Some readers may know the woman by her maiden name and not her married name. Also, in newspaper accounts, if the male survivors have the same last name as the deceased, the last name is omitted as a space saver.

Exceptions

Now for some exceptions. If a person dies and has only a niece or nephew as a sole survivor, the relative's name will be used. Rarely will it happen that a person will die leaving no relatives, just a close friend. The friend's name may be included in the obituary, but the reporter should check with the editor for the decision. If the person has been living with the friend, the common address allows for an easy tie-in. It might read: Miss Doe is survived by Mary Smith with whom she made her home at 2529 Terrace Blvd., or at the Terrace Boulevard address.

Prominent-Person Obituary

For nationally prominent persons, most local media will rely on the wire services to furnish the obituary data. If there is any local tie-in, a reporter may check the news morgue for additional information. Most people prominent locally and in the state will have an obituary file already started in the news morgue. A picture also may be on file. It is common to keep such information on hand as a time-saving measure. If the person dies, most of the research necessary to write the obituary is right at hand. Sometimes the clip files contain more data than the funeral director has.

Writing the obituary for a prominent person may fall to a news staffer who dealt with the person professionally. But, no matter who draws the writing assignment, the prominent person's obituary is written differently from the average person's obituary.

For the local prominent person, the primary identification most likely will be a professional affiliation.[1]

> Dr. Ellen Smith, 61, of 200 S. 10th St., a practicing pediatrician in Newville for 28 years, died in Mercy Hospital Monday afternoon. . . .

* * *

1. Information used in this chapter was taken from actual published obituaries and appear as the obituary reporters wrote them. Some names and locations have been changed to avoid invasion of privacy.

District Judge Charles N. Mason, 48, of 3174 Green Drive, died Tuesday at a Newville hospital after a brief illness. . . .

* * *

Harold M. Brown, 53, director of the University of Newville school of journalism from 1967–1972, died in University City Wednesday of an apparent heart attack. . . .

* * *

One newspaper managed to sneak a circulation plug in the obituary of one of its leading citizens.

William T. Bunker Sr., 106, who was born Dec. 14, 1864 in Newville, died Friday in Deaconess Hospital in St. Louis, Mo. He undoubtedly had been the oldest living Newville native. (After listing funeral data, the obituary continued . . .)

Mr. Bunker was born in a two-story frame house which stood at 150 5th Ave. S., and which now is part of the city's central business district. In addition to his longevity, he was The Newville Herald's oldest reader and its longest subscriber.

The paper had been delivered to the Bunker home for more than 100 years . . .

Obituaries, like any news story, may have as many different leads as persons writing them. When Lance Reventlow died in 1972, the two wire services wrote the following obituary leads.

(UPI)—Lance Reventlow, heir to the Woolworth five-and-dime fortune and son of Barbara Hutton, one of the world's richest women, was killed in the crash of a small plane in the Colorado Rockies, law officers disclosed Tuesday.

The Battle Creek, Mich., *Enquirer and News* ran the following wire story, with a local angle.

(AP)—"Some people are born with brown eyes. I was born with money."

That was Lance Reventlow's offhanded comment about the $50 million to $100 million he would some day inherit from his mother, the much-married Woolworth dimestore heiress, Barbara Hutton, who is a niece of Marjorie Merriweather Post, Battle Creek cereal heiress.

His mother outlived him, though. Reventlow and three other persons died in the crash of a light plane near Aspen, Colo. during a thunderstorm Monday night . . .

In this day of satellite communication, the death of a nationally known person is flashed around the world in minutes. The UPI writer assigned to write the obituary for Walter Winchell must have had this thought in mind and the educated guess that papers running the story would announce the death in the headline. For four paragraphs and 141 words, the writer eulogized Winchell before revealing his death.

> "Good evening Mr. and Mrs. America and all the ships at sea. Let's go to press."
>
> His hat on his head, his right hand triggering staccato beeps on a noisemaker telegraph key beside the microphone, his breathless delivery rushing through big news and small gossip, Walter Winchell needed no other identification. He brought Americans crowding around sets from the era of the Jazz Age through the Korean War.
>
> As the voice of the 1930s and 40s, spilling in rapid bursts from the cloth grilles of woodframe radio sets, Winchell was an American presence, from Damon Runyon's gaudy Broadway to debates of the 1950s over communism.
>
> His column, punctuated with dots and dashes and sprinkled with the words he coined called "Winchellisms," appeared at one time in almost 1,000 newspapers. He was one of the most powerful commentators of his time.
>
> Winchell died of cancer Sunday at the age of 74 . . .

Suicide Obituary

Most obituary reporters will be faced sometime with writing a suicide story. The main thing to remember in the suicide obituary is that the cause of death must be fixed by an authority—in this case, the coroner or the medical examiner. The police are not considered expert witnesses. If they were, they would be able to sign the death certificate. Only the coroner can sign the certificate stating the cause of death.

However, there are ways to get around labeling a death a suicide. Most funeral directors will ask that the word *suicide* not be used in the story, as a consideration to the family. Some will just not bother to mention the cause of death. If the police reporter isn't back before the obituary is called in and the obituary writer missed an early newscast that might have carried the death notice and called it a suicide, the funeral director will probably get away with just not explaining the cause of death.

For example, the following was the lead on the obituary of a woman who killed herself by sitting in her car in a closed garage with the motor running.

> The funeral service will be held at 3 p.m. Thursday in St. Luke's Methodist Church for Mrs. John Smith, 22, of Newville, who was found dead at her home Tuesday . . .

Most likely the funeral director played the death straight and the reporter didn't ask for the death cause. If a person under 60 dies or if the person dies some place other than at a hospital, ask for the cause of death. If the funeral director hedges or refuses to give the information, ask if death was from natural causes. If the funeral director says no or hedges again, ask if the coroner was called. The last question usually draws a yes or no answer. If the answer is yes, call the coroner for the cause of death.

Another way around labeling a death a suicide occurs when the autopsy or inquest, one of which is performed any time there is a question about the cause of death, is to be performed after the news medium's deadline. This type of obituary will read:

> Mrs. Patricia Nea, 40, of 2217 3rd St., Rock Island, was found dead Saturday in the garage at her home.
> Rock Island County coroner, James Shaw, said death was apparently caused by carbon monoxide poisoning.
> Shaw said an inquest will be held.

It is unlikely that the results of an autopsy or inquest will be made public. The circumstances under which autopsy findings are released include when the person is nationally prominent or murder is suspected, and the death was ruled from natural causes or that the person was, indeed, murdered. An example of revealing autopsy information will be given later in this chapter.

Sometimes the coroner or medical examiner will just not release the information whether the death was accidental or suicide. This was the case of a locally prominent college instructor and local politician. Note, although the death cause was determined by a medical examiner, this paper chose to attribute the death ruling to the police.

> John Doe, 45, a Community College instructor and former public works chairman of Newville County, died of carbon monoxide poisoning Monday in the garage of his home at 101 LaCrosse St., Summer Township police said.
> The cause of death was determined by an autopsy, but a county medical examiner would not rule immediately on whether the death was a suicide . . .

The obituary did carry the information that the police chief had ruled out foul play. The autopsy ruling was never made public.

Official's Choice

Carbon monoxide and drowning deaths give investigating officials some leeway in making a suicide ruling, as opposed to a death due to gunshot wounds or hanging. A case of the coroner arbitrarily ruling a drowning death as accidental occurred in an Iowa community several years ago. An elderly mother and her middle-aged, recluse daughter lived several blocks from the Mississippi River. The mother became ill and health officials decided that the woman should be hospitalized. The mother and daughter had not been separated in more than 30 years. In the afternoon, an ambulance took the mother to the hospital, leaving the daughter alone. The next morning some fishermen spotted a body floating in the river. Dragging it into shore, the victim was identified as the recluse daughter. It was the first time in years she had been known to leave her house. The official death ruling was accidental drowning. There were no witnesses. Death was fixed at about 9 p.m., the preceding evening. As one official said, there was no point in ruling it a suicide. What difference would it make?

Instruments of Death

When suicide is mentioned in the obituary, the method of death may or may not be given. If the coroner gives the information, it should be used.

> Johnny P. Dexter, 16, of 5454 N. Lansing Road, died Monday afternoon at his home from a self-inflicted gunshot wound, according to Ingham County Coroner Jack B. Holmes . . .

Sometimes additional information can be picked up from police records and used, as is the case in the Dexter obituary.

> Meridian Township deputies said the youth's body was found in an upstairs bedroom by his mother, who had been in the basement at the time of the shooting . . .

Then, there is the situation when the coroner will acknowledge that the death was a suicide but will give no more details.

> Larry L. Louis, 28, of 1906 Chester Road, took his own life Saturday, according to Jack Holmes, Ingham County coroner . . .

One obituary reporter omitted any expert ruling on a death but did include an unattributed account of the death instrument:

> Miss Mary Ellen Mitchell, 23, died Wednesday morning of an apparent overdose of pills at the Eleanor Parkway Club in Chicago, a residence for professional women.

The unsubstantiated implication is suicide—an implication that could result in a libel suit against the newspaper, because suicide is illegal. Use of the word *apparent* with *overdose* is not a defense against libel. In this case, a libel suit was not instigated.

Suicide victims often leave notes. The contents of these are seldom revealed for publication. However, an exception is sometimes made when the person is nationally prominent. Such was the case with George Sanders.

"I am bored and I have already lived long enough," George Sanders wrote in a suicide note.

Then the 65-year-old actor who had played the suave cynical cad in scores of films took an overdose of sleeping pills. His body was found Tuesday on the bed in a hotel room at Castelldefells, a seaside resort near Barcelona.

Five empty barbiturate tubes were beside the body, police said, and he left a second note in Spanish.

Translation of the Spanish note was not given.

Extraordinary Deaths

In writing obituaries dealing with extraordinary death circumstances, information given by the coroner about cause and place of death should be included in the obituary.

Mrs. Dorothy Mason, 22, of 1313 W. Main, was found dead Monday morning in an apartment on West Isaac, where she was visiting a friend, Coroner Glen Dunn said today.

The coroner said a preliminary examination revealed that Mrs. Mason may have been the victim of a drug overdose . . .

* * *

The body of John W. Winston, 18, of 4160 Tower Place, was found this morning in a back yard in the 3000 block of Tower Place.

Coroner Jack B. Holmes said the victim took his own life . . .

If the coroner gives full details on an extraordinary death, the reporter should use the information in the obituary. For example, the coroner's explanation in the following obituary proves that not all carbon monoxide deaths are suicides.

George M. Walker, 77, of 1111 Just-A-Mere, was found dead at his home Friday afternoon and Coroner Jack Holmes ruled the death accidental.

Holmes said Walker was working on his car, with the motor running, in a garage that was inadequately ventilated, and was overcome by carbon monoxide fumes. The coroner said some of the doors of the garage were open but this apparently was not adequate . . .

Unexpected Information

Sometimes details on unusual deaths are supplied by the family, as the following were.

> Terri, 5, daughter of Mr. and Mrs. Jon Wells of just south of Newville died at 10:50 p.m. Tuesday in St. Luke's Hospital during surgery to correct a lip injury inflicted by the family's German Shepherd dog.
>
> The family said Terri died of a heart condition they were unaware she had . . .

Incidentally, "just south" of anywhere is not correct identification. Every home has an address. Get it. Use it.

In deaths connected with occupations, full details, if available, should be used.

> Army Spec. 4 Jack W. Finton Jr., 19, of 919 Westmore, died Thursday in Malibu, Calif.
>
> Army authorities said he died as the result of an accidental gunshot wound while on the firing range . . .

Death and the Police

In situations where unusual circumstances, requiring police investigation, surround the death of a local person, the obituary reporter generally will not be the one to write the story. The police reporter will get most of the details, while the obituary writer will pick up the funeral and personal data from the funeral director and give it to the police reporter for incorporation in the larger story. Also, stories of this nature might run on the same page as the death notices, but they will have their own headlines. Here is one example:

Night of Fun Ends in Tragedy

An evening of fun Saturday for two Newville brothers-in-law ended in tragedy when one of them was struck and killed by at least two hit-and-run cars on the US-171 expressway about two miles north of the Martin interchange.

They had been at the drag races at Martin.

Dead is Jerry Dale Smith, 33, of 290 Helen St., William Township. State police at the Newville post said that Smith's body was found by a passing motorist at 3 a.m. Sunday. He was pronounced dead by an Everson County medical examiner.

State police said Smith and his brother-in-law, Kelly Hansen, 28, of 234 Lowland Ave., attended the races earlier in the evening. They were southbound on the expressway when Hansen's pickup truck ran out of gas.

Hansen, police said, went for gas and later became confused and forgot where he left Smith and the truck. Police assume that Smith became impatient and may have attempted to flag down a motorist for aid . . .

The obituary details followed.

Check with the Police Reporter

An obituary reporter should check with the police reporter, as well as with the coroner, for details on deaths requiring police investigation. Autopsy information should be included in the obituary, even if the same information appears in the police story. Remember, not all readers will read both stories. The following obituary lead appeared in a Monday edition of an Iowa newspaper.

The funeral service was held at 2 p.m. today in the Newville Funeral Home for Mrs. Mary M. Needles, 42, 222 15th Ave. S., whose body was found in her car Saturday afternoon in the Mississippi River . . .

About three weeks before, the woman and her car had plunged into the Mississippi River. On the previous Saturday, skin divers recovered the car. An autopsy was conducted the same day but, on Monday, the coroner said the results were not back and he would not rule on the cause of death. All this information was contained in the police reporter's story appearing on the front page of the paper. None of this information was carried in the obituary. The results of the autopsy were never made public.

Failure to make public an autopsy report may be the fault of the reporter, who just doesn't bother to check back with the coroner. As mentioned earlier, some autopsies are performed after the news media's deadlines and a follow-up is not deemed newsworthy by the editor because the persons were not prominent. However, if the autopsy is performed before the news deadline, the reporter should call the coroner and ask for the results. The author of the following obituary failed to do this:

Donald J. Coors, 45, former Newville councilman, died Tuesday night in Whalen Hospital. An autopsy was to be performed this morning to determine the cause of death . . .

Not all autopsy reports are lost to the public. While written by the police reporter, the following story is included here to show the importance of following up a story and including background information that brings the reader up-to-date. Note also that background information allows a reader seeing the story for the first time to have a clear idea of what happened.

Freezing Was
Cause of Death

Mrs. William (Mary) Smith, 2324 Ivanhoe Ave., whose frozen body was found Jan. 15, four blocks from her home, died from "freezing and exposure" according to a death certificate filed in the office of Clerk of District Court.[2]

Dr. William Meyer, county medical examiner, had waited for results of blood and chemical tests from a Chicago laboratory before ruling on cause of death.

"We are satisfied that there was no foul play involved in Mrs. Smith's death," Chief of Police H. J. Fries told The Herald today. "The results of the toxology reports give no indications that there might be anything amiss."

Police had investigated the whereabouts of Mrs. Smith and her actions from the time she was last seen walking away from The Inn parking lot about 2 a.m. Jan. 15 until a passerby found her lying near a driveway at 1215 4th Ave. N. Her car, which she reportedly could not get started early that morning, was still on The Inn parking lot when police began a probe of the death.

Out-of-Town Death

When an unusual death occurs out of the news medium's area but involves a local person, the obituary reporter will probably get the story to write. Details for the story will come from the funeral director or perhaps a wire story. If a wire story is not available, there are two alternatives for getting the details. Call the out-of-town police directly and get the information or contact the wire service office in the city and have a reporter get the details and wire them back. Either way, a story, similar to this one, may be the result.

Services will be held at 1 p.m. Tuesday in the Newville Funeral Home for a former Newville woman who was killed in Florida last week in a traffic accident.

The victim, Mrs. Wilma Brown, 22, was struck by a car Tuesday night while walking in pajamas and a coat on a fogbound county road about 2½ miles north of her home in Kissimmee, according to Tpr. D. E. Smith of the Florida Highway Patrol.

Police said they were puzzled why Mrs. Brown was walking in the area on a cold, drizzly night.

Smith said Mrs. Brown came to Florida in November and stayed briefly in Tampa before coming to Kissimmee, where

---

2. Death certificates are public records and a reporter could follow up on an autopsy any time after the death certificate was filed in the Clerk of District Court's office.

she was employed at a service station operated by Howard Gray, 35, also a former Newville resident.

Mrs. Brown, clad in bed-type pajamas and a brown wind-breaker, was walking northward in the middle of a two-lane road when she was struck by a northbound car driven by Alan Hunter of Kissimmee. Hunter, who was not held, told troopers he didn't see the victim in the fog until it was too late to avoid hitting her . . .

The obituary information followed.

Occasionally, the obituary writer will receive a death notice of an out-of-town relative of a local person. To localize the story, put the relationship of the deceased to the local resident and the latter's address in the lead. An example:

Word was received by Martha Holgate, 2222 North Ave., of the death today of her brother William Holgate, 70, of Fort Collins, Colo.

The rest of the obituary would follow.

Family Feuds

Along with suicide, most obituary reporters will meet with at least one family feud. The funeral director will call and give all the details for the funeral, all the person's personal data and the survivors. It might be noted that there were two marriages, but nothing more will be added by the funeral director. About 20 minutes later, the first wife calls, the children from the first marriage call, a sister-in-law calls, someone will call and ask that so-and-so be omitted from the list of survivors. Or, another name will be given to add to the survivors. And, most likely, the reporter will be treated to the start of a lengthy disser-tation on the family's problems.

Cut the person off immediately. Do not involve yourself one minute more in a family feud. Pleasantly, but emphatically, tell the caller that the newspaper prints only the obituary information provided by the funeral director, that the person should call the funeral director and tell him about this. Say, too, the newspaper's or broadcast station's deadline is near and so the person had better call the funeral director.

Next will come the funeral director's call. He may try to tell you the family feud in detail. Cut him off, again politely, but emphatically. You have the complete obituary information, he may add something to it, but he must contact the family if an approval, or more information is needed. Not you. Remind him that your job is to write the obituary, his is to get the information. This is the one time when the reporter should draw the line at seeking out additional information for a story.

If the reporter involves him or herself in the family feud, the story will not only be delayed in getting written, so will any other of the reporter's stories for the day. And, probably the reporter and the news medium will both end up in disfavor with the family, no matter what the decision is to print. This is the funeral director's job. Let him do it.

The Obituary Feature

Rarely, will a death so move a city editor as to assign a reporter to flesh out the obituary into a feature story. But it can happen. Two examples will be discussed in more detail in chapter 14. One story concerned a suicide of a college youth, the other a lawyer who was murdered.

13   LISTENING TO SPEECHES AND COVERING MEETINGS

People looking for 8 a.m. to 5 p.m. jobs should not enter journalism. A regular part of most city reporters' lives is the covering of meetings and speeches. Few of these ever fall between 8 and 5. Most convene around 7:30 p.m. and may ramble on well past 11 p.m. Then, like the reporter, the meeting participants want to get home.

Here, then, lies the first rule in covering meetings—the rule for covering speakers too, but they will usually stop talking before 11 p.m. —do not wait until after the meeting to talk to any participants whose quotes are needed to write the story. After the meeting, people scatter rapidly. If the reporter is caught on one side of the room and the door is on the other, there is little chance of stopping a news source, unless the person is stopped before the meeting's end.

Advance Preparation

So, to avoid this last-minute panic, let us back up to the day before or the morning of the meeting or speech that is to be attended by the reporter. The first thing the reporter should do, in preparation for the assignment, is to get the agenda for the meeting and/or a copy of the speech from the speaker.

In speech and meeting assignments, the basic techniques of interview reporting are used. Get as much information about the event as possible beforehand. For the meeting, the information needed is the agenda. Be familiar with what is going to happen at the meeting. Usually, the news media also receive a copy for advance publication. In public governmental meetings, the agenda is published 24 hours in advance to notify any interested persons of what business is expected to be transacted, allowing the public to attend the meeting and express its views.

The agenda may be sent to the news media with the announcement of the meeting. If it is not, the reporter must contact, by telephone or personal call, the person in charge of the meeting. For governmental meetings, the secretary or clerk of the group will be the person responsible for the issuing of the agenda. All members of the group that is meeting will be sent an agenda before the meeting.

If the reporter regularly covers the meeting—a part of his or her beat—the agenda is usually sent directly to the reporter. If not, the editor gets it and will pass it on to the reporter.

The reporter should get from the news medium's morgue the clippings on the last couple of meetings. Again, if it is the reporter's usual assignment, a personal clip file will probably be kept by the reporter at his or her desk. A check of the agenda will tell if there is any old business that has been carried over or is expected out of a committee for action. Back clippings will yield the information needed about these items of business when they were first introduced.

If the reporter has any questions about the agenda, a call should be made to the secretary. If such isn't possible, the reporter should arrive at the meeting early and talk to the secretary or the meeting chairperson or president *before* the meeting begins.

Most regularly scheduled city government meetings will have a press table near the front of the room. In some communities, the press will be allowed to sit at the table with the city council, the zoning commission members or the members of whatever group is meeting. A reporter in this situation should try to sit next to the secretary. As the secretary usually sits near the chairperson for the meeting, this gives the reporter the opportunity to check any missed business immediately with the secretary and to corner the chairperson or member immediately after the meeting.

Its advantages include being able to hear all that is said by the official members, getting all the handouts and having quick access to any one of the main participants in the meeting. A big disadvantage, usually, is being away from the audience. If someone makes a quotable statement from the audience, most times it will be done anonymously. If the quote is to be valid, it should be attributed. Often, the person leaves the meeting at the minute of adjournment, while the reporter is trying to get through the crowd to the door. This puts the reporter in a bind for getting names, addresses and additional information from the person.

Unethical Bluff

Bluffs may be useful in an interview (when trying to get information and pretending you know more than you do)—but not in the following way, ever!

At a public meeting in Dover, N.J., neither the newspaper nor the radio reporters covering the meeting could reach a particular person before she was lost in the crowd. Both reporters wanted to use her quote in their stories. The quote, an objection made to a proposed urban renewal housing plan, was important to the story because the person making it was a resident of the affected area. Thus, the reporters thought an identification had to accompany the quote. So, the reporters made up a name and address, and both agreed to use it in their stories. Then, they kept their fingers crossed that the person would not notice and call their bluff. It worked.

It was a bluff that could have cost both reporters their jobs had the hoax been revealed. They also might have faced a possible libel suit had someone with the same name as the one made up for the story decided to press charges. It is repeated here to show the need for the reporter to plan ahead to avoid a similar situation. If an important quote is made at a meeting and the reporter is unable to get the person's name at the time the statement is made, the reporter should attempt to stop the speaker before the person gets away at the meeting's end. If seated in the front of the room, at a press table, keep an eye on the person. As soon as the move for adjournment is seconded, immediately move to the door ahead of the crowd and head the person off.

If the person leaves early and it is impossible to follow without disturbing the meeting, try to stop someone who was sitting near the person. Ask the members of the group meeting if anyone knows the person. If the attempt is unsuccessful, the quote can be used with the explanation that the person saying it was unable to be identified. A last resort is to not use the quote.

The bluff worked for two reporters because they agreed to it. Very seldom will competing reporters agree to a common story plan. Had a third reporter been there, and not gone along, the bluff would have been dropped.

If the reporter knows in advance that an item on the agenda will bring people to the meeting, the reporter may want to sit in the audience or near the door. When the people leave, the reporter can then slip out with a minimum of disturbance.

News Sources

Clerks as News Sources

Cultivating the friendship of the meeting clerks or secretaries is a good reporting technique. These persons, if not news sources in themselves, are excellent news source leads. They know as much as their bosses, and sometimes more. The clerks will have copies of minutes for all the meetings and will be well versed in background information for any issue before the meeting members. However, confidences should be strictly respected. Clerks can give reporters leads on business that is being considered by the members or business, that is not on the agenda but that might be brought up at the meeting. Reporting any information given in confidence can bring an abrupt end to profitable news relationships. It can also lead to the blacklisting of a reporter from the meetings.

Destroying News Sources

Such was the case of a reporter in Iowa. The man had the habit of pumping the clerks for information and then publishing it ahead of the meeting. He also found it convenient to put words into people's mouths and then quote them in his paper. As a result, at least one city council literally locked the door, keeping him out of all its sessions. Another city council would not let him sit at the table with the secretary and council members and would not give him any information other than that which was given in the public meeting.

No other reporters were involved. Freedom of the press was not at issue. Had the newspaper for which the reporter worked sent another reporter to the meetings, all regular courtesies afforded the other reporters would have been offered. It was strictly a personal confrontation between the reporter and the meeting clerks and members that resulted in his being segregated from his news sources.

Covering the Meeting

If the reporter has a copy of the agenda and a working knowledge of the main issues expected to be presented at the meeting he or she is ready to attend the meeting. Covering a meeting requires use of all the basic reporting techniques discussed in the previous chapters. By being familiar with the work to be done at the meeting, the reporter can anticipate some of the meeting results.

If a map or a written plan of some sort is presented to the council or commission, the reporter should ask to see it before leaving the meeting. The reporter must understand the reason behind the presentation of the material and the material itself. If the reporter does not understand, the person reading or hearing the story will never understand.

If a group of people appear at the meeting, always try to talk to the spokesperson, or the person who tended to monopolize the conversation. This person will probably know the other people there. Contact with one person at the meeting may save a lot of checking with several persons after the meeting when there is a deadline to write against.

Off-the-record comments may be made at a meeting. How to handle this situation will be discussed later in this chapter.

In covering a meeting, the reporter should remember that even if this is his or her first meeting, it is routine for most of the persons there. The members and the clerk are used to working with the press. Never hesitate to ask the clerk for clarification of something not understood or for a look at the minutes if something was missed. Most of these people will go out of their way to help a new reporter get the information needed. A reporter who admits he or she needs some help will get a lot further with the clerk than the reporter who tries to bluff and ends up having to call the next day and get a rehash of the meeting.

Covering Speeches

Much of what was said about meeting coverage applies to covering speeches. Get as much preparation as possible done for the story before going to the speech. This includes getting the biographical information on the speaker ahead of time. If the person is sponsored by a local group or organization, the background information should be available through the sponsor. For example, if a college is having a national speaker, the person was probably booked through an agency. The college will have received full biographical data on the speaker from the booking agency. If a press release is sent to the news media and the reporter wants additional information, a call to the sponsor's public relations representatives should yield additional information or a source where it can be obtained.

The reporter should ask for an opportunity to talk with the speaker either before or after the event. Sometimes the sponsor will have a press conference. Sometimes the sponsor won't see the speaker until immediately before the event. If there is no press conference and no pre-event time to see the speaker, arrange with the sponsor to have a few minutes immediately after the speech. If the person is prominent, there will be local dignitaries whom the sponsor will want to have meet the speaker. Check on being in that group.

Ideally, the reporter will want to talk to the speaker alone. Rarely is this possible. More likely, several news media representatives will be there. Do not hesitate to ask the questions raised by the speech or prepared in advance. The length of time a person has been a reporter is not important when trying to get a story. Aggressiveness is not a sin to be shunned by new reporters. Being obnoxious is.

A common assignment is to cover a dinner-speech at which awards are to be given. Contact the person in charge ahead of the meeting date and get the list of the persons receiving awards and details on the awards themselves. Get biographical information on the people getting the awards and—if they are not surprise awards—contact the recipients for their comments on the awards. All this can be written up before the dinner. Ask for a copy of the speech. Many persons make copies in anticipation of press requests. Don't disappoint anyone—ask for a copy. It is most helpful when writing the follow-up, and if the person follows the speech, ready quotes are available. However, the reporter should avoid the temptation to over write and make the story longer than necessary.

If no advance information or speech is available, get to the dinner early. Look up the person in charge and get all the award information and biographical data then. Ask for any program and other material being distributed. If possible, see the speaker and get the speech copy then. Getting a copy of a speech does not mean that the speaker will deliver the remarks exactly as prepared. The reporter should check the copy against what is actually said. An aside comment or an answer to a question might prove to be the most quotable statement of the affair.

Writing the Story

In writing the speech and the meeting stories, the same considerations as for any good lead should be followed. What was the most important thing said or acted upon? If several things come to mind, a summary lead might serve best.

> Julian Bond had harsh words for the Nixon Administration and the Congress and a position of support for busing when he spoke here Tuesday.

A quote can start off a speech or meeting story.

> When you stand on a mud bank where no man has ever stood before and look at the indescribable rock formations in a giant cave which man has never seen before, you have a feeling which must be akin to those of the men who have landed on the moon.

This was the opening statement of a high school instructor and amateur cave explorer speaking at a Rotary meeting.

Sometimes, an incident that occurred at a meeting can be used in getting the story started.

> The light thrown on Iowa's thorny liquor-by-the-drink problem during a discussion meeting last night at the YWCA generated considerable heat.
>
> At one point two women, holding that their "dry" views were being ridiculed, stalked out of the meeting in anger. Their husbands chose to stay until adjournment.

An overall impression of the meeting or the speaker lends itself to a good story opener:

> Margaret Mead, recently named the outstanding woman of the 20th Century, Friday night assured an audience of more than 1,000 that the family of tomorrow will be far more protected and secure than the isolated families of today.

Action taken at a meeting can provide an eye-catching story lead:

> Four representatives of a citizens' committee supporting Roger Furman as basketball coach, presented a list of

school district problems to the Camanche School Board Monday night.

Or, a simple declarative sentence might be used to start the story:

Camanche is growing faster than the city's expansion plans.

The second paragraph puts the problem in perspective:

This is the argument with which city councilmen confronted Mayor Lewis Westgate when the mayor objected to the acceptance of a detailed contour map of the city . . .

Off-the-Record Comments

Dealing with off-the-record comments in covering speeches and meetings is simpler than handling the same situation in interviewing. If a public meeting is held, anything said or presented during the course of the meeting is public information. Even if a speaker says something is off-the-record, keep right on taking notes and report whatever the person says.

If the meeting participants want to hold a portion of the meeting in secret, they must officially recess the meeting, clear the meeting room of all other persons and then caucus in private. Note that all other persons, *not just the press,* must be removed from the room. If a press-only exclusion is attempted, refuse to leave. If forcefully evicted, *immediately* report the incident to an editor. Almost always, the news medium will take legal action to have the portion of the meeting, held without the reporter but with other persons representing the public present, made public.

If a recess is called, the reporter should stay nearby until the meeting reconvenes. If the outcome of the caucus is not revealed, the reporter should question individual meeting participants after the meeting to find out what went on. Sometimes, this technique pays off with a meeting participant who will share all or give a lead on what happened in the secret session.

Secret Documents

It has happened in a public meeting that a document has been referred to or shown to only members of the immediate group concerned. Like the off-the-record admonition, the mere reference of the document within the confines of the public hearing makes that a public document. The reporter should ask to see the document or to be told of its content. If the request is denied, call the editor and report the situation.

An eastern newspaper reporter faced this problem. Covering a public meeting, one of the members mentioned that a letter had been received from a person concerned with the issue that was being discussed at the meeting. The member, however, said he would disclose the letter's contents later. The reporter asked to see the letter or to be appraised of its contents and the member refused. The reporter told the newspaper's editor and a lawsuit against the civic body was instigated. The result was the public revelation of the letter contents. The courts held that the mention of the existence of the letter at the public meeting brought the letter and its contents into the public domain.

Wrap-up

In covering speeches and meetings, the reporter should apply the skills of advance preparation, interviewing, accurate note taking and attribution. And, remember, within a public meeting that has not been recessed or adjourned, there is no such thing as an off-the-record comment or document.

14 FEATURE STORIES— THE SPICE OF WRITING

Feature stories are often the fun stories of newswriting. Usually, the feature story is not written under the pressure of a tight daily deadline. These are the soft news or human interest stories. Timeliness is not an important factor in the feature story. Usually, feature stories are not dated. Those that are, are considered news features, with a hard news peg or angle.

Some feature categories include the background story, the personality story, the color story, the review story, the "do-it" story, the news feature story, made news feature and the syndication non-news packages of feature material.

Feature stories differ from straight news stories in that a slant or angle is played up in the feature story. A person's achievements may be considered, a situation explored, a play reviewed or a journey chronicled in a feature story.

Another distinguishing point between the straight news story and the feature is the exploration of all sides of a story. In straight news, the reporter learns and reports as much as can be learned about all sides of a story. The feature writer may not. One artist, in a colony of artists, may be interviewed for a personality feature. One book might be reviewed on a subject that has had four other similar novels written about it. The feature story can take a narrow view of an event or person and explore it.

The best way to illustrate the workings of a feature story is by example. Let's look at each feature story category.

Background Feature

The background feature story may appear as a sidebar story to a straight news story, or it may stand on its own. When the U.S. space program was in its infancy, news media that could locate a local tie-in with the astronauts played the story as a sidebar to any space news. One example occurred when former astronaut Scott Carpenter was active in the program. An Iowa newspaper discovered an uncle of his wife living in its publishing area. A feature, complete with pictures of the uncle, his family and a photo of Mrs. Carpenter, accompanied the next wire story on the space program in the paper.

Background stories that stand alone are those features that spring from a straight news event but have enough interest in themselves to be run independently. With the rise of the drug culture on the American scene, the media began to localize stories by assigning reporters to do in-depth interviews with local drug users and pushers, with the result that the degree of individual community involvement with the drug problem could be determined. The reporter's stories usually took the form of a series of stories on the various aspects of the local drug problem.

One aspect of a feature story is that it usually is not dated (news features being exceptions). It usually can be held for a day or a week after it is written, without losing any reader interest.

For example, there seems to be no deadline on interest in the interaction of various races. A journalism student at the University of Iowa surveyed the campus on interracial dating for an interpretive writing class. The resulting story was published by the *Des Moines Register.*

The Republic of South Africa, in which apartheid (enforced segregation of the races) is practiced, produced a feature story on the problems that two residents had when, after years of living as white citizens in the country, suddenly faced life as non-whites. One, a girl, 17, was officially certified white, but her skin turned black after surgery. The other, a man, 56, had lived his life as a white. The son of a white mother and half-Chinese, half-French father, the man, in 1961, was reclassified as non-white.

The flower children, street people, hippies were also explored in feature stories that delved into the hows and whys of their existence. What it is like to be a member of a minority group was explored by grade-school children as a classroom experiment. Student members of the minority were labeled "digits," while the other students had no label. For four days, the digits lived under strict rules of segregated conduct while at school. The total class experience and the results were documented in a newspaper feature story.

Other background feature stories have appeared on being a bill collector, interview with Studs Terkel on his books *Hard Times* and *Working,* the fundamentalist church movement among young people, what goes into preparing an auditorium, gymnasium or field house to stage *Jesus Christ Superstar,* the purpose of the organization FISH and Americans who avoided the military draft by moving to Canada.

The purpose of the background feature story is to take a deeper look at many experiences that have an impact on life but frequently are overlooked or taken for granted.

Personality Feature

The personality feature focuses on the individual. It is meant to give the audience a glimpse into the personal life of a news maker.

What the person thinks, wears, does for relaxation, how and where the person lives, these all might be contained in a personality feature. This type of feature can be subjective on the part of the writer. The reporter can stack the personality story to favor or disfavor the subject through the asking of questions aimed at ego polishing or temper raising, and then play up the person's answers and reactions.

Judy Klemesrud, a *New York Times* reporter who has conducted and written many personality features, includes in her stories any actions or reactions the person has toward the reporter. The person is expecting the interview and should be ready when the reporter arrives. According to Klemesrud, the interview begins with the opening of the door. The person's manners and actions during the interview are all a part of the personality that is being explored and probed by the reporter. If the person drinks too much, threatens the reporter or perhaps offers a homemade cookie during the course of the interview, she or he includes it in the story.

The rules of interviewing apply to the personality feature, but here the person is the most important element. The reporter is giving the audience a word portrait of the personality. It should be as complete a picture as possible.

Personality features can be written about anyone who has an interesting aspect to his or her life. It's the reporter's job to translate that interesting aspect to readable, enjoyable copy.

Subjects can range from the famous to the obscure. Following are some examples of persons in whom reporters found a personality feature.

Strother Martin is a Hollywood character actor who had an unusual co-actor in a recent movie. The movie was *Sssssss,* and the actor was a blue racer snake that sank its fangs into Martin's arm—all in the line of the story script. The feature concerned the movie and Martin's role and adaptation to his reptile cohort.

James S. Yates is a London constable who gives out his business cards to the people on his beat—an area notorious in the past for race riots. The personality sketch tells how Yates, 25 and white, interacts with the people of the racially integrated area.

LeRoy Carson is a free man after spending 36 years and three months in prison for murder. He was freed after a district judge ruled that according to admissible evidence, there was no probable reason to believe that Carson had shot and killed a 12-year-old girl as charged. His first impressions of freedom and his memories of prison made the personality feature.

Margaret Sinclair married an international politician-playboy and the press immediately immortalized her with a long personality feature on her life before and after she became Mrs. Pierre Trudeau. Her husband is the Canadian prime minister.

Ideas for personality features can be found anywhere there are people—persons marking 100th birthdays, people with unusual occupations or hobbies, such as the boy, 12, who is an expert unicycle rider, the minister who is a policeman or the nun who is a policewoman—persons who undergo radical life style changes, such as the priest who marries and has a son, or Sandy Duncan, the actress who loses the sight in her left eye. And there is no rule that personality features must be done only with people.

Take the enterprising journalist who interviewed a turtle.

Piepy Kibler is a Mexican turtle that met his Iowa family at the border. Piepy and 299 other turtles were being brought into the states illegally in the trunk of a car. Stopped at the border, the patrol officer allowed the driver to pass after giving up one of the turtles. Piepy was the one. The officer, in turn, gave the turtle, estimated to be 15 years old, to the Kibler family. Piepy is allowed to tell the story in "his own words," some of which were recorded in chapter 8 on using dialogue in a story.

Reporters should always be on the lookout for personality features. They're everywhere.

Color Story

The color-story feature is written for the benefit of the audience who missed a big event or who went and want to make sure that they missed nothing. The color story gives an overall view of what has happened. While it may contain quotes from persons involved, the story will not concentrate on any one aspect of what took place. The color story is a kaleidoscope of words describing the event, the action and the people.

Stories on cities as potential vacation spots are color stories. For example, the following was written about Montreal, Canada. The story lead sweeps the reader into the city . . .

> Montreal—the city of yesterday and tomorrow, with blocks of small, old English houses dwarfed between 70-story skyscrapers and quaint French boutiques nestled beside department stores with the latest in fashion.

Another reporter takes readers on a tour of San Francisco with a running commentary that includes the following:

> Start a morning at Powell and Market Street downtown and take the Hyde Street Cable Car line to Aquatic Park. The rickety, noisy cable cars have served San Francisco's steep hills since the horse-drawn days and are America's only moving National Historical Landmark . . .
> Up the steep hills and through the narrow streets bisected by mysterious alleys your cable car climbs to the sky. San

Francisco's sidestreets are fascinating in themselves and few tourists ever walk them. The alleys off Lombard Street (the crookedest street in the world) look like Humphrey Bogart is ready to lurk in search of the Maltese Falcon . . .

But, travel stories are not the only color stories a reporter can write. The following was co-written by two *Lansing* (Mich.) *State Journal* reporters about a fire that gutted a section of the city.

Whipped into an inferno by winds of up to 40 miles an hour, fire that broke out in a rambling, aged warehouse on Turner Street in North Lansing ravaged a two-block area between the Grand River and Center Street Saturday night . . .

An eerie orange glow across the night sky, visible as far away as Holt and Perry, drew thousands of people to the scene. A driver heading toward Lansing from Perry said it looked as if the sun had not yet set . . .

Several trucks were turned to blackened hulks along Turner Street, and a Lansing fire department truck was reported completely destroyed behind the Kish Plastics warehouse nearby . . .

There was almost a carnival atmosphere in the area, with many families, including babies in arms and heavily blanketed against the wind, out to see the fire.

Taverns and short-order restaurants in the area did a brisk business, especially those where it was possible to munch snacks or drink, and view the flames at the same time.

Firemen eventually made use of some of the hangers-on, calling on volunteers from the crowd to help spread hoses . . .

And, so, the two authors from their combined notes recreated the horror and excitement of the fire in vivid word pictures.

The Review

A review can be written about a play, book, dance, concert, art show, circus, ice show, county, state or world's fair and a number of other things.

Reviews are written by experts in their respective fields and by reporters fresh out of college. On some newspapers and broadcast stations, the review is a regularly assigned beat, while on others it might be considered a reward or punishment assignment.

The expert reviewer can judge a performance according to the criteria obtained as a student or professional in the field. But, the average reviewer is not an expert in any field. He or she is a reporter who, among other reporting chores, has drawn the lot of general reviewer. This sometimes can include writing the weekly movie column from material furnished by the individual movie studios and publicity agents.

If possible, especially in the case of the novice reviewer, an attempt should be made to familiarize oneself with the work to be performed. In reviewing the event, a chronological replay sprinkled with words such as great, fantastic, marvelous, breathtaking and inspired, should be avoided.

If a play is being reviewed, the potential audience will want to know something of the story line, but not the entire plot. If it's a musical event, the audience will want an overall impression and the concert highlights. Simply saying a performance was marvelous will not give a true picture of what took place. Saying an actor "was marvelous as his sense of stage presence held the rapt attention of the audience," gives one's readers and listeners an evaluation of the man's perform- ance.

Reviews carried in the mass media, written by working reporters for a mass audience, need not be composed in the language of a scholar of the field being reviewed. The average newspaper reader or broad- cast listener is a person like the reviewer. This audience does not expect, nor want, a highly technical appraisal of the production. What this audience does want is an honest opinion of what went on. Words such as *good* or *fantastic* are blanket adjectives that hold little meaning without further explanation.

But, if the reviewer said "the musician's fingers upon the keyboard, speaking in flats and sharps, brought the message of Chopin to an audience that responded with a standing ovation," the reader or lis- tener will get the impression that the concert was a success.

Music reviewers should include in the review a listing of the music presented. If a complete listing is impractical, include a variety of the numbers to give the audience the flavor of the musical range of the concert.

Reviewers attend opening performances. The reviews are written for the benefit of future audiences. They are not written for the first nighters, the actors or the director. Great detail on production will mean nothing to persons who have not yet attended the event. The future ticket holders are interested in the general tone of the produc- tion.

Reviewing a Play

Reading a play before attending the opening may help a reviewer judge the effectiveness of the transition of script to stage. Such was the case when a civic theater staged "No Place To Be Somebody" and the reviewer, familiar with the play, wrote:

> ... Director Gerald Brown has committed what this re- viewer, as a writer, abhors most in any production.

Brown did a wholesale butchering job on the script in an effort to play the middle of the road, trying to attract blacks to theater and at the same time second guess and soothe the sensitivities of his patrons.

He cut all sexual references except the most innocuous idioms, such as "the life," "call girl" and "bed."

This is not a statement advocating flippant use of vulgar or pornographic language in plays.

The point is that this play is set in a barroom in Greenwich Village, not Lakeview. The people who frequent it include hard and hurting prostitutes and drug freaks, and the Mafia. The owner, Johnny, is a cold, embittered pimp.

Yes, the original script has many scenes with what would be considered vulgar actions and speeches. And yes, there were some in the audience who were offended by even the diluted version Brown presented.

The fact remains that playwright Charles Gordone (who won a Pulitzer Prize for this script) spent five years creating every word, phrase and action so that his play would accurately and vividly depict a certain segment of life.

If Brown feels that the level of his audience is such that they cannot accept true-life situations that are foreign or unpleasant to them, then he should stick to "Charlie Brown" and "The Music Man" . . .

If actors blew lines or moved like wooden sticks, such should be said. But the review should not revolve around such things. Plays have directors to straighten these things out. It's not the reviewer's job.

. . . Her superficial portrayal never develops the desperately despondent state that Dee (the character) reaches . . .

. . . His portrayal of the stereotype emotional Hollywood personality is so overplayed that almost nothing he said could be understood . . .

If a performer is outstanding, in the reviewer's opinion, the audience wants to know it. It does not want to know every detail of the person's performance. For example, one reviewer painted a vivid picture of one actor's ability, using a minimum of words.

. . . He has a gorgeous, clear, deep voice. He understands everything he says and delivers it accordingly. And his delivery never falters . . .

In another three sentences, the same reviewer appraised the performance of an actress:

. . . When it comes to playing peculiar people, Barbara probably is the grandest comedienne in this area.

A peculiar person herself (in a good way), she plays a hilarious role as though she is unaware that the character is ridiculous—which is why her portrayal is right all the way. Because she has full knowledge and constant awareness of her character, so does the audience . . .

Has the actor or actress convinced the reviewer that the character portrayed was alive and well on the stage?

. . . She seemed unsure and uneasy with the insanity of her character at the beginning, but eventually settles down and gains control of the role, rather than visa versa . . .

Do the players interact so as to produce a play that moves swiftly along, advancing the plot and holding the audience's attention?

. . . He has a good stage voice and relates well to the other players . . .

Or—

. . . In calm moments of normal conversation she was okay, but when she had to interact with another character she overreacted, scurrying and screaming around the stage like she was doing "The Perils of Pauline" . . .

And, finally—

. . . The cast for the most part worked well together, although several of the minor roles received rushed, weak performances.

The reviewer should not give the plot away. In the case of reviewing a new play or one not popularly known, some accounting of the plot must be made in more detail than usual.

. . . (The House of) "Blue Leaves" is 98 percent comedy, aiming its ridiculing funny bone at everything from love, marriage, sex and families to insanity, religion, the military and movie magazines.

Beneath the laughter are some very pointed comments about humankind's eternal search for the silver lining and refusal to see and accept ourselves as we really are.

All of this develops out of one day in the life of Artie Shaughnessy (Woody Bowers), a would-be but never-will-be great songwriter.

Artie is a zookeeper, both professionally and figuratively in his private life.

His AWOL son (Noble Linn) wants to get recognition by blowing up the Pope. His girlfriend, Bunny (Whitehair), is willing to go to bed with him but fights the temptation to cook for him until they are married.

Parading through this zoo of dreamers is a caricature carnival of nuns, a deaf movie starlet, a Hollywood director, an MP and a man from the asylum.

Actually, the only one who has come to terms with reality is Artie's wife, Bananas (Joyce Midcalf), who has retreated to the sanctuary of insanity.

One more thing about the plot, it has a surprise ending but I have been sworn to secrecy about it . . .

Supposedly, the reviewer, by nature of the assignment, has seen more plays than the audience and, therefore, by sheer exposure to the theater should be in a better position to make a judgment on whether the play was worth attending. How the reviewer arrives at this decision is of less importance to the audience than the decision.

The one thing for the reviewer of any production to remember is that the person is reviewing it for people who have not yet seen or heard the production or read the book. If the review does not give this audience a clear idea of what to expect, the review fails in its purpose.

Do-It Feature

The Do-it feature story simply spotlights a project or a feat that a person or thing has done. The whammy, of course, is the undertaking and the lead should reflect this. An imaginative lead will set the stage for the story. Some examples:

Two Iowa teenagers decide to ride motor scooters to a South Dakota destination. The mother of one calls the newspaper. The story lead easily draws readers into the story:

Take two motor scooters, add two boys, throw in a dash of money, flavor heavily with a spirit of adventure and you have the recipe that two area youths used recently . . .

A dull teaser lead almost loses readers on the following sleeper. A double whammy awaits the reader, who gets a curious clue in the headline:

Sports Car's
Last Fling
Darkens City

Floyd Marvin saw his friend Richard Monia stopped on the main street of this desert town (Palmdale, Calif.) with car trouble and offered to help.

Marvin tried to start Monia's car with battery jumper cables. The aging sports car not only started but lurched off by itself at 20 miles an hour, hit a rut, turned onto another road, plunged through two chain link fences, crashed into a power pole half a mile away, caught fire and left Palmdale without power for 20 minutes.

> While police were assessing the damage, Monia sold the car to a bystander for $50.

A summary lead launches this feature on a college professor and four other travelers who took a Holy Land tour.

> Few South Central Michigan residents have swam in the Dead Sea, displayed their college banner atop the Mount of Olives, ridden a camel or sailed across the Sea of Galilee . . .

Unusual sports stories make interesting do-it features.

> While snowtime in Michigan lures thousands to swarming ski slopes or noisy snowmobile trails and scramble areas, a few hardy outdoorsmen still find their thrills in the sport of snowshoeing . . .

A ship is launched. It's a do-it feature about a family of shipbuilders:

> The Santana, a miniature Spanish galleon and 10-year family project of the Lynn Merkles of San Diego, has unfurled her sails at sea—at last . . .

Other do-it stories include a resourceful Michigan State University coed who "stumbled on a gold mine that might contain up to $5 million worth of precious metals" while on an archeology trip in the Mojave Desert; a reporter who spent a day blindfolded and was led around by a guidedog; three high school girls who spent twelve days in a mock space capsule as a school experiment; and an egg crate-looking thing that a student architect designed to give his small apartment a floor and one-half.

News Feature Story

The news feature story might be described as a straight news story that is expanded into a feature. Timeliness plays a part in the news feature since this story usually is born of a news event and, therefore, is current. This is more of a category than method of feature writing. Usually, the reporter writing the story will not give a second thought about the type of story this is. It borders closely on straight news. Some examples should make the point.

In the 1972 elections, Ayshire, Iowa, elected the nation's youngest mayor (19) and the state's third largest city (Davenport) elected a woman mayor. The Associated Press came up with feature stories on both people.

At a wine auction in Houston, Texas, a woman found an unusual Christmas gift for her husband—a $9,600 jeroboam of rare wine—Chateau Mouton Rothschild 1925. Only eight jeroboams (bottles holding four-fifths of a gallon) of it were vinted and of those only two are left. The other one sold for $9,200 in New York.

An unsuccessful rainmaker, whose contract and money ran out before he could produce the much needed moisture in a Texas community, was interviewed as he was packing his truck to move on. The story told of a group of ranchers who hired the rainmaker to produce five inches of rain in 30 days. On the thirtieth day, only .65 inches had fallen. But, the rainmaker said he could do the job and after a couple days' rest, he would return.

Follow-up Story

Another aspect of the news feature story is the follow-up story. This story is a wrap-up story. The aftermath of an occurrence or event provides material for a feature. Sometimes reporters think their job is done when they report a story that has no second-day story. Not so. Days or weeks later, if the reporter learns the outcome of a story, it should be written. For example, there is the story of a widow who was robbed . . .

> A 66-year-old Detroit widow has recovered her billfold, stolen by muggers last November. More important, she thinks she may have saved a mugger's soul.
>
> The woman, who insisted on remaining anonymous, said she was accosted by two teen-age boys as she walked home from a Detroit church last fall. They demanded her purse.
>
> "I was afraid, but I refused to hand over my purse. Instead, I opened it and gave him my billfold. I looked him straight in the eye as he grabbed it," she said.
>
> As the boys fled, the woman did an unusual and dangerous thing. She called them back and offered the boys the Bible her late mother had given her more than 25 years ago.
>
> "I hope this will save your wicked heart," she told the youth who had taken the billfold.
>
> This month, the woman found the billfold and Bible in her mailbox. An unsigned note was attached.
>
> "I had intended to shoot you . . . ," the note said. "But nobody ever said God bless you to me before . . . afterwards I kept thinking about your face, and I couldn't forget you . . .
>
> "I'm very sorry I robbed you . . . I read your Testament and I now have one of my own . . . I thought you would be glad to know I am going to church now."

A news story in a New Jersey paper told about the plight of a 5-year-old boy, who had been imprisoned in a county juvenile detention center. The youngster was there because, as an arsonist and habitual runaway, he could not be placed in a foster home or returned to his parents, both of whom were mental patients. As a result of the story, law enforcement officials hurriedly transferred the boy to another facility. A follow-up news feature was written. Its lead ran:

> Authorities cut through red tape over the weekend so a 5-year-old boy charged with being "incorrigible" can be transferred to a child treatment center for special care . . .

What happens when an entire city's electric power is cut off for an hour?

> Furnaces shut off. Overhead doors wouldn't raise. Cash registers wouldn't open. Traffic signals quit. The city's electricity supply was dead . . .
>
> . . . An act of sabotage could not have destroyed the lifeline of the city any more effectively . . .

This was the lead on a story telling the plight of a midwestern city. Some more of the results of the power failure included jammed telephone circuits, elevators that stopped and were lowered to ground floors via hand cranks. Hospitals and plants with their own generators switched over; while stores with electric cash registers "blew the dust off hand cranks and opened their cash registers manually."

Bakeries and homemakers were caught with food in unheated ovens. One commercial baker with bread in an oven salvaged the loaves but said "the delay was deemed enough to sell them at day-old prices." In another bake shop, "employes finished frosting a cake by candles and flashlights."

Hair dryers in beauty shops shut off, forcing wet-haired patrons to extend their stay as their hair dried naturally. Dental patients, with partially drilled teeth, found their appointments lengthened by 60 minutes.

> . . . Even the news media were stymied. Radio stations were put off the air, teletype and photofax machines stopped. Melted down lead for newspaper type solidified during the power failure.
>
> Police communications were knocked off the air. Police placed an officer in the city garage with a car radio to relay messages from the station to police cars operating throughout the city.
>
> All city traffic lights were off and police were sent to busy intersections to aid the flow of traffic.

The 17-inch, 15-paragraph story gave a comprehensive picture of the powerless city. How did the reporter get all the information? While one reporter wrote the story, contributions came from several sources. The police reporter picked up the information on police communications. Another reporter was one of the women caught under the dryer at a beauty shop. When regular calls to the hospitals for birth information and new admittances were placed, a check was also made on how they handled the situation. A call to the main office buildings in the city revealed how they coped with the elevators, the cash registers and the no-heat problems. But, for all the extensive reporting, one very important element was omitted from the story. Nowhere in the story did the reporter give the cause for the power failure, the most important question of all. And, it was not answered.

Obituary Feature

Unusual follow-up stories sometimes result from deaths. The two examples that follow are these kinds of features.

The headline read: "It Was a 'Strange Place to Die.' " A boxed, sidebar insert in the story layout said:

> His name was James Robert Culver and as far as Lansing was concerned, he was just about All-America everything. At Waverly High School he was a hero. "Most Outstanding" this and "Most Outstanding" that and his coaches talk of him with both love and awe. A truly super athlete. He was not less a person at Central Michigan University, but a little lost in a crowd of other good people. Soon after his 21st birthday he was hurt in the field and hurt in his own mind. He went home over Thanksgiving to recover from both injuries. He went back Jan. 15, a Sunday, went back because everyone thought he would be OK. He wasn't. This is a story about a little bit of James Robert Culver.

The story ran on Jan. 22, after James Robert Culver had committed suicide. He used a $39.95 Glenfield .22 rifle, which he had bought a few days earlier at a discount store. The store's owner described the gun as "just a piece of crap." He shot himself through the heart and the bullet pierced his lungs. He bled to death on the muddy wooden floor of a building once known as "State's Cabins." He was found four days later. An almost empty bottle of Jim Beam was lying in the corner. The cabin sits off a dirt road that's near the highway leading into the city. It's about a quarter of a mile from the university dormitory where Culver lived. It was once "The Community Showers and Bath" cabin. It was where Culver told his mother he wanted to live. It was where his mother told the police to look, after her son was reported missing from the university.

The 56-inch story contained interviews with the youth's mother:

> He took the Jim Beam from our house and I'm glad he had something to help him. You see, he just could not stand not

being a strong, healthy person. That bothered him . . . But
he was a good boy. He was a good boy.

The reporter also talked with Culver's friends, the store personnel who
sold him the rifle, and the police. From these sources he built a very
personal, very intimate profile of a dead man.

Murder snuffs out lives every day. In a large city, a one-column,
several-inch story might carry the news. In a small town, the newspaper's front page might be splashed with the story. But, seldom do
follow-up stories on the victim appear. A story on the apprehension
of the killers, their trial and sentencing will be run. But, once the victim
is dead and buried, little else about the person is given to the public.
Now and then, there is an exception. Two Detroit reporters wrote the
exception story.

The victim was a criminal lawyer, Gerald Franklin. At 43, he was
shot five times in the back. He died on the street next to his $12,000
Citroen car. It looked like a professional job. The day before he died
he told a friend he had heard there was a contract out on his life.

The story opened at the dead man's funeral.

> It was a strange sort of funeral. At times the eulogy sounded
> like an indictment . . .
>
> The dead man, the rabbi said, did not have any very close
> friends. His life-style was "overstated." Most people either
> instantly liked him, or instantly hated him. Franklin wanted
> it that way.
>
> "People who need attention prefer hatred to indifference,"
> declared the rabbi.
>
> Franklin had a horrible temper, but he loved his four chil-
> dren. He was, on occasion, lavishly generous. He was a big
> tipper.
>
> He was concerned about his appearance. He was, in Yid-
> dish, "shpilkadick"—always in motion, hyperkinetic.
>
> Underneath the glib, provocative exterior "he was a child,"
> said the rabbi, "who went home to his wife to get his back
> rubbed."
>
> "He died," said Rabbi Wine, "in the style in which he
> lived."

The feature went on to review Franklin's life, his birth, early childhood, education, early business ventures, his marriage, his enjoyment
of being in criminal law—"of rubbing shoulders in the halls of justice
with all sorts of clients, attorneys and hangers-on."

The reporters detailed a list of offenses Franklin's partners charged
him with and which led to the dissolution of the business partnership.
It was not his first. They interviewed a former friend:

> He knew what was going to happen to him—he always said
> he was living on borrowed time.

They interviewed the maitre d' from the restaurant that Franklin frequented:

> He was one of the most gentle men I've ever met. A very, very pleasant man.

His barber:

> Gerry used to come in here sometimes three times a week, and then it was a dependable every other Saturday morning at 7:30. I'm telling you he really dug his family. Sometimes he would bring his boys down for haircuts, manicures, the whole bit.

The headline for the story was *Slain Lawyer Led Fast, Flashy Life;* this life was laid bare in the story for all to see.

While some story follow-ups may not be anticipated, most can be. The reporter should keep a future file in which any stories that require a follow-up are placed. The future file should be arranged in chronological order, so that each day when the reporter checks the file, the stories due for further current checking will be on top or in the front of the file.

Made News

Made news is just what the name implies—non-news items that reporters make into news stories. This is the one area that the technician journalists skip over. Only reporters make news stories, because it means going out of one's way to get the facts that make the story news.

Remember the discussion earlier of the reporter who spotted the lowered flag or the curious sign and, once at the office, investigated its meaning? This is an example of a reporter making a news story. In themselves, neither of these items was news—with a little digging, both were.

Made news can come from almost as many sources as the mind can imagine. If someone handed you a telephone book and said, "Dig a feature story out of here," could you? Neil Hunter, writing a column in the *Lansing State Journal,* did. And here it is.

The Onlooker
By Neil Hunter

> You've probably had time by now to peruse through your new telephone directory and enjoy its interesting cast of characters, though the plot isn't much to speak about.
>
> Those who have strong eyes and plenty of free time can find an unbelieveable tome of printed information ranging from the fact that Greater Lansing has most of the presidents from Washington (12) and Adams (114) to Johnson (410) and Nixon (12).

Unfortunately for the lovers of peace there are more Hawks (6) than there are Doves (2).

And if you like nursery rhymes there is always Mary (5) Haddad (4) Little (31) Lamb (13).

Alexander (43) Graham (54) Bell (62) would be proud of this compendium with its white pages that list about 75,000 names and varied other entries starting with AAA and going to Zzek.

There are more Smiths (521) than there are Jones (243) and there are more Goods (18) than there are Bads (0).

You can find such Birds (10) of a Feather (2) as Robbins (37) and Wrens (3) and if you are really interested in wildlife there are plenty of Wolves (21), Foxes (89) and Deer (1) along with Bass (13) and Trout (6). There are even Hunters (37).

In the directory you can find a Doll (11) House (21) and such handy building materials as Irons (2), Steel (3), Stone (38) and Wood (94).

Greater Lansing has the same number of Highs (1) as it does Lows (1) but there are more Youngs (124) than there are Olds (15).

The seasons are all there: Summer (1), Winter (9), Spring (4) and Fall (1). And for just plain seasoning there are such tasty entries as Salt (2), Pepper (5), Sugar (2) and Spice (2).

If your eyeballs are still in their sockets you can splash an array of colors across your pallet such as Brown (305), Black (39) and White (137).

The directory has its Coats (7), Hats (18) and Suits (2).

Going on: Hills (93), Dales (6), Valleys (12), Glenns (6), Meadows (4), Sands (1) along with Sandy (3) Beach (29).

Strong (19), Meek (1), Long (47), Short (9).

North (28), East (34), South (2), West (64).

Faith (5), Hope (6), Charity (0), Golden (8) Rule (8), proving that they must go together.

Star (1), Light (1), Trump (3), Card (8).

Flood (7), Waters (21).

Wright (161), Foote (42).

Winters (18), Knight (29).

Lotus (1), Budd (4) and if you can take this one: Lotz (1) Moore (144) Luck (1).

They are all there! Happy phonebooking when you're not reading The Onlooker!

While weather stories are usually dull to write and read, occasionally an enterprising reporter will turn out an interesting feature on the subject. Such was the story of a *Los Angeles Times* reporter who visited the wettest city in America—Aberdeen, Wash.

Aberdeen averages between 80 and 113 inches of rain per year. It even holds an annual rain derby to guess how many inches will fall each year. Cities as close as eleven miles from Aberdeen often have sunny days, while in Aberdeen it is raining most of the time—62 days in a row once, the reporter found.

How are the people of Aberdeen? According to the story, the city has more grouchy people per capita than any other town in the world. It also has the highest suicide rate per capita in the west. But, the nearby forests and the sea provide lumber mill jobs, and the hunting and fishing are good for the city's 18,489 residents. The city holds the dubious distinction of having been the last city in Washington to outlaw prostitution.

An interesting, fact-filled feature sprinkled generously with quotes from the people of Aberdeen was the result of the work of a reporter who was sparked by an interest in the weather.

Ever spot a rock with a plaque on it? Did you stop and read it or walk right on by? A reporter walking on the Michigan State University campus stopped, read and wrote a feature story about the rock, its plaque and its history. It was put near Spartan Stadium in memory of four members of the MSU Varsity Club who died during World War I, according to the story. The names of the men were on the plaque, and the reporter checked the records of the MSU Alumni Association for their identification and backgrounds, all of which was carried in the story.

Sometimes a reporter will pick up a story lead while covering another story. A midwestern reporter, while assigned to cover a state banking commission hearing on an application from a small bank in the newspaper's circulation area that was seeking state charter, learned that a page in the state senate was from the city of the newspaper. Giving up a lunch hour during the commission hearings, the reporter sought out the young man and interviewed him. The result was a feature story that detailed the young page's senate duties, including hours, wages and how he got the job. It also provided readers with a peek into the workings of one branch of state government.

Feature story ideas need not always come from reporters. A Michigan photographer on an assignment at a civic center spotted a little girl astride a pony in the basement of the building. She took a picture and returned to the newspaper office. The result was that a reporter was sent to get the story.

The little girl's parents owned the pony, which was part of a circus appearing at the civic center. The story became a personality feature on the youngster, who was learning math by correspondence and hating it and wanted to become an animal trainer when she grew up.

Made-news story ideas can come from a variety of sources. A survey of birth records, on file at the county court house, will tell a reporter what names are most popular for boys and girls this year. Almanacs will tell a reporter if the news media's immediate area is the home of any endangered wildlife. Almanacs, encyclopedias, statistical abstracts, city directories and telephone books—all found in any newsroom—yield enough facts to write enough story facts to fill several newspapers or news broadcasts.

And, don't forget the local library. What is the oldest book in it? What current books are circulating the most? Are any books not allowed on the library shelves? How many books a year are given to the library? What are some of the unusual requests librarians are asked? One librarian was asked how long is an elephant's pregnancy—(20 to 22 months).

Take a look at the city map. See any unusual names? What's the story behind them? What does it take to change a street name? Unusual spellings, longest and shortest names and streets, all are facts that might be used in a feature story. And, how old is the map? Are the new subdivisions included on it? There's probably more facts and questions that could be found while looking at the map, but you get the idea. And, an idea is all a reporter needs to write a feature story.

Three News Sources

Three treasure boxes of feature story leads are the classified advertisements in the newspaper, the Action Line type columns and letters to the editor. A feature could be written on the messages in the personal columns of the classified alone.

Here's an example of a classified ad that led to a story and a follow-up picture.

DOG BODYGUARD NEEDED for AKC Registered dog. No pedigree necessary for job. Hours: 10 to 11:30 a.m. and 4:30 to 6 p.m. 5 days. 963-9289.

A reporter saw the ad and followed it up, and the following story appeared before publication of the ad. The story lead was the classified ad. The rest of the story read:

The dog that needs protection is Penelope Theodora Jane III, an 8-month-old platinum blonde cocker spaniel, almost an extinct strain of the breed, according to her owner, Mrs. Lyle Kizer, of 11 Neward Ave.

Her dog, which will be entered in shows this spring, has been stolen and recovered once, and another attempt to steal her was made Thursday, said Mrs. Kizer.

"I'll take any means necessary to protect this dog," she explained when placing the above classified advertisement, which is to appear in Sunday's newspaper.

For a bodyguard, Mrs. Kizer wants the services of "a dog that will bite, but will be gentle with 'Penny.'"

When Penny is outside, she's on a 25-foot chain inside a three-foot-high fence with the gate wired shut.

> Taken from the yard about three weeks ago, she was returned the following night, jammed between a storm door and an inner door, said Mrs. Kizer.

On the following Tuesday, Penny had her bodyguard and the paper had a great picture of a huge St. Bernard standing in back of the small cocker spaniel. The cutline read:

> Try to take Penny at your own risk!
> Penelope Theodora Jane III, has a bodyguard. Because "Penny," a rare blonde ascot cocker spaniel, has been nearly stolen twice, her owner, Mrs. Lyle Kizer of 11 Newark Ave., advertised for a bodyguard for her when she's outdoors. The advertisement ran in Sunday's Enquirer and News and Penny had her bodyguard on Monday. He is Col. Brandy Alexander, a 3-year-old St. Bernard owned by Miss Ilene Head of 115 Overton St. The giant St. Bernard will watch over Penny from 9:30 a.m. to 6 p.m. daily. Mrs. Kizer will pay Miss Head for the gasoline needed to transport her pet. Mrs. Kizer received 18 responses to her appeal.

A plea to the *Detroit Free Press* Action Line produced results for a worried mother and a follow-up story:

> My son joined the Marines five weeks ago. Since then the drill instructors at the San Diego Recruit Depot have turned him into a nervous wreck. He says they beat him so often it's a living hell. Can Action Line help?—Mrs. V. S., Detroit.

The Action Line reply:

> Your son arrived home Thursday evening with a general discharge (honorable) and horror tale about boot camp life. Marines told Action Line the youth was "unable to adjust" to rigors of Marine training. Your son says he was singled out because he failed his first attempt at an obstacle course (climbing, jumping, crawling). Things got worse when he wrote home and you complained to his commanding officer. When Action Line and Senator Phil Hart's office called San Diego, his discharge came through in a hurry. Marines say they're investigating his complaint.

And, the story was there. Headlined: *Detroiter Charges Brutality in Marines,* the story identified the youth and reiterated in detail the complaints as stated in the Action Line letter. It also told of the added treatment the youth received after Action Line had intervened. His story, told in his own words, is in chapter 8.

The victim of a purse snatching wrote a long *letter to the editor* of the local newspaper. In it, the writer told of the day's events. It was her birthday and in the afternoon, at her husband's suggestions, she walked the few blocks to the downtown area from her home. She was to spend the afternoon browsing and picking out an inexpensive gift that would be her husband's gift to her. Instead, the woman spent the money from the household budget on needed necessity items and began her walk home. It was as she neared her home that she saw two boys, one 14 or 15, the other eight or nine. They saw her, too. A few blocks later, the older boy grabbed her purse. The woman held onto the strap, but she was pulled along with the running boy. She let go. The younger boy ran after the other youth. The woman wrote that the hard part was telling her husband, who was paralyzed from the neck down. The woman's identity was not released.

As soon as the letter was published, reader response began to pour into the newspaper office. Two days after the letter appeared, the first follow-up story appeared telling of the donations and offers of help, such as offering transportation to the couple. A few days later, the second story ran. This story carried a lead telling that $119 had been sent in by readers to aid the couple. The identity of the people was never released—and the young thieves were not caught.

A curious omission from the letter and the follow-up stories was the absence of any mention of the police being notified of the robbery or of any subsequent investigation. The reporter assigned to flesh out a human interest story should not neglect to follow up on all story aspects. The police should have been contacted and a report on the investigation, or the lack of an investigation, included in the story. Also, in the follow-up stories, no reaction of the people involved was given. There was not even any indication if, when or how the money and service offers would be forwarded to the couple. It is apparent that a journalist-technician wrote the stories. Only the information that was placed before the reporter—either by the editor or the mail deliverer —got into the story.

In building the story, however, the writer did include excerpts from the letters offering help. These excerpts added a human-interest angle and credibility to the story. A few of these letter fragments follow:

> My deepest sympathy to her as it has happened to me twice, and I shall never enjoy being out alone again.

* * *

> We pray that the boys that did this will find the Lord before it is too late—prayer changes things.

A retired couple with limited means promised a check for a small sum, adding:

> We wish it could be much, much more.

Watch Out For the Hoax

The neglect of the reporter, following up the purse snatching story, to check with the police or the woman could have been a serious mistake had the whole incident been a hoax. The woman's letter mentioned an unusual circumstance. She wrote:

> Now, you no doubt ask: Why doesn't her husband drive her to the store?. . . . Well, my husband has been issued a Michigan driving license, but we cannot afford to buy a car and the equipment he needs.

Two paragraphs later, she added:

> Telling my husband was one of the hardest things I've had to do in a long time. How do you choose words to tell a man who is paralyzed from the neck down . . .

Question: How does a man paralyzed from the neck down get a driver's license? Perhaps he received the license before he became paralyzed and it had not yet expired, but the reader is never told.

Question: Could a man paralyzed from the neck down drive a car, even with special equipment on that car?

Question: Is there any such equipment available and if so what, and how does it work?

A reporter should have thought of these questions and sought the answers. A call to the woman would answer the first and maybe give a lead on the other two. A future feature story could be written on the equipment available for installation on a car to allow handicapped persons to drive.

But the point is that unless those first two questions are answered, the possibility of a hoax was there. The omission of any police investigation was another questionable aspect of the story.

Hoaxes do occur and the news media do get sucked in, just like the rest of a gullible public. A classified ad in a college town newspaper read:

> Wanted and desperately needed: Husbands for four senior girls who have only 15 weeks left to hook one, since that's what we're here for.

An Associated Press reporter contacted the ad placers—four coeds.

> We took out the ad to help us in our search. We're setting up appointments and are going to question all the applicants and then go from there. We aren't interested in whether they are rich or anything like that. We're just looking for eligible bachelors who are our type and are interested in becoming engaged in a serious relationship. Then, we'll just have to see how things work out . . .

The story got national play and resulted in 60 responses and calls from cities around the country, according to the following day's AP story which also carried the admission that the ad was a hoax—

One of the coeds said it was "an effort to get even with a male-chauvinist friend" who claimed the only reason women attended college was to find a spouse . . .

The following story originated in Grand Rapids, Mich., but concerned bad check passing in another Michigan city, Kalamazoo—some 54 miles distant. For want of a phone call by the reporter to the Kalamazoo police to verify the story, the Grand Rapids newspaper printed the following story, which the Associated Press then moved over its wires.

I. M. Slick cashes 12 forged checks

Would you cash a check for more than $100 payable to I. M. Slick and signed by U. R. Stuck?

At least 12 Kalamazoo area food stores did.

Milo Schuiteman, a Grand Rapids police detective, returned from this month's meeting of the Michigan Association of Check Investigators in Lansing with the tale of the obvious forger.

"I've never seen anything so obvious," Schuiteman said about the checks.

He said the checks, drawn on the nonexistent Muskegon State and Savings Bank, actually are copies of a sample used in teaching supermarket cashiers to spot forged checks.

One of the checks Schuiteman displayed is drawn for $186.95 against the payroll account of the National Paperhangers Co. of Lansing. Schuiteman explained that "paperhangers" in this context is slang for forgers.

Schuiteman said none of those cashing the checks required identification from the passers. But the cashiers in each case obtained the culprit's thumbprint under the Identiseal system, a method of catching bad check passers subscribed to by many retailers.

Five days later, the follow-up story was carried by the AP. This time the dateline was Kalamazoo. And, the 12 checks turned out to be one check.

Phoney check story
proves to be hoax

"It's strictly a joke," says a party store owner whose actions led to a report that a dozen Kalamazoo area food stores cashed checks for more than $100 each payable to I. M. Slick and signed by U. R. Stuck.

Alvin Daane, owner of Daane's Market in suburban Portage, said he slipped a copy of the check drawn on the account of the National Paperhanger's Co. of Lansing at the nonexistent Muskegon State and Savings Bank into the day's receipts for another store owned by a friend of his.

The friend was supposed to discover the phoney check, laugh and then destroy it, Daane said. "Paperhanger" is slang for forger.

But something went wrong, and the other store owner sent the check to American National Bank, where its amount was added to the store's balance, Kalamazoo police reported. Eventually, the check wound up at Union Bank & Trust Co. in Grand Rapids because the check bore genuine routing numbers Union used in the Federal Reserve System.

James Devereaux, an assistant vice president at Union, said the check came to his bank three times before it was detected and also passed through two Chicago banks and one in Detroit without comment.

Finally, Devereaux sent the check back to the Federal Reserve System saying there was an error and it should be returned to American National where it entered the banking system.

Devereaux took a photostat of the check to a meeting of the Michigan Association of Check Investigators in Lansing. There Milo Schuiteman, a Grand Rapids detective, picked up the story that a dozen such checks had been cashed around Kalamazoo. Schuiteman relayed the story to a newsman as did an officer in suburban Wyoming to a second newsman.

The story was picked up by The Grand Rapids Press and the Associated Press.

But the Lansing-based check reporting service which monitors bad check activities in Michigan said it had no reports of any such check being cashed.

Devereaux said he believes the check still is somewhere in the Federal Reserve System.

Kalamazoo police said they do not intend to prosecute Daane because there was no criminal intent and American National Bank officials said they cannot do anything until the phoney check comes back to them.

Remember, in chapter 10, the discussion on accuracy and attribution of facts to experts in the area being reported on? The Grand Rapids detective was not the expert in the case. He just passed along a second- or third-hand story. Yet, one reporter took him at his word and filed the story.

An idea for a background feature story lies in the follow-up of the hoax story. Just what is the route that a check follows from the time it is written and submitted in payment of a debt until it is returned to the writer in a banking statement?

Syndication Feature

Some readers of Ann Landers' column probably think she is a staff writer for their local newspaper. She is, if the local paper is the *Chicago Sun Times.* Her column is distributed to all other newspapers through Field Enterprises, Inc.

The comics, cartoons, opinion columns, crossword puzzles, bridge tips, knitting hints, do-it-yourself projects, home building blueprints —all these are bought by the newspaper in packages for use locally.

Broadcast stations also buy syndicated features. Dear Abby, pet tips, commentaries and interviews, cooking tips and recipes are several of the five-minute feature shows being marketed.

Some of the members of the syndicate market include B P Singer Features, Inc., Bell-McClure Syndicate, The Hollywood Informer Syndicate, King Features Syndicate, Newspaper Enterprise Association, Inc., and North American Newspaper Alliance. Some large newspapers also have syndicates including Field Enterprises, Chicago Tribune-New York Times Syndicate, Inc., the Register and Tribune Syndicate, Toronto Star Syndicate and the Los Angeles Times Syndicate.

Most syndicates sell several different features in their packages. For example, a newspaper could not buy the publication rights for only the Peanuts comic strip. Along with *Peanuts,* the newspaper might have to take a crossword puzzle, sewing column, an opinion column and bridge tips. The package cost would be figured to include all these features, some of which the paper may already be using. The average newspaper would find it financially impossible to buy the package and use only one of the features.

The Associated Press and United Press International wire services also offer features, as well as news stories. And, several newspapers and newspaper owners also have their own wire services that move feature stories written by their own reporters and transmitted to all papers and stations that subscribe to the wire service. Among newspapers and newspaper groups having their own wire services include the *New York Times,* the *Los Angeles Times/Washington Post,* Scripps-Howard, Gannett, Knight, Newhouse, Hearst and Copley.

There are also more than 30 syndicates specializing in pictures. The United Press International, Black Star and Wide World Photos are among the better known.[1]

---

1. For a more complete listing of news, feature and picture syndicates, see the *Editor and Publisher Yearbook.*

15 AFTER THE STORY IS WRITTEN—SOME BASIC EDITING SKILLS

Some Problems and Solutions

The story is written—but is it ready to give to the editor? Right, it's the editor's job to edit copy but, given enough mistake-ridden copy from a reporter, and the reporter may find his or her name edited off the company payroll.

There are a few things that the reporter should look for in reading over that copy before letting it leave the desk. Spelling, long sentences, wordiness, incompleteness, clarity and dirty copy are some check points. Let's look at them one by one.

Spelling

Spelling is still the number-one problem with copy, according to editors. Winning the county spelling bee is not a prerequisite for being a reporter, but being able to use a dictionary is. Double check every name in the story for correct spelling. As one editor said concerning the misspelling of names: "... It lowers that newspaper's reputation for reliability, not only in the eyes of the offended party, but also in the eyes of his friends."[1]

Long Sentences

Short sentences are the best sentences. The longer the sentence, the more likely the reporter is to introduce confusion, not clarification, of facts.

For example:

> An export workshop will be held on Friday, Jan. 25, at Webers Inn in Ann Arbor for Ypsilanti area businesses and industries not presently active in exporting to consider selling their projects abroad, according to Gary Hawks, Greater Ypsilanti Area Chamber of Commerce president and vice president of university relations at Eastern Michigan University.

1. John R. Brown, "Why Can't They Spell? (Or Know That They Can't?)," *Editorially Speaking, Gannetteer Magazine,* April, 1974, p. 3.

The sentence is 54 words, of which 17 were explaining Hawks' titles. There are several exit points in the sentence.

> An export workshop will be held Friday, Jan. 25, at Webers Inn, Ann Arbor, for Ypsilanti area businesses and industries.
>
> Purpose of the workshop will be to explore the possibilities of export selling for companies not currently doing so.
>
> Plans for the session were released by Gary Hawks, Greater Ypsilanti Area Chamber of Commerce president.

The change is from one sentence containing 54 words to three sentences containing a total of 55 words.

Wordiness

Wordiness can lead to long sentences. It also can cause fact repetition and overly long stories. Take the reporter who had the notorious newsroom reputation of never writing an interview story in fewer than five pages. In answer to the editor's query of why, the reporter said she couldn't determine the important things the subject told her so she just wrote everything.[2]

Redundancy is the editing error of a sloppy reporter.

> Hamilton police are seeking a strong-armed robber who forced his way into a woman's car, stopped for a traffic light, and robbed her . . .

Of course, the robber *robbed*.

> Mrs. Pat White, widow of the late astronaut Edward White III . . .

"Widow of the late" is redundant.

Cutting out non-vital words will also shorten sentences.

> They will meet on Wednesday.

Can become—

> They will meet Wednesday.

Incompleteness

News reports should answer questions, not raise them or leave them unanswered. Some examples will prove the point.

An Associated Press story about a mine disaster used the term "primer cord." The reporter then explained that a primer cord is a ropelike explosives detonator, which is forbidden in underground mines because it flashes and flames.

2. Ibid.

Another AP story on the labor union-automobile industry negotiations reported that a four-day work week might solve the problem of industry absenteeism. But, the story failed to tell how. A later insert for the story explained that Chrysler, General Motors and Ford all complained of Friday and Monday absenteeism.

Clarity

Does a story make sense? If it contains any of the errors thus far discussed, the story is not going to be clear and easily understood by the readers. The following story lead drew an irate letter from a reader:

> An apparent attempt by two men to kidnap members of three families was foiled Saturday night when a former state legislator exchanged gunfire with the pair when they tried to take him from his home.

The letter read, in part—

> ... Please tell me that my inability to comprehend your leading news story today ... without resorting to pencil and paper to make a list of characters in order of appearance ... is not due to creeping senility. Please tell me that this story, while not the only confusing one you have ever printed, is perhaps your best effort so far at making news incomprehensible ...[3]

Reporters write for readers and listeners. Those are the people out there who know less about the topic being discussed than the reporter. A reporter should not write down to a reader, but the story should not be written as though the reader has done as much research as the reporter. As city editor John R. Brown of the *Huntington* (W. Va.) *Advertiser* said:

> A good reporter is one who can find the material, correlate it, then put it together into a readable story.

Words That Clarify

Any word can be extra baggage in a story or it can be necessary to the sense of the sentence. Here is an example in which the word *that* is vital to the sense of the story, but the reporter left it out.

> In a surprise major ruling, the Supreme Court said Thursday election law changes by federal courts ...

Are all elections held on Thursday? Without *that* preceding the word *election*, it reads as if they are.

3. Associated Press Managing Editors, "Writing/Editing Committee Report No. 2," Shreveport, La., 1971, p. 16.

Dirty Copy

Dirty copy does not refer to stories dropped on the floor and stepped on. Dirty copy is copy that has been xxx-ed out, scratched over and written on to the point that reading it is impossible. If copy reaches the point of being unreadable, the editor will throw it back at the reporter for a rewrite. Save time by cleaning up the copy the first time. Retype the page, if necessary.

The day of the video display terminal (VDT) is here. Whereas an editor might have strained to read dirty copy, the computer will refuse it outright. The world of the CRT (cathode ray tube), VDT and OCR (optical character recognition) newsroom will be explored in chapter 17.

The Editor's Prerogative

Besides the job of catching misspelled words, noting unanswered questions and shortening sentences, the editor also has the right to change reporters' copy. Novice reporters, who think that every word they write should be copyrighted for untouched preservation, will be shocked rudely into reality almost immediately.

The case for copy changes is presented nicely in the following excerpt from the book *A Day In The Life of the New York Times. Times* Middle East correspondent James Feron was writing a story on the funeral of Premier Levi Eshkol in Jerusalem and said:

> "Levi Eshkol was buried today with the nation's founders atop Mt. Herzl after a simple, but moving, state funeral in the Israel capital."
>
> It pleases him. It gives the picture he wants. (The fact that it was changed slightly by the copydesk in New York to read: "Levi Eshkol was buried with Israel's founders atop Mount Herzl today after a simple and moving state funeral" didn't bother him. He believes there are many ways to reach the reader, and if the copyreader thinks he has a better way, that's fine with Feron. Many reporters do not have such a benign attitude toward the copydesk. Certain copyreaders, they readily admit, improve and embellish the stories they handle but, traditionally, reporters are inclined to feel that every copydesk alteration—except for a factual or grammatical error—is for the worse.)
>
> Feron continues at the typewriter:
>
> "The Premier, who died Wednesday at the age of 73, was laid to rest next to Yosef Sprinzak, whose personal inspiration drew Mr. Eshkol here five decades ago." (The copydesk changed this sentence to read: "The grave of the Premier, who died of a heart attack Wednesday at the age of 73, is

next to that of Yosef Sprinzak, whose personal inspiration drew Mr. Eshkol here five decades ago." Feron thought the change good. It removed "laid to rest," which he hadn't liked much anyway, and it added the information that Eshkol died of a heart attack.)

The next three paragraphs, which complete the point he wanted to make, were printed as he wrote them, except for one or two word changes . . . [4]

Veteran reporters, like Feron, expect that minor editing revisions will be made in their copy. However, reporters have been known to do battle with editors who completely revise a story, leaving the reporter's byline on it. Most reporters agree that to change a story's lead and body copy is to change the story and it then becomes the editor's work. The reporter's byline after such editing is more of a mockery than a credit, according to reporters.

Newspapers that have newsroom unions are working to insert into new contracts the right of review by reporters of any major copy changes inaugurated by the desk. Members of The American Newspaper Guild also want the right of removing the byline if the reporter thinks the story is so changed as to not reflect the original material submitted.

Editors Aren't Perfect

Another reason for close copy editing by the reporter is that copy editors are not perfect in the execution of their jobs. If they were, there would be fewer mistakes in the newspaper or on the air, and all the bad examples of stories used in this book would not have been available. The editor who read the story lead about the nun who had a "face that beams of gentleness and an invitation to a hanging" (see chapter 9) would have spotted the misplaced modifier and made the correction. Or, the editor who read the feature about the aftermath of the electricity failure in the midwestern town (see chapter 13) would have tossed the story back at the reporter and shouted: "What caused the whole thing?"

Editor Aids

Reporters can help editors in ways other than just copy reading. George R. Venizelos, managing editor of the *Binghamton* (N.Y.) *Press*, listed some:

The reporter should never assume the desk already knows about an event. Every city editor would rather hear a tip 10 times than not at all.

4. From *A Day in the Life of the New York Times* by Ruth Adler. Copyright © 1971 by the New York Times Company. Reprinted by permission of J. B. Lippincott Company.

A reporter should always contribute story and photo ideas —on and off his beat—and develop stories on his own, not simply wait for assignments.

Reporters should keep their own file of stories to follow, and other story possibilities.

Reporters should make certain they check regularly with sources, even if there is not an immediate story to talk about.

A reporter should feel free at all times to consult with the city desk on approaches to stories.

A reporter should constantly keep the city desk aware of what he or she is doing. Reporters should never surprise the city desk with a complete story that had not been discussed in advance. Lack of prior discussion can lead to time-wasting duplication.

A reporter who comes upon a fire, an accident or other spot-news event should notify the city desk immediately. Reporters should not take it upon themselves to cover the story and then call. That, too, can lead to unnecessary duplication and waste of time.

A reporter assigned to a story should always be alert for the unexpected. If, for example, a reporter finds pickets at a meeting, the city desk should be notified immediately so a photographer can be sent.

A reporter should be thinking constantly of ways to improve or expand an assignment . . .

A reporter assigned to an interview should prepare for it by checking the files, or reading about the subject.

A reporter should read the newspaper—in part, at least to have the background if he or she is moved into any assignment on short notice.

A reporter should, whenever possible, approach sources in person rather than rely on the telephone . . .

A reporter should take the initiative in suggesting sidebars, especially those that can be broken out of a long story.

A reporter should be conscious of deadlines, and plan his time accordingly.

In writing a story, a reporter should remember that even one error—including misspelling—can raise a question about credibility . . .

And editor Venizelos adds one more very important editing requirement—this one for the city desk editors:

And it is incumbent on city desks to communicate regularly with their staffs, to guide, advise and lead.

The end result should be a factual, lively, attractive newspaper that is on top of, or ahead of the news.[5]

Picture Editing

The selection and sizing of photos for publication is an editor's job. The reporter will usually write the cutline for pictures. Photographers will sometimes accompany reporters on story assignments but, even if the photographer takes the story pictures at a later time, the reporter will almost always work with the photographer on deciding what will be photographed.

Once the pictures are taken and printed, the job of the photo editor begins. In determining what pictures will appear with a story or as wild pictures, the impact and importance of the subject in the picture are considered. Of almost equal importance is the space available for the picture.

If a close-up of the person's face will show the reader the impact of the story being told, a full-length body and background shot would lessen the impact. The two-column-by-five-inch picture may become

5. George R. Venizelos, "First Instinct Should Be To Tell the City Desk," Editorially Speaking, *Gannetteer Magazine,* April, 1974, p. 6.

While staff photographers handle the local news assignments, most newspapers also have Wirephoto machines leased from Associated Press/ United Press International to bring the national and international picture events to their newsrooms.

National and international news copy is brought to the local newsroom via the major news services' wire teletype machines . . .

. . . and both video and print units are housed in an area separate from the newsroom because of the constant clacking noise of the machines as they type out the news 24 hours a day.

a one-column-by-two-and-a-half inch picture. And, of course, the reverse editing could be more effective in another picture situation. In some cases, the reducing of a picture in size might give more impact to the picture and allow a second picture to also be used in the space that one larger picture might have taken.

Dick Sroda, director of photography for the *San Bernardino* (Calif.) *Sun-Telegram,* believes there are no rules for good photo editing. "Nor should there be any. Each picture has to be judged on its own."[6]

According to Sroda:

> Pictures should not be used to break up the type or to take care of pesty promotion chairmen who keep nagging the editor. Nor should a picture be used to illustrate a story unless it provides additional information. It should not be used as a graphic device intended to draw the reader's attention to a story he wouldn't otherwise read.[7]

Defending Photo Selection

Occasionally photographs, like news stories, will bring a public outcry of invasion of privacy. An example of this occurred when a

6. Dick Sroda, "Picture Editing—Who Needs It?" Editorially Speaking, *Gannetteer Magazine,* February, 1974, p. 1.
7. Sroda, "Picture Editing," p. 1.

photographer for the Battle Creek (Mich.) *Enquirer and News* shot a series of pictures showing a local man perched on a window ledge in a downtown office building, threatening to jump. The *Enquirer and News* ran the picture spread on the front page of the day's paper with a story, including the man's identification and the fact that he was talked out of the jump.

Public response in the form of letters to the editor accused the paper of poor taste in using the pictures, of adding to the man's problems by using the pictures and of forcing the man to move from Battle Creek because of the publicity. One writer wrote "there should be a law against it (publishing the photos and story on the front page) even if it's only a moral one."[8]

Enquirer and News Managing Editor Paul LaRocque answered the letters in a column Behind the News. The rationale he used is applicable to the news judgment demands of most photo editors.

Behind the photo decision
By Paul LaRocque
Managing Editor

It has often been said that the newspaper is a mirror of its community. That is, it portrays life as it is in the community in which it is published. And this, in turn, means that a newspaper, in order to accurately reflect its community, must publish the good and the bad and all that falls in between.

Newspapermen have been called insensitive to human feelings and we have been criticized for "always looking for the sensational."

We also have been told that we interfere with private lives and publish information that is none of our business.

And we have been told many times that we are concerned only with selling more papers and making more money.

Recently, the *Enquirer and News* was accused of all of the above after it published on page one of the June 5 newspaper a series of pictures of police rescuing a man who apparently was threatening to jump from a downtown building. Some letters of complaint are published on this page.

The decision to publish the series of pictures was not made lightly and it was not made without consideration of the complaints that we would receive from readers. It was made after discussion and thought by several *Enquirer and News* editors.

8. Letter to the Editor, Battle Creek, Mich. *Enquirer and News,* June 16, 1974, p. B–2.

A Battle Creek, Mich., man threatened to jump from a window in a local downtown office building. An *Enquirer and News* photographer shot a series of pictures of the man perched on the ledge. The problem—should the newspaper run the pictures, including one clearly showing the man's face, with the accompanying story. The decision and its repercussions are discussed in this chapter. Two of the pictures—the man perched on the ledge (a) and a police officer's successful attempt to talk the man down (b)—are reprinted here. A third picture, which clearly shows the face of the man, was not released by the newspaper for reprint on the grounds that when the incident occurred it was news and the man's suicide threat brought the police, causing the incident to become public record. Thus all three pictures were news at that time and were not an invasion of the man's privacy. However, today no such circumstances exist, and to visually identify the person in this book would be an invasion of his privacy and possibly could prove the basis for a lawsuit.

Here are some of the factors we considered before making the decision to use the series of pictures across the top of the front page:

—The action took place in a public building on a public street. Police were called to the scene and the incident is a matter of public record in police files. And there was an outside possibility that others could have been injured. Recently, in Detroit, a pedestrian was killed by a body falling from a downtown building.

—The pictures are a dramatic record of alert and calm police officers saving the life of a distraught person. Lt. James McLaughlin and Capt. Robert Houghtaling talked to the man on the window ledge and pulled him to safety. A life was saved—a very positive reason for running the pictures.

—Why did we use so many pictures, thus giving the incident prominent display? We looked at all the pictures. One picture would not have told the story. The first picture showed the precarious position. The second showed an officer talking to the man on the ledge. The third showed that he had been saved.

One complainant was angered because we were "splashing an emotionally ill person's picture all over the front page." Another said because of the pictures "that man is going to have to move out of town."

Emotional illness is no different than any other illness. It requires treatment and it can be cured. I wonder what reader reaction we would have received had we given the same pictorial display to a police officer jumping into a runaway car, the driver of which had suffered a heart attack at the wheel. The situations are quite similar.

The man on the ledge in our June 5 pictures is now receiving medical attention. We sincerely hope that he will not have to move out of town. If he does, it will not be because of our pictures but because of a narrow-minded community attitude toward mental illness.

As for the profit motive: The *Enquirer and News* did not sell more papers June 5. About 95 per cent of the circulation of the *Enquirer and News* is home delivered. Most of our customers buy the newspaper regardless of what is on the front page. It is very likely that a continued overplay of sensational stories would cause the *Enquirer and News* to lose customers. Sensationalism and profit did not enter into our decision to use the pictures.

We do not enjoy being the messenger with bad news, but if we are to accurately reflect the community we must print the bad along with the good.

The bad news will not go away if we ignore it. In fact, it could possibly increase because of public ignorance and apathy.

And there is another positive aspect other than a life being saved by police and a person in need receiving medical attention. A family, which is in desperate need of help, may receive it now that public attention has been called to its plight.

Putting It Together

Editing is the job of the reporter as well as the editor. Reading, correcting and cleaning up copy is the job of the reporter before handing it to an editor. Looking for ways to improve a story, digging up news leads, spotting potential stories and keeping the editor informed of developments in all these areas is the reporter's job. Suggesting photo assignments and working with the photographer to get the best picture to illustrate a story are also a part of the reporter's assignment.

Teamwork is the key to running a productive, accurate, informative news operation.

16 THE HEADLINE AND THE CUTLINE

Headlines

No matter how great a product is, if the producer doesn't find a way to tell the public about it, no one is going to buy it.

So it is with a news story. The most sparkling lead, the carefully constructed body copy and all the greatest transitions to carry the reader from point to point in the story are for naught if a dull or misleading headline is written. Few reporters are ever called upon to write a headline. This is one of an editor's jobs.

But, in most cases, if the story does have a lead that adequately reflects the story content, a headline that will draw readership should fall off the tip of the editor's pencil.

If the headline is drawn from within the body copy, then the reporter probably missed the real story lead. The headline is a mini-lead. In a few words, the headline should give the reader a clear idea of what to expect in the story. The exceptions to this, of course, are the suspended interest leads and sometimes the teaser leads. If the headline writer blows the story whammy, the reporter would be justified in breaking every pencil the editor owns.

Misleading Headlines

Headline writers build up expectations that readers want fulfilled in the story. Remember the World Football League story in chapter 9? Not only did the writer mislead the reader with the reference to the priest-player, but the headline writer picked up the lead reference and played it.

WFL Drafts Priest, Ex-NBA Star

And the reader was left to wonder how a word as broad as "ministry," as used in the sentence—

> The back led the Canadian Football League in rushing in 1972, but sat out last year after entering the ministry.

could be interpreted as having the man enter a priesthood.

Misleading headlines are often written by editors who did not read the entire story. Take the case of the headline:

Students Get Shortchanged
at College, Says Graduate

The 26-inch story, in fact, extolled the virtues of college as witnessed by the author, a summer intern with a New York state paper and recent journalism graduate.

The headline was taken from the fourth paragraph.

> . . . not only do I think college is worth the time and money,
> but I think I shortchanged myself the first time around . . .

A careless editor completely misread it and obviously stopped reading there.

The use of an incomplete title in a headline can cause some reader confusion if the person is not familiar with the nature of the story. Again, a sports story example:

Saldivar Gets
Nod; Regains
Feather Title

The story lead explains the headline.

> Vicente Saldivar of Mexico regained the world feather-weight championship tonight by pounding out a 15-round decision over Australian Johnny Famechon.

A misleading headline might be the result of an editor's error in assigning type to the headline and byline. The following was set in capitals, using the same type family, style and size.

7 MORE KILLED
by THE ASSOCIATED PRESS

Sexism in Headlines

Remember the sexist lead in chapter 9?

> The Republican party's new co-chairman is a pretty blonde
> who fits the image of All-American girl.

Here is the headline for that story:

GOP Co-Chairman
Is Pretty Blonde

But some editors have to search further than the lead to come up with the sexist tie-in. The next headline was taken from the second following paragraph of a story about three women attorneys who opened a law office.

"Women are superior to men in every way," she added with a chuckle. "They are smarter, prettier and nicer, and they smell better too."

The headline:

> 3 Women Set Up
> Pretty Law Firm

Well, at least it wasn't written:

> 3 Women Set Up
> Smelly Law Firm

In searching for the snappy headline, the writer should avoid extremes in references to sex.

Headline Tells the Story

A headline does its job when it gives an accurate clue as to the story's content. Here is a sampling of headlines that summarize the story and are good eye stoppers.

> Dog Guards
> Unconscious
> Master, 83

* * *

> An Unusual Hotel:
> Residents Dead

* * *

> "I'll Stay Gone Forever"
> Woman Defies Order to Give Child to Natural Mother

* * *

> CPA Is Suing
> Telephone Co.
> As a Ding-A-Ling

* * *

> Unwed Father
> Sues for Baby

A danger for the headline writer when he does not take the headline from the lead lies in having the headline reference completely edited from the story. Take this headline:

Dubuque KC's
Rap 2 Movies

And the story—edited to one paragraph:

Three Dubuque County Knights of Columbus
organizations have demanded an end to what
they call "trash" movies in the Dubuque area.

End of story. So where are the two movies referred to in the headline? On the cutting room floor, where an editor with a small news hole— just one paragraph deep—snipped it off the story.

Take a Second Look

After a headline is written, rewritten and rewritten again to fit an allotted column width, the editor can be so weary of working with it that he neglects to take a last look at what finally fits. The result can be often humorous and sometimes ridiculous, as the headline writer of the following found out after publication:

Wharton Gets
Pat on Back
From Rear

The lead was taken from the first paragraph of the story that carried the dateline, Wharton.

County Superintendent of Schools Leslie V. Rear gave the
board of education a pat on the back at last night's meeting.

In sports reporting, the rules of good writing are sometimes tossed to the winds. The sports writer and editor simply assume that their readers need only clues to recognize the sport being discussed. Witness the headline:

Freeland
Shakes Off
Shepherd

Not once in six paragraphs does the writer mention the sport. But, there are clues. The lead:

Freeland's size was just too much for game Shepherd to
overcome in the finals of the B eckenridge Class C district
here Friday night, the Blue Jays dropping a 72-69 decision.

Then, there are phrases such as: *floors a front line that averages 6-5, outscored from the field by 14 points, done in by a 28-11 deficit at the free-throw line* and *a blazing 26-point performance.* But not once is the word *basketball* used in the story.

Sensational Headlines

Some newspapers take a more sensational slant on the news presentation. Their headlines reflect the story color as well as give a condensed version of the story. Two examples are:

Grab Biz Man
As Pot Seller

A Bronx businessman was arrested in New Rochelle yesterday after he allegedly sold three pounds of marijuana to a cute blonde who turned out to be a lady cop . . .

The staccato use of slang in the headline catches the reader's eye and curiosity. Read on.

Sues Shrink
Says That He
Couched Her

A prominent East Side psychiatrist is being sued for $1,250,000 by a brunette former patient on charges that he made love to her as part of her treatment, according to papers on file yesterday in Supreme Court . . .

Cutlines

The picture cutline[1] or caption is sometimes a miniature story in itself.

This occurs when the picture is run wild, that is, without an accompanying story, and also when the editor has the room and directs the reporter to write more than a name line or a teaser line for a picture. The longer cutline should answer the questions the reader might ask if he or she were witnessing the scene. Writing this picture cutline is like writing the lead for a news story but with the reader exiting after the first paragraph. The reporter must get all the pertinent facts into the cutline. Here is an example of a reporter who did that. The picture showed a man walking alone on bridge girder spans. It was run wild.

1. The word *cutline* stems from the newspaper letterpress process of etching a picture on a zinc plate and then cutting the plate so that the picture could be fit into the page layout with the type. A line (s) of type identifying the picture ran beneath the zinc plate. Thus, the term *cutline* was born.

Jeremy Krauss, 21, walked the high iron girders of Golden Gate bridge for two hours while highway patrol officers and bridge employes tried to talk him out of leaping. Then he fell—into nets spread to protect bridge painters. Later, he walked to safety.

Questions with No Answers

But not all picture cutlines are complete. Some, like the following, leave a big question for the reader. The picture showed an infant, with one leg in a cast, lying in a crib. The cutline read:

It's not a cast of thousands, nor a baby cast in a new role, but maybe 28-day-old Norman Mansfield can have the cast on his broken leg bronzed when he gets older. Norman, who barely tips the scales at five pounds, broke his right leg Tuesday in Toronto, but is resting fine.

All those details on Norman and not a clue as to how the 28-day-old child broke his leg.

Some sports writers are as obtuse at naming games in cutlines as they are in revealing them in stories. Eleven girls stand in a cluster, smiling at the camera. They are wearing jeans and sweatshirts. The cutline listed all the girls' names and opened with:

The Comets were undisputed champions of the city recreation sponsored Women's League this past season, posting an 8-0 record.

The cutline did not tell what competition these champions participated in.

Story and Pictures

When a picture accompanies a story, the main message of the story sometimes is played in the cutline. For example, a story on a civic play will include the play opening dates, where it is opening, the play times and ticket information, along with details on cast members and play preparations. In the accompanying pictures, the vital information of location, times, opening date and ticket information should also be given. If several pictures are used, this information may be spread among the cutlines. Readers will sometimes look at the pictures on a page and skip the story. These readers should get the pertinent information about the play in the cutline, just as readers who read the complete story do.

If space is limited, or at the editor's discretion, a story picture may carry only the nameline of the person shown. Sometimes if more than one picture accompanies a story, teaser lines will run under each picture. The lines may read independent of each other or they may be written to be read together as the reader scans the pictures.

Cutlines Can Draw Readers

Sometimes the cutline information can be used as a drawing card for the story. This occurs when the picture has a reference to the story. For example, a picture shows a huge Saint Bernard dog in the foreground and two small boys standing alongside the dog. The cutline:

> The little Heineys, Robert and John, and their 200-pound defender, Battle.

The accompanying story tells of an attempt by two men to break down a storm door at the Heiney home in Detroit. Mrs. Heiney screamed and Battle rushed to the door and, according to Mrs. Heiney, "scared the wits out of the two of them and they fled to their car screaming."

Here, the use of the word *defender* in the cutline catches the reader's eye and curiosity and results in reading of the story.

Summary

As a newswriter, you can help draw readers to your story by writing a lead that contains the pertinent story facts. This gives the headline writer material that will catch the reader's eye and lead the person right into your story.

17 TYPEWRITER VS. COMPUTER

The milestones of print journalism include the invention of type, the invention of movable type and, now, the introduction of computer type. Will the computer replace the reporter? No, but reporters must be capable typists and learn a coding language that is used to denote story identification, copy start, paragraphs, corrections and story end. Will the computer replace editors? No, but they must acquire new editing skills. Will the computer replace the print shop? No, but computer journalism is giving the back shop a face lifting and the printers second thoughts about job insecurity.

Newspaper union contracts are beginning to contain job security clauses. And, letterpress or hot-type printing methods are becoming extinct. Hot-metal line-casting machines sales numbered only 55 in 1972, while 4,100 phototypesetters, used in computer type composition, were sold worldwide the same year.

The arrival of the computer newsroom operation has not been an overnight affair. Nor has it been limited to only large newspapers. In 1971, the *Breeze Courier* (circulation 8,567) in Taylorville, Ill., installed an optical character recognition scanner (OCR), a video display terminal (VDT) and a couple of phototypesetters.

The cost of the changeover inhibits a swift, national switch to VDT, OCR, and CRT (cathode ray tube) journalism. Systems run from several hundred thousand dollars to well over a million.

Computer Operations

VDT-OCR Operation

Some newspapers are taking the first steps in the conversion through the use of optical character recognition units (OCR or the scanner system) and electric typewriters. The system consists of giving electric typewriters to all reporters and OCRs to the composing room. Reporters also receive special blue ink pens and the editors black ink pens. The reporter types the story and makes the preliminary editing marks in blue ink, which the OCR scanner cannot read. The copy then goes to the editor, who does the final editing deletions in black ink,

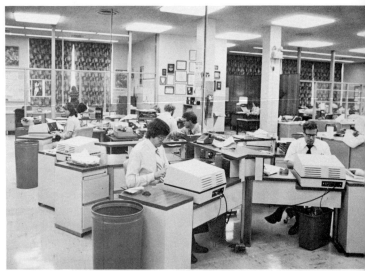

Two views of typical news-rooms: the traditional . . .

. . . and the computer-converted operations.

In a non-computerized news-room, the reporter rolls a sheet of paper into a manual typewriter and writes the news story.

In a computerized news operation, the manual typewriter and paper are traded for a video display terminal (VDT).

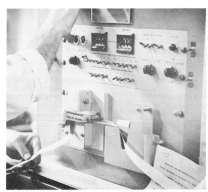

On the non-computer news-paper, typesetting is done on a Linotype machine. The reporter's typed copy is given to the operator who sets it into lead letters.

In some news operations a preliminary step to a computerized operation is the use of the compugraphic system. The operator first translates the reporter's typed copy into a punched tape . . .

The tape is then fed into a compugraphic machine . . .

. . . along with direction on how many unit counts of type per column is to be set.

. . . and the result is a sheet of copy ready to be pasted on a makeup sheet.

In a totally computerized news operation, an optical character recognition scanner reads the reporter's typewritten copy and translates it into a series of electric impulses that, in turn, are fed into a typewriting computer that produces the sheet of copy, set and premeasured to the news column width.

which the scanner can read. If an insertion of copy is to be made, it must be typed in by the editor.

Copy is next sent to the scanner where it is read and fed into the computer as electronic impulses. Then, with the push of a button, the story is sent to the typesetting machine, which feeds out the printed copy on paper ready to be pasted up, photographed, made into an offset plate and sent to the press.

CRT/VDT, OCR and CAM Operation

Some newsrooms have already switched to the all-electronic news operation. The first was the Richmond (Va.) *Times-Dispatch and News Leader.* The electric typewriters have been replaced with cathode ray tube/video display terminal (CRT/VDT). The CRT/VDT resembles a typewriter keyboard attached to the base of a television screen. A reporter can type a story, giving it an identification code, and have the copy appear on the CRT screen. Then, with a push of a button, the story is sent into a computer storage unit. The editor, as the copy is needed, can call up the reporter's story by typing out the story identification code on his or her CRT/VDT, edit it and write a headline. The story can then be sent back to the storage unit or on to the OCR.

With the use of computers, even page layout can be completed on composition and makeup terminals (CAM). Using the CAM, the compositor operator can call up on a video screen, line drawings or the story copy. The operator may then compose, edit or review the copy and art, using the CAM data-entry facilities for manipulation, with immediate display of the results. When satisfied, the operator can send the completed work to a storage computer for its eventual call-out to a full-page output device capable of setting both copy and graphic material. The CAM may be used for page layout, advertising composition and advertising page makeup.

The Associated Press and United Press International both are using the video display terminals for editing. Other newspapers using the various computer systems include the *Detroit News, Milwaukee Journal, Davenport* (Iowa) *Democrat, Today* (Cocoa, Fla.), *Daytona Beach* (Fla.) *Journal and News,* the *Richmond* (Va.) *Times-Dispatch* and *News Leader,* the *Baltimore Sun* and The *Merced* (Calif.) *Sun-Star.*

Reader Benefits

What does all this electronic journalism mean to the reader? A good computer newspaper system provides greater flexibility and speed, coupled with offset printing, to produce a higher quality reproduction.

Newspaper budgets can be increased for news as costs go down in production. Paper costs will decline with the increase of the reporter operated CRT/VDTs. And with the switch to video computers in the newsroom, the concept of the newspaper subscriber having a VDT in the living room has taken a step closer to reality.

Objections to the Computer

With technological advances come status quo protests. Some reporters and editors find their attention tied more to the computer operation than to the production of news copy. In the early changeover phases, mistakes in computer copy production slip through. Making the corrections for the scanner system demands more time and care since, in some cases, the copy must be fed back into the typewriter to make a correction.

A more serious objection is the compromise of journalistic excellence in copy editing. For example, if it is near deadline and a piece of copy that has the lead buried in the fourth paragraph comes across the editor's desk, the job of moving the fourth paragraph to the first paragraph position (an easy job with a pair of scissors and a paste pot for the pre-computer news copy) now requires a retyping of the whole page. A second thought by the editor may be that the present lead isn't that bad and the story is passed as is.

The Union Problem

The concern of newspaper production unions for job retention for composing room employees is apparent in most contract negotiations. In some instances, newspaper printers walking off the job in protest of the computer installations, found that the paper was being printed anyway, using the computer installations already on hand. As a result, longer contract periods are being agreed to by printers and newspapers, with the guarantee of job security for these employees.

The 1974 labor contracts agreed upon by the publishers of the *New York Times* and the *New York Daily News* and the International Typesetters Union give the present printers a lifetime job guarantee that cannot be revoked. A printer may be put on suspension but cannot be permanently discharged. A mandatory retirement age was not specified, but the publishers agreed to give a $2,500 incentive bonus to printers who requested early retirement within the first six months of the agreement.

All printers on both papers were given a six-month productivity leave with full pay, to be taken between 1975 and 1984. The early retirees also received the six-month leave.

Some of the newspapers plan to meet the decreasing composing room employment demands by not filling jobs that open up through retirements, reassignments or resignations.

While the total transition of the newspaper industry, large, medium and small dailies and weeklies, will take a number of years to realize, students in journalism schools today will most likely work for a news-room computer operation one day. The question, then, is how to prepare students today for those jobs? The cost of computer installation, prohibitive for many newspapers, is within few journalism school budgets. Some large university journalism schools have begun computer journalism training. But, other colleges, located in areas that have newspaper computer operations, will have to let field trips provide the introduction to the computer journalism.

The Gannett Van

Most large university journalism schools, and certainly any other colleges within commuting distance of the university campus, will have the opportunity for an up-close, hands-on training session with a fully equipped computer newsroom on wheels. The Gannett Newspaper Foundation of Rochester, N.Y., has outfitted an oversize moving van, with side expansion to 17 feet, as a mobile computer newsroom. Costing $280,000 to construct and furnish, the van has an annual operating budget of nearly $170,000.

The van's newsroom contains the electronic equipment to allow students to write and edit copy and assemble and print entire newspaper pages without using traditional hot metal methods. The van's equipment includes the following:

Electric Typewriter
Computerized optical character reader (OCR scanner) and video display terminals (VDTs) for the generation of paper tape for the laboratory's phototypesetter.
Keyboard photo headline machine.
Darkroom with camera able to reproduce an entire newspaper page or pre-screen photos before page formatting.
Small offset press capable of printing a tabloid-size newspaper page.

The van, labeled "Newspaper Technology . . . On The Move A Service of the Gannett Newspaper Foundation," visits journalism schools, for ten-day to two-week visits.

The Future

Electronic computer journalism is here and the future will see its growth and expansion into all areas of print journalism. The journalism student today who is postponing that typing course would be well advised to get into it now. Learn the journalism computer language. Job applications and/or employment tests soon may have questions concerning the CRT/VDTs and OCRs. If the Gannett van is in your area, get over to see it and use its facilities. If it's not a class project, do it on your own. Read the journalism trades magazines, especially *Editor and Publisher, Matrix* and *Quill,* to keep up with the electronic revolution. Try to get part-time or summer jobs with newspapers that have the computer equipment in operation. The difference between knowing and not knowing how to prepare computer copy may be just the difference needed in getting that first reporting job.

18 THE JOURNALISM JOB MARKET

The journalism job market is tight and the squeeze is going to get tighter. The reason lies with the simple laws of supply and demand. Journalism school enrollments are soaring. There were 10,793 graduates in 1973; the 1974 prediction was 11,700; and the 1978 college graduations are expected to find 20,500 students receiving journalism degrees.[1]

"J" Student Explosion

According to figures compiled by the Newspaper Fund of Princeton, N.J., journalism enrollments will continue to grow at an average of 13.1 percent a year, based on previous growth patterns, while media job projections, through 1978, show only a 6.7 percent average annual increase. Translated into students and jobs, it means that 20,500 journalism college graduates in 1978 will be competing for 5,600 available media jobs, including newspapers, broadcasting, wire services, magazines, advertising and public relations.

What is the attraction for journalism jobs? In an article appearing in the *Chicago Tribune*,[2] Robert Haiman, managing editor of the *St. Petersburg* (Fla.) *Times,* gave his opinion.

> Journalism is sort of where it's at now. I hear these kids say the same kinds of things kids were saying about the Peace Corps five or six years ago.
>
> There's no doubt in my mind the whole Watergate thing— Woodward and Bernstein (The Washington Post's two young Pulitzer Prize-winning investigative reporters)—has a lot to do with it.

Employers' Market

The current job outlook makes the media market an employers' utopia. Media employers will have many applicants to choose from for

1. Newspaper Fund, "Competition in Journalism Employment Market," Princeton, N.J., 1973. Reprinted with permission.
2. Jan Schaffer, "Hard fact—journalism market glutted," *Chicago Tribune*, March 24, 1974.

every job opening. Who will get the job? It will be the person who wisely uses the college years to combine education with job experience. Internships with local news and non-news employers should be looked into. Basic newswriting skills and disciplines are needed in the other media fields of advertising, public relations, magazines and company communications. Some colleges offer internships as a part of the journalism curriculum and the student can earn college credit while getting professional media experience.

Smaller colleges, especially the two-year schools, have the advantage of fitting the internship into the college program. Here, the smaller number of journalism students to be placed lends itself to local media jobs. Most media employers will sponsor internship programs with the colleges. Two-year journalism students who transfer to a four-year college and major in another field graduate with two major areas of study, such as journalism for the Associate Arts degree, and sociology, psychology, anthropology, political science or history for the Bachelor of Arts degree. Any internship(s) or summer media jobs held by the graduate add to the possibility of the person's job application surviving the initial weeding out by an editor or media personnel executive.

Getting Writing Experience

Most newspaper, radio stations and television stations can use correspondents or stringers. These are reporters who take part-time assignments with a news operation. Many newspapers also accept freelance articles and photographs. To check out the job possibilities, follow the advance preparations learned in interviewing techniques. Find out as much as you can about the news operation of the paper or broadcast station where an application is to be made. Study what kind of local stories it runs. If many feature stories are used, chances are some of them are freelance contributions. Get the name of the news editor and call for an appointment. Take along your clip book (samples of your writing) and a few ideas for articles you might write. Offer to submit an article without payment, the topic to be selected by the editor, as a sample of the work you can do for the editor. Chances are good that if the editor takes you up on the offer and accepts the story for publication, you will be paid stringer rates. And, more important, you'll have a story for your clip book.

The Clip Book

The clip book is an important possession for a news reporter. It is a folio of the reporter's best news and feature stories. These writing samples are a part of a reporter's job application. The student should start a clip book with the first story published in the school newspaper.

As better stories are written, the clip book is updated. Any stories written professionally by the student should be included. Broadcast reporters should keep copies of the stories written, noting the date of broadcast.

What Editors Look For

What does it take to get a news job? What qualities does an editor look for in a reporter? Steve Ahrens, news editor of the (Boise) *Idaho Statesman* answered the question by listing the qualities he expects in a newswriter:

1. A reporter who values his or her own professionalism and can respect it in others, in spite of differences of opinion;
2. A reporter who makes just one more phone call to get one more side of the issue even after he/she thinks the whole story is in hand;
3. A reporter who can listen to those with doctorate degrees and then write for those without doctorate degrees to read and understand;
4. A reporter who has a genuine interest in improving the whole newspaper and works for constructive gains;
5. Staffers who submerge personal preferences or egos in the interest of putting out the best possible product for the reader.[3]

Reporters' Salaries

Salaries will vary among media jobs, public relations ranking among the highest and newspaper reporters among the lowest. In the area of news, the size of the newspaper or broadcast market affects salaries, as does the experience of the reporter. Publications that have contracts with The Newspaper Guild usually provide the best salaries for beginning reporters. At papers without Guild units, management will set the wage scale and it may vary considerably, even within the same area.

The average starting salary in 1974 Newspaper Guild contracts for reporters with no experience was about $150. Experience is spelled out in the Guild contract at one medium-sized (circulation 38,000) midwestern daily newspaper as full-time employment—40-hour week —with a daily newspaper having a circulation of more than 20,000. The paper's management also has the prerogative to accept any expe-

---

3. Steve Ahrens, "Miami Dolphins Theory of Journalism," *Editorially Speaking, Gannetteer Magazine*, April, 1974, p. 5.

rience gained on a publication of less than 20,000 circulation, daily or weekly, and any part-time news experience the reporter might have.

Guild contracts are negotiated with individual newspapers, so the experience definition may change somewhat from newspaper to newspaper.

Another 1974 salary survey taken among metropolitan newspapers showed that more than three-fourths of the reporters, writers and copy editors, were paid $15,000 to $25,000 a year, or $288 to $480 a week. Within that salary range, the greatest proportion of journalists made $15,000 to $18,000 a year. Reporters at a Guild paper in Chicago with five years' experience made a minimum of $317 a week, or $16,500 a year.[4]

The First Job

A journalism graduate's first job is important. It should be in the news field, regardless of the eventual career goal. Newswriting experience will be valuable in any field. The discipline of deadline pressure can be applied in advertising, public relations, company publications and magazines. Any writer who submits copy to a news medium has to know the requirements. These include copy and publication deadlines, copy preparation, how to write and edit a news story, picture requirements and specifications and to whom to send the story.

Large metropolitan papers rarely, if ever, hire a reporter straight from the campus with a B.A. Besides, the metro papers are large and specialized—reporters assigned to only one area—and the best reporter training comes from being assigned to a variety of beats. The middle-sized and smaller dailies and weekly papers are the places to get this kind of experience. The college and summer-job writing experience will be appreciated and considered at these papers. The job outlook for broadcast media jobs in large markets is also limited, and the best beginning job opportunities lie in the smaller city markets.

A reporter with basic newswriting experience can move freely among the various job offerings in the journalism field. It is not unusual for a person to work as news reporter, advertising copywriter, public relations writer and squeeze in some radio news and on-air time before trying the television field. Magazine and wire service reporters can come from just as diverse professional background.

Company Journalism

Many corporations, companies and industries, with a large number of employes, have their own communications offices. A weekly or monthly newspaper is published for employes and sometimes a maga-

4. Schaffer, "Market glutted," *Chicago Tribune,* March 24, 1974.

zine is published solely for the company's customers. Many times, the communications people work with the company's outside public relations or advertising agencies in preparing advertising campaigns or employe incentive programs.

Large corporations will have communications people in several departments. Public relations and marketing are two examples. Many corporation executives climb the company ladder through public relations assignments. A public relations person must be familiar with the entire operation of the corporation. Knowing and understanding company policies, chain of command and most executive duties are all part of the job. Like the news reporter, if the public relations person does not understand the company and its workings, he or she cannot handle the relations—public and employe—job for the company. Extensive travel is sometimes required of the public relations writer and this familiarity with all facets and holdings of the company also contributes to job advancement possibilities.

Starting salaries, while they will vary between companies, may be higher than those of the comparable news media. Large companies with their own public relations and communications departments often hire new graduates. Some can even get into the management training programs. The company personnel door is not one to be overlooked by the journalism job seeker.

A Final Word

Whatever goal a journalism student has, the basic newswriting course is the foundation for future college journalism work and job training. The basics of all news jobs—style, writing principles, deadline pressures—are met in this course. A student turned off by the requirements and demands now is best advised to seek another profession. The student who thrives under the demands of the course has just turned the key in the door that opens to an exciting, interesting and varied career, which is limited only by one's imagination. WELCOME.

APPENDIX

NEWSWIRE STYLEBOOK

UNITED PRESS INTERNATIONAL

UNITED PRESS INTERNATIONAL

STYLEBOOK

UNITED PRESS INTERNATIONAL

220 East 42nd Street   •   New York, N.Y. 10017

REVISED EDITION 1968
TENTH PRINTING 1974

N O MANUAL in the world can produce good writing. Some of the ingredients are not definable. Among those that are, some stand out with particular importance—a questioning mind, imagination, command of language and, above all, a passionate regard for balance and accuracy.

The best story in the world can only suffer if its presentation does not adhere to the proper style. Thus this stylebook, to help both writers and editors achieve uniformity in one area where uniformity is an asset.

The advent of the Teletypesetter made it essential that the two basic news services arrive at a common style to facilitate the handling of their copy at subscribing newspapers.

The first joint UPI-AP stylebook was published in 1960. Now comes this second edition, revised and updated to reflect as closely as possible the consensus of the industry.

Countless editors have assisted in this revision over the past few years with their suggestions and we are grateful for the guidance they have given to the editors from the two services.

United Press International

Capitalization I

1.1 CAPITALIZE titles preceding a name: Secretary of State John Foster Dulles. LOWER CASE title standing alone or following a name: John Foster Dulles, secretary of state. EXCEPTION: Incumbent president of the United States is always capitalized. Do not capitalize candidate for president, no president may seize, etc.

1.2 CAPITALIZE government officials when used with name as title: Queen Elizabeth II, Premier Debre, etc. LOWER CASE when standing alone or following a name: Debre, premier of France.

1.3 CAPITALIZE Pope in all usage; pontiff is lower case.

1.4 CAPITALIZE foreign religious leader titles Imam, Patriarch, etc., but LOWER CASE standing alone or following a name. EXCEPTION: Pope and Dalai Lama, capitalized in all usage. (See Section VIII)

1.5 CAPITALIZE titles of authority before name but LOWER CASE standing alone or following a name: Ambassador John Jones; Jones, ambassador; the ambassador. (See 1.12, 3.31)

1.6 Long titles should follow a name: John Jones, executive director of the commercial department of Blank & Co. Richard Roe, secretary-treasurer, Blank & Co. (See 6.5)

1.7 LOWER CASE occupational or "false" titles such as day laborer John Jones, rookie left-handed pitcher Bill Wills, defense attorney John Jones. (See 2.14)

1.8 CAPITALIZE Union, Republic, Colonies referring to the United States; Republic of Korea, French Fifth Republic. (See 2.12)

1.9 CAPITALIZE U.S. Congress, Senate, House, Cabinet; Legislature when preceded by name of state; City Council; Security Council. LOWER CASE when standing alone: The legislature passed 300 bills.
   The building is the Capitol, the city is capital.
   Do not capitalize "congress" when it is used as a synonym for convention. (See 1.20)

CAPITALIZATION

1.10 CAPITALIZE committee in full names: Senate Judiciary Committee, House Ways and Means Committee, etc. LOWER CASE "subcommittee" in titles and standing alone, also "committee" standing alone.

In some shortened versions of long committee names, do not capitalize: Special Senate Select Committee to Investigate Improper Labor-Management Practices often is rackets committee, not capitalized.

1.11 CAPITALIZE full titles: Interstate Commerce Commission, New York State Thruway Authority, International Atomic Energy Authority, etc., LOWER CASE authority, commission, etc., standing alone. (See 2.1)

1.12 CAPITALIZE Supreme Court, Juvenile Court, 6th U.S. Circuit Court of Appeals, etc. (See 4.2) Specify which U.S. Court such as district, patent, tax, etc. It is Juvenile Court Judge John Jones and not Juvenile Judge John Jones.

1.13 CAPITALIZE Social Security (Administration, Act) when referring to U.S. system: He was receiving Social Security payments. LOWER CASE use in general sense: He was an advocate of social security for old age.

1.14 CAPITALIZE U.S. armed forces: Army (USA), Air Force (USAF), Navy (USN), Marines (USMC), Coast Guard, National Guard but LOWER CASE all foreign except Royal Air Force (RAF) and Royal Canadian Air Force (RCAF); French Foreign Legion, no abbreviation.

CAPITALIZE Marine, Coast Guardman, Swiss Guard, Evzone, Bengal Lancer, etc. LOWER CASE soldier, sailor, etc. NOTE: It is Coast Guardman (no "s") if member of U.S. Coast Guard.

CAPITALIZE Irish Republican Army (political). (See 1.20)

1.15 CAPITALIZE Joint Chiefs of Staff but LOWER CASE chiefs of staff.

1.16 CAPITALIZE holidays, historic events, ecclesiastical feasts, fast days, special events, hurricanes, typhoons, etc. Mothers Day, Labor Day, Battle of the Bulge, Good Friday, Passover, Christmas, Halloween, National Safety Week, Hurricane Hazel, Typhoon Tilda, New Year's (Day, Eve) but LOWER CASE: What will the new year bring? At the start of the new year, etc.

CAPITALIZATION

1.17 CAPITALIZE Antarctica, Arctic Circle but not antarctic or arctic.

1.18 CAPITALIZE specific regions: Middle East, Mideast, Middle West, Midwest, Upper Peninsula (Michigan), Southern (Illinois, California) Texas (Oklahoma) Panhandle, Orient, Chicago's near South Side, Loop, etc.

1.19 CAPITALIZE ideological or political areas: East-West, East Germany, West Germany. LOWER CASE mere direction: Snow fell in western North Dakota.

1.20 CAPITALIZE political parties and members but not "party." Democrat, Democratic, Republican, Socialist, Independent, Nationalist, Communist, Congress (India) etc. LOWER CASE democratic form of government, republican system, socialism, communism, etc.
CAPITALIZE Red when used as political, geographic, military, etc., descriptive.
LOWER CASE nationalist in referring to a partisan of a country.
CAPITALIZE Algerian Liberation Front (FLN) and Irish Republican Army (IRA). (See 1.14)

1.21 CAPITALIZE names of fraternal organizations: B'nai B'rith (no abbreviation), Ancient Free & Accepted Masons (AF&AM), Knights of Columbus (K. of C. as departure from 2.1). (See 2.5)

1.22 CAPITALIZE Deity and He, His, Him denoting Deity but not who, whose, whom. CAPITALIZE Talmud, Koran, Bible and all names of the Bible, confessions of faith and their adherents. (See Section VIII)
CAPITALIZE Satan and Hades but not devil and hell.

1.23 CAPITALIZE Civil War, War Between the States, Korean War, Revolution (U.S. and Bolshevik), World War I, World War II, etc.

1.24 CAPITALIZE names of races: Caucasian, Chinese, Negro, Indian, etc. LOWER CASE black, white, red (See 1.20), yellow. Do NOT use "colored" for Negro except in National Association for the Advancement of Colored People. Colored is correct in African usage.
Identification by race should be made when it is pertinent.

CAPITALIZATION

1.25 CAPITALIZE common noun as part of formal name: Hoover Dam, Missouri River, Barr County Courthouse. LOWER CASE dam, river, courthouse, etc., standing alone. CAPITALIZE Empire State Building, Blue Room, Carlton House (hotel), Carlton house (home), Wall Street, Hollywood Boulevard. (See 4.1)
Plurals would be: Broad and Main streets.

1.26 CAPITALIZE species of livestock, animals, fowl, etc., but LOWER CASE noun: Airedale, terrier, Percheron, horse; Hereford, whiteface, etc.

1.27 CAPITALIZE names of flowers: Peace rose, etc. If Latin generic names are used CAPITALIZE the genus (camellia, Thea japonica).

1.28 CAPITALIZE trade names and trademark names: Super Sabre Jet, Thunderjet, but Boeing 707 jet (jet descriptive, not part of name), Pan Am Clipper.
"Coke" is a registered trademark of Coca-Cola and is not a synonym for soft drinks. "Thermos" is a registered trademark. Use vacuum bottle (flask, jug) instead.
Use generic, or broad, term preferably in all trademark names.

1.29 Some proper names have acquired independent common meaning and are not capitalized. They include paris green, dutch door, brussels sprouts, etc. Check dictionary.

1.30 CAPITALIZE titles of books, plays, hymns, poems, songs, etc., and place in quotation marks: "The Courtship of Miles Standish." (See 3.26)
The words a, in, of, etc., are capitalized only at the start or end of a title: "Of Thee I Sing" and "All Returns Are In" as examples.

1.31 CAPITALIZE first word of a quotation making a complete sentence after a comma or colon: Franklin said, "A penny saved is a penny earned." (See 3.16)

1.32 CAPITALIZE names of organizations, expositions, etc., Boy Scouts, Red Cross, World's Fair, Iowa State Fair but LOWER CASE scout, fair standing alone.

CAPITALIZATION

1.33 CAPITALIZATION of names should follow the use of preference of the person. In general, foreign particles are lower case when used with a forename, initials or title: Charles de Gaulle, Gen. de Gaulle, but De Gaulle without forename or title. (See 3.5, 6.4)

In anglicized versions the article usually is capitalized: Fiorello La Guardia.

It is E. I. du Pont de Nemours and Du Pont; Irenee du Pont but Samuel F. Du Pont (his usage).

1.34 CAPITALIZE fanciful appellations: Buckeye State, Leatherneck, Project Mercury, Operation Deep Freeze (Deepfreeze, one word, is trademark.)

1.35 CAPITALIZE decorations, awards, etc. Medal of Honor, Nobel Peace Prize.

Abbreviations II

2.1 First mention of organizations, firms, agencies, groups, etc., should be spelled out. Exception: AFL-CIO. In names that do not have commonly known abbreviations, the abbreviation should be bracketed after the spelled name. Thereafter in the story the abbreviation may be used. Example:

The desire was expressed in the Inter-American Economic and Social Council (IA-ECOSOC) of the Organization of American States (OAS) in considering the European Economic Cooperation Organization (ECCO).

Distant Early Warning line (DEW line).

General Agreement of Tariffs and Trade (GATT).

2.2 ABBREVIATE time zones, airplane designations, ships, distress call, military terms, etc. EDT, CST, MIGI7, B60, Military Police (MP), absent without official leave (AWOL), SOS (but May Day), USS Iowa, SS Brasil. (See 3.3, 10.12, 6.15)

2.3 ABBREVIATE business firms: Warner Bros.; Brown Implement Co.; Amalgamated Leather, Ltd.; Smith & Co., Inc. (See 3.40)

2.4 ABBREVIATE St., Ave., Blvd., Ter., in addresses but not Point, Port, Circle, Plaza, Place, Drive, Oval, Road, Lane. Examples:

16 E. 72nd St. (single "E" with period); 16 Gregory Ave. NW (no periods in "NW"); Sunset Boulevard, Main Street, Fifth Avenue (no addresses. (See 1.25, 4.1)

2.5 Lower case abbreviations usually take periods. The rule of thumb is if the letters without periods spell words, periods are needed. Examples: c.o.d., f.o.b., etc. However, m.p.h., a.m., p.m.

Periods are not needed in 35mm (film), 105mm (armament), ips (tape recording).

In news stories first mention of speed should be "miles an hour" or "miles per hour" and thereafter in story use m.p.h.

ABBREVIATE versus as vs. (with period).

A B B R E V I A T I O N S

2.6 ABBREVIATE states which follow cities (towns, villages, etc.), airbases, Indian agencies, national parks, etc. (See 3.23)

2.7 Standard abbreviations for states (rule of thumb is abbreviate none of six letters or less except Texas):

Ala.	Ill.	Miss.	N.M.	Tenn.
Ariz.	Ind.	Mo.	N.Y.	Tex.
Ark.	Kan.	Mont.	Okla.	Vt.
Calif.	Ky.	Neb.	Ore.	Va.
Colo.	La.	Nev.	Pa.	Wash.
Conn.	Md.	N.C.	R.I.	Wis.
Del.	Mass.	N.D.	S.C.	W.Va.
Fla.	Mich.	N.H.	S.D.	Wyo.
Ga.	Minn.	N.J.		

Do not abbreviate Alaska, Hawaii, Idaho, Iowa, Ohio, Maine or Utah. All states are spelled standing alone: He went to Minnesota at the turn of the century.

2.8 ABBREVIATIONS:

C.Z.	P.R.	V.I.	Alta.	B.C.	Man.	N.S.
Que.	Ont.	Sask.	Nfld.	N.B.	B.W.I.	P.E.I.

but obscure ones should be spelled in story, such as Prince Edward Island, etc.

2.9 B.C. as abbreviation of Canadian province must be preceded by town name; B.C., the era, must be preceded by a date.

2.10 ABBREVIATE U.S.S.R. and U.A.R. in datelines.

2.11 ABBREVIATE United Nations and United States in titles: U.S. Junior Chamber of Commerce (Jaycees as exception in abbreviation by letters), U.N. Educational, Scientific and Cultural Organization (UNESCO). (See 2.1, 3.3)

2.12 Spell United States and United Nations when used as a noun. U.S.A. and U.N. as nouns may be used in texts or direct quotations.

2.13 ABBREVIATE and capitalize religious, fraternal, scholastic or honorary degrees, etc., but lower case when spelled: B.A., bachelor of arts. (See 8.4)

ABBREVIATIONS

2.14 ABBREVIATE titles and capitalize: Mr., Mrs., M., Mlle., Dr., Prof., Sen., Rep., Asst., Lt. Gov., Gov. Gen., Supt., Atty. Gen., Dist. Atty., in titles before names but not after names. Do not abbreviate attorney in: The statement by defense attorney John Jones, etc. (See 1.7)

2.15 Mr. is used only with Mrs., or with clerical titles (except in texts or verbatim quotes). (See 8.4, 8.9, 8.10)

2.16 Do NOT abbreviate port, association, point, detective, department, deputy, commandant, commodore, field marshal, general manager, secretary-general, secretary, treasurer, fleet admiral or general of the armies (but Adm. Nimitz or Gen. Pershing is correct). (See 2.21)
Do NOT abbreviate "guaranteed annual wage" and do NOT abbreviate Christmas.

2.17 ABBREVIATE months when used with dates: Oct. 12, 1492; but spell out otherwise as October 1492. Abbreviations for months are Jan., Feb., Aug., Sept., Oct., Nov., Dec. Do not abbreviate March, April, May, June or July except in tabular or financial routine where the abbreviations are Mar, Apr, Jun, Jly and spell May.

2.18 Days of the week are abbreviated only in tabular matter or financial routine where they are Mon, Tue, Wed, Thu, Fri, Sat, Sun. The proper word division for Wednesday is: Wednes-day.

2.19 ABBREVIATE St. and Ste. as in Sault Ste. Marie, St. Louis, St. Lawrence, etc. (except Saint John, N.B.). Abbreviate the mountain but spell the city: Mt. Everest, Mount Vernon; Abbreviate army post but spell city: Ft. Sill, Fort Meyer.

2.20 Do not abbreviate Alexander, Benjamin, Charles, Frederick, William, etc., as Alec, Alex, Ben., Benj., Chas., etc., unless person does so himself. Follow person's preference.

ABBREVIATIONS

2.21 Military abbreviations:

ARMY

General	Gen.
Lieutenant General	Lt. Gen.
Major General	Maj. Gen.
Brigadier General	Brig. Gen.
Colonel	Col.
Lieutenant Colonel	Lt. Col.
Major	Maj.
Captain	Capt.
Lieutenant	Lt.
Chief Warrant Officer	CWO
Warrant Officer	WO
Sergeant Major	Sgt. Maj.
Specialist Nine	Spec. 9
Master Sergeant	M. Sgt.
First Sergeant	1st. Sgt.
Specialist Eight	Spec. 8
Platoon Sergeant	Platoon Sgt.
Sergeant First Class	Sgt. 1.C.
Specialist Seven	Spec. 7
Staff Sergeant	S. Sgt.
Specialist Six	Spec. 6
Sergeant	Sgt.
Specialist Five	Spec. 5
Corporal	Cpl.
Specialist Four	Spec. 4
Private First Class	Pfc.
Private	Pvt.
Recruit	Rct.

NAVY, COAST GUARD

Admiral	Adm.
Vice Admiral	Vice Adm.
Rear Admiral	Rear Adm.
Commodore	Commodore
Captain	Capt.
Commander	Cmdr.
Lieutenant Commander	Lt. Cmdr.
Lieutenant	Lt.
Lieutenant Junior Grade	Lt. (j.g.)
Ensign	Ens.
Commissioned Warrant Officer	CWO
Warrant Officer	WO
Master Chief Petty Officer	M.CPO
Senior Chief Petty Officer	S.CPO
Chief Petty Officer	CPO
Petty Officer 1st Class	PO 1.C.
Petty Officer Second Class	PO 2.C.
Petty Officer Third Class	PO 3.C.
Seaman	Seaman
Seaman Apprentice	Seaman Appren.
Seaman Recruit	Seaman Rct.

MARINE CORPS

Commissioned officers are abbreviated the same as Army, warrant officers the same as Navy. Noncommissioned designations are the same as Army except specialist and:

Master Gunnery Sergeant	Mgy. Sgt.
Gunnery Sergeant	Gunnery Sgt.
Lance Corporal	Lance Cpl.

AIR FORCE

Air Force commissioned officers are abbreviated the same as Army. Noncommissioned designations include:

Chief Master Sergeant	CM. Sgt.
Senior Master Sergeant	SM. Sgt.
Master Sergeant	M. Sgt.
Technical Sergeant	T. Sgt.
Staff Sergeant	S. Sgt.
Airman 1st Class	Airman 1.C.
Airman 2nd Class	Airman 2.C.
Airman 3rd Class	Airman 3.C.
Airman Basic	Airman

The Air Force also may designate certain other descriptions as radarman, navigator, etc., but such designations are not abbreviated.

The Navy has numerous ratings such as machinist, torpedoman, etc., and they are not abbreviated.

The Army, Coast Guard and Marine Corps also may describe personnel by specific duty in addition to rank.

Note: The period is used in several abbreviations, such as Spec. 1.C., in Teletypesetter in the absence of the diagonal or slash mark.

Punctuation III

Punctuation in printing serves the same purpose as voice inflection in speaking. Proper phrasing avoids ambiguity, insures clarity and lessens need for punctuation.

THE PERIOD

3.1 The period is used after a declarative or imperative sentence: The facing is Vermont marble. Shut the door.

The period is used after a question intended as a suggestion: Tell how it was done.

The period is used in summary form:

1. Korean War. 2. Domestic policy. A. Punctuate properly. B. Write simply.

3.2 The period is used for ellipsis and in some columnist material. Ellipsis: The combine . . . was secure.

Column: Esther Williams gets the role. . . . John Hay signed a new contract. Rephrasing to avoid ellipses is preferable.

3.3 The period is used in abbreviations: U.S., U.N., c.o.d., etc. (See Section II for variations)

3.4 The period separates integer and decimal: 3.75 per cent; $8.25; 1.25 meters. (See 7.1, 7.2, 7.5, 7.7)

3.5 The period is omitted after a letter casually used as a name, and where a person omits the period in his name:

A said to B that he was not watching.

Herman B Wells (his usage). (See 1.33)

THE COMMA

3.6 The comma separates words or figures:

What the solution is, is a question.

Aug. 1, 1960.   1,234,567

The comma serves in a series:

The woman was short, slender, blonde, well-dressed and old.

x, y and z.   1, 2 and 3.

The Selma, Ala., group saw the governor.

PUNCTUATION

3.7 Do not use comma before "of": Brown of Arkadelphia.

3.8 Newspaper usage has, in most cases, eliminated the comma before "and" and "or" but this practice does not lessen the need for the mark in: Fish abounded in the lake, and the shore was lined with deer.

3.9 The comma is used to set off attribution: The work, he said, is exacting. It is used in scores: Milwaukee 6, St. Louis 5.

3.10 The comma is used to separate in apposition or contrast: Smithwick, the favorite, won handily.
But: The car that failed had been ahead.

3.11 The comma is omitted before Roman numerals, Jr., Sr., the ampersand, dash, in street addresses, telephone numbers and serial numbers: Louis XVI, John Jones Jr., Smith & Co., ORegon 3-3617, 12345 Oak St., A1234567. (See 4.4)

THE SEMICOLON

3.12 The semicolon separates phrases containing commas to avoid confusion, and separates statements of contrast and statements too closely related:
The draperies, which were ornate, displeased me; the walls, light blue, were pleasing.
The party consisted of B. M. Jordan; R. J. Kelly, his secretary; Mrs. Jordan; Martha Brown, her nurse; and three servants. (Without the semicolons, that could be read as nine persons.)

THE APOSTROPHE

3.13 The apostrophe indicates the possessive case of nouns, omission of figures, and contractions.
Usually the possessive of a singular noun not ending in "s" is formed by adding the apostrophe and "s"; the plural noun by adding the "s" and then the apostrophe: boys' wear, men's wear.
The apostrophe also is used in the plural possessive "es"; Joneses' house.
The "s" is dropped and only the apostrophe used in "for conscience' sake" or in a sibilant double or triple "s" as "Moses' tablet."
In single letters: A's.

PUNCTUATION

3.14 The apostrophe is used in contractions: I've, isn't; in omission of figures: '90, '90s, class of '22. (See 4.3)

3.15 The apostrophe use or lack of should follow the official name of group, institution, locality, etc.: Johns Hopkins University, Actors Equity Association, Court of St. James's (variation of possessive ending).

THE COLON

3.16 The colon precedes the final clause summarizing prior matter; introduces listings, statements and texts; marks discontinuity, and takes the place of an implied "for instance":
The question came up: What does he want to do? (See 1.31)
States and funds allotted were: Alabama $6,000; Arizona $4,000, etc.

3.17 The colon is used in clock time: 8:15 p.m. (See 4.9)

3.18 The colon is used in Bible and legal citations:
Matt 2:14. Missouri Statutes 3: 245-260.

THE EXCLAMATION POINT

3.19 The exclamation point is used to indicate surprise, appeal, incredulity or other strong emotion:
How wonderful!   What!   He yelled, "Come here!"

THE QUESTION MARK

3.20 The question mark follows a direct question, marks a gap or uncertainty and in the latter use is enclosed in parentheses:
What happened to Jones?
It was April 13 (?) that I saw him.
The mark also is used in public proceedings, interviews, etc.:
Q. Were you there? A. I don't recall.
Exception: Where, in interviews, the question or answer is of some length, it is preferable to paragraph both Q. and A.

PARENTHESES

3.21 Parentheses set off material, or an element of a sentence.
It is not the custom (at least in the areas mentioned) to stand at attention.

3.22 Where location identification is needed but is not part of the official name: The Springfield (Ohio) Historical Society edition, etc. It is not necessary to bracket: The Springfield, Ohio, area population, etc.

PUNCTUATION

3.23 Parentheses are not used around political-geographical designation: Sen. Theodore Francis Green, D-R.I., and Rep. Charles A. Halleck, R-Ind., were invited. (See 2.6)

3.24 Parentheses set off letters or figures in a series: The order of importance will be (a) general acceptance, (b) costs, and (c) opposition.

3.25 Where part of a sentence is parenthetical and the punctuation mark comes at the end of the sentence it goes outside:
He habitually uses two words incorrectly (practical and practicable).
Ordinarily the mark goes inside: (The foregoing was taken from an essay.)
Several paragraphs of parenthetical matter start with the opening mark on each paragraph and the final paragraph is ended with a closing parenthesis with the punctuation inside.

QUOTATION MARKS

3.26 Quotation marks enclose direct quotations; are used around phrases in ironical uses; around slang expressions; misnomers; titles of books, plays, poems, songs, lectures or speeches when the full title is used; hymns; movies; TV programs, etc. (See 1.30, 10.14)

3.27 Use quotation marks instead of parentheses around nicknames apart from the name: Smith, who weighed 280, was called "Slim."
Harold "Red" Grange.
The comma and period are placed inside the quotation marks. Other punctuation is placed according to construction:
Why call it a "gentlemen's agreement"?
The sequence in multiple quotations:
"The question is 'Does his position violate the "gentlemen's 'post-haste' agreement" so eloquently described by my colleague as "tommyrot"?'"

THE DASH

3.28 The dash indicates a sudden change. Examples:
He claimed—no one denied it—that he had priority.
It can be used instead of parentheses in many cases: 10 pounds—$28—paid.
If that man should gain control—God forbid!—our troubles will have only begun.
The monarch—shall we call him a knave or a fool?—approved it.

3.29 The dash is used after the logotype and before the first word of a story:
NEW YORK (logotype)—Mayor, etc.

3.30 The dash also is used as the minus sign in temperatures to indicate below-zero temperature: Duluth −12.

PUNCTUATION

THE HYPHEN

3.31 The hyphen is one of the least correctly used, and most abused, marks. It is used properly to form compound words, to divide words in composition, in figures, in some abbreviations, and to separate double vowels in some cases.

The general rule for hyphens is that "like" characters take the hyphen, "unlike" characters do not.

A-bomb, U-boat, 20-20 vision, 3D, B60, MIG17, 3-2 (odds and scores), secretary-treasurer, south-southwest, north-central.

Exception: 4-H Club.

3.32 Adjectival use must be clear. (See 5.6)

The 6-foot man eating shark was killed (the man was).

The 6-foot man-eating shark was killed (the shark was).

3.33 Suspensive hyphenation:

The A- and H-bombs were exploded.

The 5- and 6-year-olds attend morning classes.

3.34 Ordinarily in prefixes ending in vowels and followed by the same vowel, the hyphen is used: pre-empt, re-elect. (Check dictionary for exceptions such as cooperate, coed, coordinates, etc.)

3.35 NEVER use the hyphen with adverb ending in "ly" such as badly damaged, fully informed, newly chosen, etc.

3.36 The hyphen also serves to distinguish meaning of similarly spelled words: recover, re-cover; resent, re-sent.

3.37 The hyphen also separates a prefix from a proper noun: pre-Raphaelite, un-American, etc.

3.38 The prefix "ex" is hyphened: ex-champion.

3.39 The hyphen has been abandoned in newspaper usage in weekend, worldwide, nationwide, etc.

THE AMPERSAND

3.40 The ampersand is used in abbreviations and firm names: Jones & Co., AT&T, etc. (See 2.3)

Numerals IV

In general, spell below 10, use numerals for 10 and above.

4.1 Numerals are used exclusively in tabular and statistical matter, records, election returns, times, speeds, latitude and longitude, temperatures, highways, distances, dimensions, heights, ages, ratios, proportions, military units, political divisions, orchestra instruments, court districts or divisions, handicaps, betting odds and dates (Fourth of July and July Fourth acceptable).

Use figures in all man or animal ages. Spell under 10 for inanimates: four-mile-trip, four miles from the center, etc.

Exceptions Fifth Avenue, Fifth Republic of France (See 1.25, 2.4), Big Ten, Dartmouth eleven.

The forms: 3-year-old girl, the girl is 3, 5 feet 2, 5-foot-2 trench, Washington won, 6-3; $10 shirt, seven-cent stamp, eight-hour day, five-day week, 60 cents (See 4.6), .38-caliber pistol.

6:30 p.m. or 6:30 o'clock Monday night (never 6:30 p.m. Monday night, or 6:30 p.m. o'clock). (See 6.15)

The vote was 1,345 for and 1,300 against.

The ratio was 6 to 4, but the 6-4 ratio.

It is 20th century but Twentieth Century Limited (train).

In series, keep the simplest related forms:

There are 3 ten-room houses, 1 fourteen-room house, 25 five-room houses and 40 four-room houses in the development.

$4 million but four million persons—the $ is equivalent of second numeral.

4.2 Numerals: 6th Fleet, 1st Army, 2nd Division, 10th Ward, 22nd District, 8th U.S. Circuit Court of Appeals.

Arabic numerals for spacecraft, missiles, etc.

4.3 Casual numbers are spelled:

A thousand times no! Gay Nineties. (See 3.14)

Wouldn't touch it with a ten-foot pole (but: The flag hung from a 10-foot pole—an exact measure).

4.4 Roman numerals are used for personal sequence, Pope, war, royalty, act, yacht and horse: John Jones III (some may prefer and use 3rd), Pope John XXIII, World War I, King George V, Act II, Shamrock IX, Hanover II. (See 3.11)

NUMERALS

4.5 Highways: U.S. 301, Interstate 90, Illinois 34.

4.6 In amounts of more than a million, round numbers take the dollar sign and million, billion, etc., are spelled. Decimalization is carried to two places: $4.35 million.

Exact amounts would be: $4,351,242.

Less than a million the form: $500, $1,000, $650,000, etc.

The same decimalization form is used for figures other than money such as population, automobile registration, etc. (See 4.1)

Spell "cents" in amounts less than a dollar. (See 4.1, 7.5)

See Section VII for exceptions in market routine.

In ranges: $12 million to $14 million (or billion) not $12 to $14 million (or billion).

4.7 The English pound sign is not used. Spell "pounds" after figures and convert to dollars. (See 3.28)

4.8 Fractions in Teletypesetter are confined to matrices of 8ths: ⅛, ¼, ⅜, ½, ⅝, ¾, ⅞. Other fractions require the hyphen 3-16, 9-10, 1-3, etc.

Fractions used alone are spelled: three-fourths of a mile.

If the diagonal or slash (/) is incorporated in Teletypesetter operation, that symbol will replace the hyphen in fractions other than 8ths. The "plus" sign now occupies that casting-machine channel in the agate font and the hyphen will continue to be used in the agate font for fractions other than 8ths.

Stories dealing with percentages use figures; an isolated one-time reference under 10 is spelled as: four per cent of the population is illiterate.

4.9 Time sequences are given in figures: 2:30:21.6 (hours, minutes, seconds, tenths). (See 3.17)

4.10 Metric measurements use the comma in three-figure sequences except that kilocycles and meters in electronics are printed solid unless 10ths are included and the 10ths are set off by a period.

4.11 Serial numbers are printed solid: A1234567.

4.12 Write it No. 1 boy. No. 2 candidate, etc.

Spelling V

The first preference in spelling is the short version in Webster's New International Dictionary with exceptions as given in this section; the U.S. Postal Guide; The U.S. Board of Geographic Names and National Geographic Society with exceptions as given in this section. The news services have agreed on some spellings where authorities do not agree.

5.1 The following list includes agreed spellings:

Algiers	Cologne	Kingstown	Romania
Antioch	Copenhagen	Kurile	Rome
Antwerp	Corfu	Leghorn	Saint John, N.B.
Archangel	Corinth	Lisbon	St. John's, Nfld.
Athens	Dunkerque	Macao	Salonika
Baghdad	Florence	Madagascar	Sofia
Bangkok	Formosa Strait	Marseille	Taipei
Basel	Frankfurt	Mt. Sinai	Tehran
Bayreuth	Genoa	Mukden	Thailand
Beirut	Goteberg	Munich	Tiflis
Belgrade	Gulf of Riga	Naples	Turin
Bern	The Hague	North Cape	Valetta
Brunswick	Hamelin	Nuernberg	Mt. Vesuvius
Bucharest	Hannover	Peking	Vietnam
Cameroon	Hong Kong	Pescadores I.	Warsaw
Cape Town	Jakarta	Prague	Wiesbaden
Coblenz	Katmandu	Rhodes	Zuider Zee

5.2 Where old and new names are used, or where quoted material uses a different form, one is bracketed: Formosa (Taiwan); Gdansk (Danzig), etc.

5.3 In Chinese names, the name after the hyphen is lower case: Chiang Kai-shek, Mao Tse-tung.
It is Peking People's Daily, People's Republic, etc.

SPELLING

5.4 Often used and frequently misspelled: (*preferred spelling)

adviser	consul	hitchhiker	restaurant
accommodate	copilot	homemade	rock 'n' roll
anyone	copter	home town	schoolteacher
Asian flu	council	impostor	sit-down
ax	counsel	ionosphere	skillful
baby-sit	disc	isotope	strait jacket
baby sitter	drought	judgment	strong-arm
baby-sitting	drunken	jukebox	subpoena
baritone	employe*	kidnaping	swastika
blond, male	embarrass	likable	teen-age
blonde, female, hue	eyewitness	machine gun	under way
box office	fallout	missile	vacuum
box-office sales	fire fighter	naphtha	wash 'n' wear
cannot	fulfill	old-timer	weird
cave-in	goodby*	per cent	wheel chair
chauffeur	good will, noun	percentage	whisky
cigarette	goodwill, adj.	permissible	wiretapping
clue	hanged	post office	X ray, noun
consensus	harass	propeller	X-ray, adj.

Disc is a phonograph record, National Council of Disc Jockeys is the trade organization.

It is drunken driving.

Be sure of words ending in ise, ize, and yse.
It is GI and GIs for persons, GI's and GIs' for possessive.

A consonant after a vowel and ending in a final accented syllable is doubled: corral, corralled; transfer, transferred; canal, canalled.

A consonant is not doubled when the accent falls on an earlier syllable: total, totaled; kidnap, kidnaped; channel, channeled; cancel, canceled.
It is bus and buses—buss is not a vehicle.

5.5 In compounding, meaning should be the guide. A great grandfather means he is great; a great-grandfather is lineage. Three-piece suits at $100 a piece would be $300 each; three-piece suits at $100 apiece would be $100 each.

It is right-hander, right-handed, left-wing group, left-winger but the left wing of the party.

SPELLING

5.6 "Air" is solid in airplane, airline, airport, airwave, airship, etc. Some corporate names divide airline: Eastern Air Lines (EAL), United Air Lines (UAL).

5.7 Some of the general rules for prefixes and suffixes:

all (prefix) hyphenated: All-Star.

ante, anti (prefix) solid: antebellum, antiaircraft—except in proper noun usage which is anti-American, etc.

bi (prefix) solid: biennial, bifocal.

co (prefix) usually solid: copilot, coed, etc.

counter (prefix) solid; counterfoil, etc.

down (prefix and suffix) solid: downstroke, touchdown.

electro (prefix) solid: electrolysis.

ex (prefix) hyphenated: ex-champion.

extra (prefix) solid: extraterritorial.

fold (suffix) solid: twofold

goer (suffix) solid: churchgoer.

in (prefix): insufferable; (suffix) hyphenated: stand-in

infra (prefix) solid: infrared.

inter (prefix) solid: interstate.

intra (prefix) solid: intrastate, intramural.

multi (prefix) solid: multimillion, multifaced.

non (prefix) solid: nonpartisan, nonsupport.

out (prefix) hyphenated: out-talk, out-box.

over (prefix and suffix) solid: overcome, pushover.

post (prefix) solid: postwar (but it is post-mortem).

pre (prefix) solid: predetermined, predawn.

self (prefix) hyphenated: self-defense.

semi (prefix) solid: semiannual.

sub (prefix) solid: subzero.

super (prefix) solid: superabundance, superman.

trans (prefix) solid: transatlantic, transcontinental (but trans-Canada with proper noun of country).

tri (prefix) solid: trifocal.

ultra (prefix) solid: ultraviolet.

un (prefix) solid: unshaven, unnecessary (but un-American with proper noun).

under (prefix) solid: underground, underdog, undersold.

uni (prefix) solid: unicolor.

wide (suffix) solid: worldwide, nationwide.

Miscellaneous VI

6.1 Engine is correct, not motor, in aviation; twin-engine, six-engine, etc. Exception: Trimotor, an obsolete plane but it still occurs in news stories. In railroading, power plants are locomotives—electric, steam, diesel. Diesels also may be called units, or engines.

6.2 Jet planes are driven solely by turbine engines. If the jet engine turns a propeller, it is a turboprop. True jets include the Boeing 707, Douglas DC8, Convair 880, de Havilland Comet, French Caravelle and numerous military (naval) planes. Turboprops include Lockheed Electra, Fairchild F27, Bristol Britannia, Vickers Viscount.

Propeller-driven planes include Super Constellation C, Douglas DC6B, Boeing Stratocruiser.

Flier is an aviator, flyer is a train.

6.3 A wife becomes a widow on the death of her husband. It is redundant to say "widow of the late."

"John Jones is survived by his widow" (not wife).

6.4 Include in first reference the first name and initials, or names or initials according to preference of person: Sen. Theodore Francis Green, D. H. Lawrence. (See 1.33, 9.7)

Correct spelling: Randolph McC. Pate. Howard McC. Snyder.

6.5 Long titles: (See 1.6)

International Brotherhood of Teamsters, Chauffeurs, Warehousemen and Helpers is shortened to Teamsters Union, and in subsequent references to Teamsters.

Cemetery Workers and Green Attendants Union of the Building Service Employes International Union is shortened to Cemetery Workers Union.

6.6 An automatic is not a revolver and vice versa, but "pistol" describes either. A bullet is the metal projectile of a cartridge which includes the propellant powder, casing and primer.

Shell describes military and naval or shotgun ammunition.

6.7 Weather: See Webster for Weather Bureau wind scale which has replaced the Beaufort wind scale.

Be certain in the use of tornado, cyclone, typhoon, monsoon, hurricane, etc. The U.S. Weather Bureau defines a blizzard:

"Generally when there are winds of 35 m.p.h., or more which whip falling snow, or snow already on the ground, and temperatures are 20 degrees above zero Fahrenheit, or lower.

"A severe blizzard is where winds are 45 m.p.h. or more, temperatures 10 degrees above zero or lower, and great density of snow either falling or whipped from the ground."

Neither is a hard and fast rule, the bureau says, because winds and temperatures may vary but blizzard-like conditions may prevail.

Rule of thumb: Do not call a snowstorm a blizzard unless the Weather Bureau describes it as such.

In weather stories, with addition of Alaska and Hawaii as states, it is incorrect to refer to highest or lowest temperatures "in the nation" if figures from those two states are not included. The Weather Bureau has a phrase to cover the omission: It refers to minimums and maximums in the "48 contiguous states."

6.8 There are policemen, detectives, deputies, investigators, etc., but not "lawmen."

MISCELLANEOUS

6.9 Avoid making verbs out of nouns: shotgunned to death, suicided, etc.

Avoid trite phrases of dialect, especially "Sure and it was" and "begorra" etc., in March 17 stories.

If a record is set it is new—"new record" is redundant.

6.10 In describing someone or something from Washington, make clear it is the state or District of Columbia.

6.11 Fahrenheit is used most frequently to measure degrees of heat and cold. If centigrade occurs in foreign, or scientific, copy conversion to Fahrenheit is nine-fifths times centigrade plus 32.

The Kelvin scale of temperature will come into use oftener. Temperatures are referred to in this scale as "degrees absolute" or "degrees Kelvin." Absolute zero in the Kelvin scale is 460 degrees below Fahrenheit zero; 273 degrees below centigrade zero.

6.12 A knot is a unit of speed and is equivalent to 6,076.10 feet an hour. The knot is a nautical mile computed as the length of one minute of the meridian. To convert knots into approximate statute miles per hour, multiply knots by 1.15. It is incorrect to say "sailed 14 knots an hour."

6.13 Gross tonnage is a necessary part of any story dealing with commercial shipping as the accepted basic measurement of size. Naval vessels list "displacement tonnage."

6.14 Red-headed means a red head; red-haired means hair of that color. A person may be called a "redhead" jocularly but is not properly described as "red-headed."

6.15 It is not necessary to bracket time zones in ordinary happenings such as accidents, shootings, etc. It is sufficient to say something occurred at 11 p.m. (See 4.1)

Zone should be included in earthquakes, radio and TV broadcast times. Convert to EST.

Informative notes to editors giving times should include the zone.

6.16 G, G-force, is gravitational pull equal to about 32 feet per second, a second, in acceleration. Thus a flier (plane, rocket, etc.) subjected to a force of 5 G's is accelerating at five times the force of gravity at the earth's surface, or roughly at a 160-foot-a-second, per-second, rate.

6.17 Mach numbers refer to the speed of a body (aircraft, missile, etc.) in relation to the speed of sound. Mach 2 would be twice the speed of sound. A rule of thumb for speed of sound is 750 miles an hour at sea level, and 660 miles an hour at 30,000 feet.

6.18 Thrust is the measure of a driving force, or power, expressed in pounds. Jet engine and rocket powers are expressed in pounds. Thrust in pounds times speed in miles per hour divided by 375 converts thrust to horsepower.

Markets VII

7.1 Commodity routine consists of quotation material, stripped to barest essentials with most punctuation omitted. Dollar signs are not used in this routine. When quotations are less than a dollar, the decimal is not used. Range is indicated by the hyphen. The form:

Salable hogs 8,000; active and uneven, generally 75-1.00 higher on all weights; sows 50-75 higher; top 23.75 for short load; most good and choice 180-240 lb 23.00-23.50; 250-275 lb 22.00-22.75.

Wheat 1,534 cars; 1 lower to 3 higher; No 2 hard and dark hard 2.20½-2.30 (new) No 3 2.21-2.27 (new); No 2 red 2.19½-2.25N.

7.2 In newspage stories, the dollar sign is used, also decimal:

Stock advances ranged from $2 a share to more than $5.50 in brisk trading. At the opening, some shares were down $1 to $1.25 but a surge of buying which put the ticker several minutes behind trading sent prices up.

Market page leads do not use the dollar sign. Increases or losses are told in points as: Brown Bros. was up 1 at 82¼.

Bonds are designated: 3s, 4½s, etc.

7.3 Abbreviations in routine, but not used in newspage, roundups or market leads:

pt qt gal pk bu bbl lb

Letter designations in routine do not take periods: N (nominal); No (number); B (bid); A (asked).

7.4 Stories are carried when there is a change in dividend declarations — increased or decreased, passed or declared after having been passed. However, regular dividends of the large corporations are news — AT&T, U.S. Steel, General Motors, Ford, etc.

7.5 In reporting dividends, use the designation given by the firm (regular, special, extra, increased, interim, etc.) and show what was paid previously if there is no specified designation such as regular, quarterly, etc.

The story should say if there is a special, or extra, dividend paid with the regular dividend and include amount of previous added payments. The form:

Directors of the New Way Products Corp. voted a special dividend of $1.90 a share, in addition to the regular $1 dividend, both payable Sept. 15 to shareholders of record Aug. 25. A special dividend of 75 cents was paid June 15. (See 4.6)

When the usual dividend is passed, or reduced, some firms issue an explanatory statement, the gist of which should be included in the story.

7.6 News of corporate activities, and business and financial news should be stripped of technical terms. This does not apply to routine.

There should be some explanation of the firm's business (plastics, rubber, electronics, etc.) if there is no indication in the name of the nature of the business. The location of the firm should be carried.

Names of corporations are as important as those of individuals. Check New York Stock Exchange lists or Standard & Poor's Directory of Directors for correct names and spelling.

MARKETS

7.7 Corporate earnings are interesting chiefly because of net earnings, or losses. Net per common share always should be carried with comparison to the previous period specified. The form:

The ABC Co., automotive parts makers of Detroit, reported its net income for six months ending June 30 was $18,456,301, equal to $1.67 a common share. In the similar period last year net income was $12,412,006 or $1.03 a share.

Newsworthy earnings are carried in tabular form where several are available (after a dateline introduction). The form:

XYZ Corp. for six months ended June 30:

	1960	1959
Net income	$ 1,378,933	x-452,881
Share	74 cents	
Sales	24,114,396	16,513,662

x-net loss

Religious VIII

There is only one way to refer to confessions of faith and members and officials of them—the correct way. While general usage and correct titles of some of the faiths are listed in this section, some are not. In case of omission, or doubt, consult authoritative sources.

8.1 Members of communions of the National Council of the Churches of Christ in the United States of America—the official title which may be shortened to National Council of Churches—and others:

African Methodist Episcopal Church
African Methodist Episcopal Zion Church
American Baptist Convention
Antiochian Orthodox Catholic Archdiocese of Toledo, Ohio,
    and Dependencies
Armenian Church, Diocese of America, Diocese of California
Christian Churches (Disciples of Christ), International Convention
Christian Methodist Episcopal Church
Church of the Brethren
Church of the New Jerusalem
The Episcopal Church
Evangelical United Brethren Church
Exarchate of the Russian Orthodox Church of North and South America
Friends United Meeting
Greek Orthodox Archdiocese of North and South America
Hungarian Reformed Church in America
Lutheran Church in America
The Methodist Church
Moravian Church in America
National Baptist Convention, U.S.A., Inc.
National Baptist Convention of America
Philadelphia Yearly Meeting of the Religious Society of Friends
Polish National Catholic Church of America
Presbyterian Church in the U.S.
Progressive National Baptist Convention, U.S.A., Inc.
Reformed Church in America
Romanian Orthodox Episcopate of America
Russian Orthodox Greek Catholic Church of America
Serbian Eastern Orthodox Church
Seventh Day Baptist General Conference
Syrian Antiochian Orthodox Church
Syrian Orthodox Church of Antioch
Ukrainian Orthodox Church of America
United Church of Christ
United Presbyterian Church in the U.S.A.

RELIGIOUS

8.2 Other communions:
Roman Catholic Church
Church of Jesus Christ of Latter-day Saints (Mormon)
Church of Christ, Scientist
The Lutheran Church—Missouri Synod
Seventh-day Adventists
Southern Baptist Convention
Churches of Christ
Jehovah's Witnesses
Unitarian Universalist Association
Unity of the Brethren
The American Lutheran Church

8.3 Jewish groups are:
Union of American Hebrew Congregations (Reform)
United Synagogue of America (Conservative)
Union of Orthodox Jewish Congregations of America (Orthodox)
Rabbinical groups:
Central Conference of American Rabbis (Reform)
Rabbinical Assembly (Conservative)
Rabbinical Council of America (Orthodox)
Union of Orthodox Rabbis (Orthodox)

The Synagogue Council of America represents both congregational and rabbinical groups of Reform, Conservative and Orthodox Judaism.

Terminology of each group should be followed, also in naming the place of worship as a temple or synagogue. The generic term: Jewish house of worship.

RELIGIOUS

8.4 In general, in writing of clergymen, the form:

The Rev. John Smith, the Rev. Mr. Smith. Do NOT use Rev. without "the" preceding it.

The Rev. Dr. John Jones, Dr. Jones.

8.5 Roman Catholic usage:

The Rev. John Smith, Father Smith.

The Rt. Rev. Msgr. John Jones, Msgr. Jones.

The Most Rev. John Jones, bishop of the Denver diocese: Bishop Jones.

Francis Cardinal Spellman, Cardinal Spellman.

A sister whose name is Jones is called by her church name, Sister Mary Joseph (or whatever) and never referred to as Sister Jones.

Mass is celebrated, said or read. High Mass is sung—never held. The Rosary is recited or said—never read.

8.6 Episcopal usage:

A deacon or priest is referred to as the Rev. John Jones or the Rev. Mr. Jones.

A dean is the Very Rev. John Jones, the Rev. Mr. Jones, or Dean Jones.

A bishop is the Rt. Rev. John Jones, the Rev. Mr. Jones or Bishop Jones.

Note: An Episcopalian is a member of the Episcopal Church. Some priests use the term "Father" which is permissible but not generally used.

8.7 Jewish usage:

Rabbi James Wise, Rabbi Wise, Dr. Wise (where degree is held).

Cantor Harry Epstein, Cantor Epstein.

Do not identify a rabbi as a "Reverend Doctor."

See dictionary for spelling of Jewish holidays.

8.8 Christian Science usage:

Practitioner, Lecturer, Reader. Do not use Rev. in any form.

Reader John Jones of the First Church.

The Mother Church (Boston church only).

8.9 Methodist usage:

Pastor, Minister, Preacher, Bishop. Mr. with surname is acceptable. (See 2.15)

8.10 Lutheran usage:

In the United States: Pastor John Jones, Pastor Jones, Mr. Jones.

Scandinavian Lutheran usage follows the Episcopal form.

8.11 Latter-day Saints (Mormon) usage. (See 8.2 listing)

President David O. McKay, President McKay.

Elder Harold B. Lee, Elder Lee.

Presiding Bishop LeGrand Richards, Bishop Richards.

Bishop Joseph L. Wirthlin of the Presiding Bishopric, Bishop Wirthlin.

Members of the church may be called Mormons.

8.12 It is incorrect to apply the term "church" to any Baptist unit except the local church. The organization of Southern Baptists is the Southern Baptist Convention.

Other faiths have diocese, archdiocese, area, synod, presbytery, etc. Check official source for accurate designation.

8.13 Check, rather than follow listings in 8.1, 8.2.

RELIGIOUS

8.14 Abbreviations of the Bible:

Gen.	1 and 2 Kings	Song of Sol.	Obad.
Exod.	1 and 2 Chron.	Isa.	Jonah
Lev.	Ezra	Jer.	Mic.
Num.	Neh.	Lam.	Nahum
Deut.	Esther	Ezek.	Hab.
Josh.	Job	Dan.	Zeph.
Judg.	Ps. (Psa. plural)	Hos.	Hag.
Ruth	Prov.	Joel	Zech.
1 and 2 Sam.	Eccl.	Amos	Mal.

New Testament:

Matt.	Rom.	Col.	Heb.
Mark	1 and 2 Cor.	1 and 2 Thess.	James
Luke	Gal.	1 and 2 Tim.	1 and 2 Pet.
John	Eph.	Titus	1, 2 and 3 John
Acts	Phil.	Philem.	Jude
			Rev.

Sports IX

9.1 BASIC SUMMARY:

Name of event—athlete's full name, his affiliation, performance (given in time, distance, points scored, or whatever performance factor is appropriate).

Observe punctuation. It calls for dash after event and commas. Semicolons are not used. Time follows the colon usage, but the word "time" is not used. The word "points" should be used with first listing only, where applicable to the event.

Example:

Mile—1, Ron Delany, Ireland, 4:06. 2, Derek Ibbotston, Britain, 4:05.5. 3, Don Bowden, United States, 4:08.2.

Include the colon before seconds in times of less than a minute, :10.2 or :50.6.

Condensed summary:

100—1, Jones, SMU. 2, Brown, Rice. 3, White, Texas. :09.7.

In the condensed summary, performance is given at end of listings of each event. If a record is broken, the former record is given immediately following the record performance in the expanded summary —but at the end of the condensed summary.

Tabular Summary:

Yacht	Elapsed Time	Corrected Time
1. Seagull	12:05.00	9:21.13
2. Comanche	11:18.20	10:12.12
3. Etc.		

Match Summary:

Althea Gibson, New York, N.Y., defeated Sally Moore, Bakersfield, Calif., 8-6, 2-6, 6-0.

9.2 BASEBALL:

The box score:

MINNESOTA	ab	r	h	bi
Oliva rf	4	0	1	0
Ward lf	1	0	0	0
Rollins ph	1	0	0	0
Hall cf etc.				
Totals	**30**	**3**	**6**	**3**
LOS ANGELES	**ab**	**r**	**h**	**bi**
Piersall cf	3	0	1	0
Smith lf	4	0	1	0
Rodgers pr	0	1	0	0
Totals	**31**	**1**	**7**	**1**

Minnesota	000	000	201—3
Los Angeles	000	000	001—1

E — Clinton, Satriano. DP — Los Angeles 1. LOB—Minnesota 7, Los Angeles 5. 2B—Oliva. 3B—Torres. HR—Hall (12). SB—Piersall. S—Knoop. SF—Hall.

	IP	H	R	ER	BB	SO
Pascual W 15-11	8 2-3	7	1	1	1	6
Worthington	1-3	0	0	0	0	0
Newman L 13-10	8	5	2	2	2	5
Latman	1	1	1	0	1	0

Newman faced 2 men in 9th.

HBP — By Pascual (Rodgers). Balk — Worthington. WP — Pascual. T—2:09. A—15,615.

In a game where the home team scores winning run in final inning, the explanation is given just before the linescore.

The above box is the standard used for all regular season games. It is transmitted in half-column agate in Teletypesetter. Longer player names are abbreviated, and only one position is shown for any player.

SPORTS

For All-Star and World Series games, headings may be expanded to full-column measure:

AB   R   H   BI   PO   A

Footnotes are listed separately instead of being run together:
a—Flied out for Spahn in 4th.
b—Singled for Narleski, etc.

The summary starts with DP. The hitting summary, starting with 2B (or whatever extra-base hit) should include description of any score that is not batted in:

SF—Aaron. Musial scored on a wild pitch in 1st; Fox scored on a double play in 6th, etc.

The pitching summary is reduced to four categories:

IP   H   R   ER

Bases on balls and strikeouts are listed and paragraphed:

BB—Turley 2 (Thomas, Spahn). Narleski (Aaron). SO—Turley 3 (Banks, Mazeroski, Jones). Spahn 2 (Mantle, Williams).

Umpires in final paragraph carry league designation:

—Rommell (A), Gorman (N), etc.

Bare linescore form:

Detroit   241 200 003—12 13 0
New York   000 000 221— 5 10 0

Lary, Aguirre (8) and Wilson; Monroe, Trucks (3), Sturdivant (8), Kucks (9) and Howard. W—Lary, 4-3. L—Monroe, 8-1. HRs—New York, Mantle (24). Detroit, Kaline 2 (16).

Schedule, result, standings, probable pitcher summary form:

BASEBALL
AMERICAN LEAGUE

	Won	Lost	Pct.	GB
New York	48	26	.649	—
x-Kansas City	38	37	.507	10½

etc.

x—late game not included.

Monday's Scores
Chicago 7, Boston 4
Cleveland 12, New York 2, night
Detroit at Baltimore, rain.

Today's Games
Cleveland (Grant 6-6 and Bell 3-2) at New York (Ditmar 3-1 and Maas 4-7), 2, Twi-night.

Wednesday's Games
Cleveland at New York
Chicago at Boston, night
Only games scheduled.

Afternoon paper headings say "today" and spell prior and subsequent days. Morning paper headings spell all days.

Standings are moved separately after afternoon games and repeated after night games.

The baseball forms should be followed on minor leagues.

In lists of results give winner first, except:

Where there are line, period, inning or box scores, home team is last, win or lose.

SPORTS

9.3 FOOTBALL:

All football games, whether using the two- or one-point conversion, will use the same summary style.

Army	8	6	15	6—35
Stanford	16	7	3	2—28

Army—John 6 run (Chambers run)

Stan—Temple 2 run (Central pass from Temple)

Stan—Powers 26 run (Powers run)

Army—Tennyson 11 run (kick failed)

Stan—Lutz 22 pass from Chambers (Chambers kick)

Stan—FG Lutz 23

Army—Tennyson 34 pass interception (Lutz kick)

Army—Brandt 22 punt return (Lutz pass from Tennyson)

Stan—Safety Doaks tackled in end zone

Army—Halmark 16 pass from Tennyson (run failed)

A—26,571.

Field goal is abbreviated to FG. Safety is spelled. It is not necessary to give any symbol for touchdowns or conversions.

In both college and professional football, the distance of a field goal is from the point the ball was kicked —not the line of scrimmage. Also, goal posts in college football are 10 yards back of the goal line. That distance must be included.

Football Statistics:

STANFORD, Calif. (logotype) — Statistics of the Army-Stanford football game:

	Army	Stanford
First downs	7	5
Rushing yardage	153	172
Passing yardage	71	62
Return yardage	69	51
Passes	4-9-0	4-7-1
Punts	4-37	5-44.2
Fumbles lost	2	3
Yards penalized	60	30

(Note—Return yardage includes punt returns, pass interception returns and fumble returns, but not kickoff returns.)

EASTERN CONFERENCE

	W	L	T	Pct.	Pts.	OP
New York	5	2	1	.714	205	105

Ties do not figure in percentage.

9.4 BASKETBALL—The box score form:

SEATTLE

	G	F	T
Taylor	8	2-4	18
Totals	**22**	**12-19**	**67**

KENTUCKY

Beck, etc.

Halftime: Seattle 30 Kentucky 27.

Note—In both NBA and ABA score by periods is carried in place of halftime score as follows:

Seattle	10	17	15	14—56
Kentucky	15	15	15	15—60

No positions are given after player name, but five starting players should be listed first and substitutes in order of appearance.

Add after linescore:

Fouled out—Seattle: Jones. Kentucky: Green.

Total fouls—Seattle 42, Kentucky 37.

(Note—In the American Basketball Association which has both 2-point and 3-point baskets, footnotes are used to explain as follows:

(3-point goals: Brown 1, Smith 2, etc.)

A—15,601.

SPORTS

Expanded football standings are headed by the name of the conference. The form then:

	Conference					All Games				
	W	L	T	Pts.	OP	W	L	T	Pts.	OP
Michigan	6	0	0	126	34	9	1	0	141	48

The form for basketball:

	Conference				All Games			
	W	L	Pct.		W	L	Pct.	Pts.	OP
Bradley	5	0	1.000		14	1	.933	1260	975

Basketball box scores in TTS are moved in half-column measure and carry only G F T headings.

Standings are the same as football except that points column is not carried. The headings are Won, Lost, Pct.

The form for standings:

EASTERN DIVISION

	W	L	Pct.	GB
Boston	30	15	.667	—
New York	25	25	.500	7½

9.5 HOCKEY—The lineups:

New York—add NHL

Toronto: Goal—Bower, Smith. Defense—Stanley, Horton, Baun, Brewer, Douglas. Forwards—Bathgate, Keon, McKenney, Armstrong, Pappin, Shack, Kelly, Mahovlich, Pulford, Stewart.

New York: Goal—Plante, Greene. Defense—Howell, Neilson, Brown, Johns, Seiling. Forwards—Gilbert, Goyette, Henry, Nevin, Ingarfield, Duff, Mikol, Marshall, Hadfield, Ratelle.

Referee—Udvari. Linesmen—Papelich, Hayes.

(Both goalies are listed under goal. Starting goalie is listed first.)

(Please note we list the entire front line as forwards, and therefore no spares are listed. Do not use first names of officials).

Where the lineups are held until after the first period is completed, the first period scoring summary should be attached to the lineups. Otherwise it is sent separately. It takes this form:

New York—add NHL

First period—1, New York, Henry 21 (Goyette) 2:15. 2, Toronto, Bathgate 16 (Keon, McKenney) 8:19. Penalties—Duff 2:43; Mikol 7:26.

(Please note that each score is numbered, and the figure after a man's name represents his total goals for the season to date. This, however, applies only to the National Hockey League. Shots on goal are sent with period summaries and at the end.)

Example of summary:

Third period—None. Penalties—Baum 4:15; Neilson, major, 17:00; Duff 18:12.

Shots on goal by:

New York	8	9	4—21
Toronto	6	8	6—20

A—14,520.

(Only major penalties are so designated.)

The final score is sent as a bulletin.

Standings:

NATIONAL HOCKEY LEAGUE

	W	L	T	Pts.	GF	GA
Montreal	50	9	1	101	245	113

S P O R T S

9.6 HORSE RACING.

NEW YORK (logotype)—The field for Saturday's $75,000-added Wood Memorial, 1⅛ miles, at Aqueduct:

PP	Horse	Jockey	Prob. Odds
1.	Sacred River	Sellers	10-1
2.	Traffic	Adams	4-1
3.	Chieftan	Rotz	8-1

Owners—1, Mrs. Ethel Jacobs. 2, Rokeby Stable. 3, Cambridge Stable. etc.

Weights—All carry 126 pounds. Gross value—$89,250 with nine starters; $58,012.50 to winner, $17,850 to second, $8,925 to third, $4,462.50 to fourth. Post time—4:50 p.m. EST.

(If weights are not all same, weights should be included after the name of horse.)

Results:

THISTLE—9

9th—$1,600 clmg 4 & up 1 1-16 mi off 547½ time 1:48 3-5.

a—Mr Action 118 R. Borg	4.40	3.20	2.60
Blimey 116 T. Fortune	—	5.20	3.80
Pirro 120 G. Smithson	—	—	5.80

Also: Gem Cutter, f-Baseball, a-Paris Fleet, Geo K.

f-Field; a-Jones entry.

(after final race)

A—6,256

Total handle $420,071.

After a second race, if there is a daily double, the form:

Daily Double:

Commendation and Lucky Ballot—9 & 11—paid $36.20.

HARNESS RACING—Same as running race results except where trotting or pacing events are in heats, when position and finish of each heat is required. Where there is betting, prices precede the heat tabulation.

S P O R T S

9.7 BOXING—Match style summary:

Eddie Lynch, 152, New York, outpointed Johnny Saxton, 154, Philadelphia, 10.

If a knockout, use "knocked out." If a technical knockout, use "stopped."

If two officials vote for one boxer and the third votes for the other, it is a split decision.

If two officials vote for one boxer and the third votes a draw, it is a majority decision.

In championship fights, "Tale of The Tape" form:

	Olsen	Langlois
Age	26	29
Weight	160	160
Height	5-10½	5-9
Chest (normal)	39	40
Chest (expanded)	42	42
Reach	70	68
Biceps	13	14
Forearm	11½	12
Waist	32	33
Thigh	22	22½
Calf	16	13
Fist	12	11½

Facts and Figures:

SAN FRANCISCO (Logotype)— Facts and figures of the world middleweight championship fight between champion Carl "Bobo" Olson of San Francisco and Pierre Langlois of France:

Date—Wednesday, Dec. 15.

Place—San Francisco Cow Palace, capacity 18,000.

Distance—15 rounds.

Television—Nationwide, CBS, with blackout 100-mile radius of San Francisco.

Radio—Nationwide, CBS.

Time—10 p.m. EST

(Other pertinent information may be included such as estimated attendance, estimated gate, shares of the purses, etc., as available.)

When a fight is scored by rounds, the form:

NEW YORK (logotype)—Scorecards of the Carmen Basilio-Billy Graham 15-round welterweight title bout:

Rd.	Ref. Tom Swift	Judge John Jones	Judge Phil Cook	Logo.
1	B	B	B	B
2	B	B	B	B
3	B	B	B	B
4	G	E	G	G
5	G	G	G	G
6	G	G	G	G
7	B	B	B	B
8	B	B	B	B
9	B	B	B	B
10	B	B	B	B
11	B	B	B	B
12	G	G	G	G
13	G	G	G	G
14	G	G	G	G
15	B	B	B	B
	9-6	9-5-1	9-6	9-6

Scoring by points:
(Basilio-Graham)

Rd.	Ref. Phil Harris	Judge Dick Smith	Judge Joe Hunt	Logo.
1	10-10	10-10	10-10	10-10
2	10-9	10-9	10-9	10-8
3	etc.			

Totals 147-132 145-134 etc.

SPORTS

9.8 GOLF: Summaries are medal or match play.

Medal play: At the end of each day's play, low scores and ties are cumulatively given:

Ben Hogan   70-70-66—206

On the final day when money winnings are reported, the amount is inserted:

Ben Hogan, $2,800 70-70-66-64—270

Home towns are given only in major amateur tournaments with home town on second line.

Match play:

Ben Hogan defeated Gary Player 4 and 3.

Arnold Palmer won from John Snow by default.

The form for pairings—Match:

8 a.m.—Ben Hogan vs. Gary Player.

Medal:

8 a.m.—Ben Hogan, Gary Player, Arnold Palmer.

The form for cards:

Par out	454	343	454—36
Par in	443	545	344—36—72
Hogan Out		444	333	etc.
Hogan In		444	445	etc.
Snead Out		434	343	etc.
Snead In		444	454	etc.

9.9 TRACK AND FIELD—Use basic summary, either condensed or expanded, depending on value.

Where the winning time, or distance, is a record, the form:

Mile—1, Ron Delany, Ireland, 3:52, world record; old record 3:53.6, Herb Elliott, Australia, Dec. 15, 1958. 2, Don Bowden, etc.

In summaries, record is given in the same form.

Team standings are given at the end of summaries in conference meets. The form:

TEAM SCORING—Michigan 97, Illinois 67, Iowa 63½, etc.

Use yards or meters as indicated in summaries in listing track events and include "hurdles" and "relay" after distances as indicated.

Full names of relay team winners should be listed:

Mile relay—1, Manhattan: Vern Jones, Joe Dixon, Lou Carty, Ed Thomas, 3:15. 2, Syracuse, 3:16. 3, Brown, etc.

9.10 SWIMMING—The same form as track summaries except events are identified by distances and style and points are included in diving: 100 freestyle, breaststroke, backstroke, individual medley, medley relay. Distance precedes each style.

Platform diving—1, Bob Clotworthy, Ohio State, 60.41 points. 2, Bob James, Yale, 59.71. 3, Tom etc.

SPORTS

9.11 TENNIS, badminton, table tennis—Use match summary form. The form for scores: 6-4, 6-3, 6-2.

9.12 ROWING—Basic summary.

9.13 FENCING—Match summary for dual and small meets and divide into epee, foil and saber classes.

In major meets where competitors meet in round-robin competition and divided into "pools" the form:

EPEE—First round, four qualify for semifinals:

Pool 1	W	L
Smith, U.S.A.	4	1
Lopez, Chile	3	2

Footnotes may be needed where a tie is decided on number of touches, or some such means.

9.14 CROSS COUNTRY—(Marathon) Tabular summary in meets giving 10 or more places; basic summary for less than 10 places.

9.15 DOG SHOWS—Summaries by groups have five places. The form:

SPORTING GROUP—Pointers: 1. Ch Magic of Mardomere, owned by Mardomere Kennels, Glen Head, N.Y. 2, etc.

The same form applies if judging is by breeds.

9.16 LACROSSE (soccer, polo, water polo)—Give scores by chukkers (periods) and list goals scored by individuals in paragraph form by teams.

9.17 AUTO RACING — Tabular summary with driver, car make, owner and average speed. Basic summary will suffice on lesser contests or where there are few drivers.

9.18 SHOOTING—(rifle, pistol, etc.)—Tabular summary with name, hometown, hits, handicap and total.

9.19 SKIING—Tabular summary for jumping, cross-country, downhill and slalom races. Jumping table should give distance of each jump and point total. Cross-country table should give time and handicap if used in event.

9.20 BOBSLEDDING — Tabular summary.

9.21 BOWLING—There are several forms. They are:

Jones	161	161	174
Smith	208	etc.	
Totals	802	903	887

In singles matches a fourth tabulation is added, giving the bowler's total for the three games. Handicaps are figured with the totals.

The Peterson summary:

	W	L	Pins	Pts.
John King, Cleveland	20	8	5886	137.36
Carmen Salvino, Chicago	16	12	5816	132.16
Tony, etc.				

9.22 WEIGHTLIFTING—Tabular summary with table for each weight class, giving name, affiliation, pounds lifted in each of three lifts, and total pounds lifted.

9.23 FIGURE SKATING—Tabular summary.

9.24 SPEED SKATING—Basic summary.

9.25 GYMNASTICS—Basic summary, events by name (sidehorse, horizontal bar, etc.) with points scored.

9.26 CYCLING—Basic summary.

9.27 WRESTLING—Match summary. Key words are "pinned" and "outpointed." Point scoring should be given after name and affiliation of loser if a decision match.

Teletypesetter X

Teletypesetter copy must meet requirements of conversion to metal.

Revision of material must retain, or regain, line justification. It is preferable to transmit an entire paragraph where a revision means casting several lines.

See current directives for transmission of material that is not to be cast, or changing type fonts.

All material must be transmitted in justified lines. Informative material, not for publication, must be justified but quads may be dropped instead of dividing words.

Numerical sequence and continuity must be observed.

10.1 Datelines are capitalized, light face, and except for major cities should carry the state. (See 2.7) There is no spacing in state abbreviations. Abbreviations should not be divided at the end of a line.

10.2 Dates are omitted from datelines. Days of the week are spelled throughout the AMS report. In the PMS report, the use is "today" and spell prior and subsequent days.

10.3 Notes to editors take several forms.

Nonpublishable: EDITORS–The following dispatch contains material which may be objectionable to some readers.

EDITORS–developing, top expected about 11 a.m. EST.

Such nonpublishable notes are followed by a 3m dash.

10.4 Current cycle advances, where release time is not fixed by source, carry only: Adv for 6:30 a.m. EST, or Adv for 6:30 p.m. EST. In Daylight Saving Time the slug is EDT.

Advance for a subsequent cycle carries a slug: Adv Tues PMS May 24. It also carries a closing note: End Adv Tues PMS May 24 (or AMS).

Current cycle advances do not require visible caution in tape.

Subsequent cycle advances carry in visible tape: MAY 24 at start of each take.

10.5 Identify leads, inserts, adds, revisions plainly. Give understandable pickup lines and precise location in story. Avoid duplicating key subject words in slugs where more than one story deals with the same field. This insures proper matching of leads, adds, etc.

10.6 Absence of parentheses on monitor printers requires special handling of parenthetical matter.

Where parenthetical matter occurs it must be indicated. In stories, where part is embargoed for later use, it either is separated in the story by 3m dash (in its proper sequence) and boldface caution **Adv for 00.00** time and **End Adv** followed by 3m dash, or may be sent as add at end of story under 3m dash with advance slugs and notation where to insert.

Within paragraphs, a parenthetical word or phrase usually is evident by the extra spacing which occurs on the monitor in place of the parenthesis.

TELETYPESETTER

10.7 Where a name is unusual and occurs only once, add note under 3m dash repeating name and saying it is correct. Check monitor to insure correctness.

10.8 In long lists of names, or similar compilations, break into paragraphs (with appropriate punctuation) after each six or eight lines, with next to last paragraph including the word "and" without punctuation after "and."

10.9 In textual matter, the signature should be flush right. Title, date and other descriptive matter are on a second line. Where signatures are multiple and of equal importance, set one flush left and other flush right and if names are too long to permit spacing, divide name and run over (right or left) under each.

10.10 In Teletypesetter, put addresses in separate paragraphs.

Instead of saying John Doe of 125 W. 71st St., Kansas City, Mo., was among those cited, make separate paragraph read: Doe lives at 125 W. 71st St., Kansas City, Mo.

That form permits deletion of the address by a distant or uninterested point without having to set a paragraph over.

10.11 Avoid transitional paragraphs except in introduction of lists, introduction to statistics or recital of events.

"Production," he said, "will equal, if not exceed, that of the past year." He added:

"The current outlook indicates a better growing season."

The above form means setting over if last paragraph is deleted.

In the following form, the paragraph may be deleted without new composition:

"Production will equal, if not exceed, that of the past year." he said.

"The current outlook indicates a better growing season."

10.12 Time zones are needed only in informative notes, release time of advances, radio or TV programs, or stories in which a time zone is part of required information. Where mention is made in a story that a conference, session, meeting, etc., is to be held at a certain hour, that information should be in a separate paragraph.

When zone is included it should be converted to EST or EDT.

It is NOT necessary to include time zones in accidents, fires, etc. A wreck at 3 a.m. gives the reader the clear picture without a time zone.

TELETYPESETTER

10.13 Weather table:

Temperature and precipitation in inches for the 24-hour period ending at 7:30 a.m., March 20:

	Temp.		Precip.
	High	Low	(T-trace)
Aroostook	80	70	T
Beaumont	92	72	.30

Aroostook and vicinity: Generally fair and warmer today. High 80-85. (Form for AMS would spell the day.)

Short form:

NEW MEXICO: Partly cloudy and warm today, mostly cloudy and continued warm with showers and possibly thunderstorms Sunday. (Change "today" to "Saturday" for AMS report.)

10.14 Play listings:

FABLE

"Rashomon": Music Box—A Japanese fable of brutality as seen by four witnesses. Clair Bloom and Rod Steiger head the cast.

10.15 Land description:

SE¼NW¼, Sec. 2 T. 10 S., R2E. Lot 3, NW¼ Sec. 2, T. 9S, R2W. S½ Sec. 10, T. 9S, R6E, sixth principal meridian.

10.16 Book review:

I WAS THERE. By John Doe, Scranton, Pa. County Press. $4.50.

John Doe has been around and his observations have been put into a readable volume. Travelers will find many things in this book that they have overlooked in their travels and will give them a guide for their return.

John Henry

News Circuit Styles

Style on TTY (page teleprinter) circuits of United Press International will conform to TTS (Teletypesetter) style in abbreviation, punctuation, figures, spelling and general usage.

In many respects procedures for identifying copy are the same on TTS and TTY circuits. There is expanding use of circuitry which permits TTY copy, read by subscribers on monitor printers in capital letters, to be reproduced in capitals and lower case, with justified lines, on TTS monitors and in TTS tape.

In the following section, both similarities and differences of style will be described.

News is transmitted on all UPI circuits in the order of its importance and urgency. Slugs indicate priority.

FLASH—Dateline, dash, no date or logotype, limited to one or two lines depending upon whether it appears on a TTY or a TTS monitor. Originating bureau comes onto wire immediately to send. Used seldom and only on biggest news.

FLASH
    DALLAS—PRESIDENT
    KENNEDY DEAD
                JT104PCS

The flash must be followed immediately by a publishable bulletin expanding the story.

BULLETIN—One paragraph of 50 words or less. It must be a self-contained report of a major development and should be followed without interruption by an add developing the story. On stories of great importance there should be no interruption between adds until the story is cleaned up.

URGENT—Used on dispatches meriting faster wire movement than ordinary copy. Aids in delivering good stories in one or two takes instead of breaking them up into a bulletin and several short adds. Must not exceed 200 words.

ADDS—A story is completed or developed by moving adds. They are slugged to indicate exactly where they fit on previous copy.

BULLETIN PRECEDE—Used to report a major development before a new lead is ready. Must be followed within a few minutes by a lead or insert incorporating the new information into the story.

USE OF BELLS—A flash takes 10 bells, which follow it. A bulletin uses five bells, an urgent four. When designated by desk, copy may be given four bells and urgent priority without the use of the urgent slug.

A news dispatch carries a three-digit number, in most cases followed by a letter for circuit designation. It carries a slugword, the month and day in digits, and either call letters of the sending bureau or the operator's initials.

Examples following show how the copy would appear on a TTY circuit, except that lines would be longer. The TTS version would be in capital letters and lower case, and each line would contain only the wordage which would fit into an 11-pica body type line. Slugwords, bureau and operator initials, pickup lines, etc., would be in lower case.

107A
    JOHNSON 3/2 WA
BULLETIN
    WASHINGTON (UPI)—PRESIDENT JOHNSON ANNOUNCED TODAY THAT SOVIET PREMIER ALEXEI KOSYGIN HAD AGREED TO SOVIET DISCUSSIONS WITH THE UNITED STATES ON LIMITING THE ARMS RACE IN DEFENSIVE AS WELL AS OFFENSIVE NUCLEAR MISSILES.
    (MORE) TM1152AES

NEWS CIRCUIT STYLES

108A

JOHNSON 3/2 WA

URGENT

1ST ADD JOHNSON WASHINGTON 107A XXX MISSILES.

JOHNSON MADE THE ANNOUNCEMENT AT A HURRIEDLY ARRANGED NEWS CONFERENCE SHORTLY BEFORE HE LEFT THE WHITE HOUSE FOR APPEARANCES AT HOWARD UNIVERSITY AND AT THE DEPARTMENT OF HEALTH, EDUCATION AND WELFARE.

JOHNSON WROTE KOSYGIN ON JAN. 27 SUGGESTING DISCUSSIONS WHICH MIGHT LEAD TO AN AGREEMENT ON LIMITING ANTI-BALLISTIC SYSTEMS.

(MORE) TM1156AES

The add carries its own number but the same slugword, date and initial of sending bureau. The pickup line repeats the slugword, dateline and number of the lead paragraph, and the closing word of the preceding paragraph, as a help to the telegraph editor.

LEADS—New developments in an existing story often require a new "top" which picks up in the previous copy as high as possible. Example:

104A

VIET 1/25 NX

URGENT

1ST LD 036A

SAIGON (UPI)—THE UNITED STATES TODAY MOVED ITS FIRST 1,000 COMBAT TROOPS INTO THE MEKONG DELTA, THE START OF A BIG PUSH WHICH THE U.S. EXPECTS WILL EVENTUALLY WIN THE WAR IN VIETNAM. ELSEWHERE IN BATTLE AREAS THERE WAS LOSS OF LIFE IN PLANE CRASHES.

U.S. MARINES CONDUCTED A LIMITED OPERATION IN A 10-SQUARE-MILE SECTION OF THE DELTA A FEW WEEKS AGO AND THE UNITED STATES MOVED IN ENGINEERS AND CONSTRUCTION TROOPS EARLY THIS MONTH TO BUILD A BASE. BUT TODAY'S WERE THE FIRST COMBAT TROOPS IN THE VIET CONG STRONGHOLD DOMINATED BY THE COMMUNISTS FOR 20 YEARS.

PICKUP 2ND PGH 036A: THE TROOPS

F1215PES

In some cases, paragraphs below the highest picked up may be outdated or superseded by information in the new lead. Then the pickup would read:

PICKUP 2ND PGH 036A: THE TROOPS, AND ELIMINATE 7TH AND 8TH PGHS: THE CHINOOK

(giving the first word or two of the first of the paragraphs to be dropped).

When an earlier dispatch is superseded by a new lead, the instruction line at the bottom of the new lead reads:

INCLUDES PREVIOUS 036A

Fast-breaking developments often produce inserts, substitutions and scattered adds in a story; these may call for a write-through lead, a self-contained dispatch replacing all previous copy.

Erroneous information in a dispatch, requiring a corrective lead, is preceded by a note to editors explaining the "correct" notation in the lead slug. Example:

NEWS CIRCUIT STYLES

225A

ADVISORY 12/16 NX
EDITORS:
WE WILL CARRY A NEW
LEAD GERMAN 204A ELIMINA-
TING REFERENCES TO A
PLANNED CONFERENCE AT
WASHINGTON. SITE OF THE
PROPOSED MEETING HAS NOT
BEEN APPROVED.
UPI NEW YORK
AF352PES

227A

GERMAN 12/16 NX
2ND LD CORRECT 204A
BONN (UPI)—etc.

At times, the dateline of a new
lead may be changed from that of
an earlier dispatch.

245A

GERMAN 12/16 NX
3RD LD 227A PREVIOUS BONN
FRANKFURT (UPI)—CHAN-
CELLOR WILLY BRANDT TO-
DAY ADDRESSED PARLIA-
MENT AND THEN FLEW HERE
TO CONFER WITH NATO OFFI-
CIALS.

If such material picked up into a
earlier lead, reference to the dateline change remains in the pickup
instructions:

PICKUP 2ND LD 227A BONN
3RD PGH: THE MEN

Material may be added to a lead
after it has been picked up on an
earlier. Example:

122A

VIET 1/25 NX
1ST ADD 1ST LD VIET SAIGON
104A XXX YEARS.
U.S. DESTROYERS COVERED
THE LANDINGS WITH FIRE
FROM THEIR FIVE-INCH
RIFLES AND FROM ROCKET
LAUNCHERS.
PICKUP AS BEFORE 2ND PGH
036A: THE TROOPS
HR120PES

(If there has been considerable
lapse of time since original pickup
instructions were sent, it may be
preferable to send such an add as an
insert.)

Secondary material may be added
at the bottom of earlier stories that
have been topped with a new lead.
The guide word "running" is used
in the slugline.

124A

VIET 1/25 NX
4TH ADD VIET SAIGON 036A
RUNNING XXX PLANE.
MACHINEGUN FIRE WAS
HEARD AT THE CENTER OF
SAIGON DURING THE NIGHT
BUT AUTHORITIES SAID IT
WAS POLICE FIRE DIRECTED
AT PROWLERS AROUND A
WAREHOUSE FULL OF RICE.
HR125PES

INSERTS—Fresh material may
be inserted:

213A

FRANCE 11/28 NX
INSERT 2ND LD FRANCE
PARIS 207A AFTER 3RD PGH
XXX JUSTICE.
DE GAULLE ACCOMPANIED
WILSON TO HIS PLANE. BOTH
MEN WERE SMILING AS THEY
SHOOK HANDS IN FAREWELL.
PICKUP 4TH PGH: WILSON
SAID
CM345PES

NEWS CIRCUIT STYLES

CORRECTIONS—All errors must be corrected swiftly and fully. Corrections are sent with bulletin priority and they must show what is being corrected and why. Because copy is reproduced in justified lines and a correction in wording brings a change in line justification, correction by entire paragraph is indicated:

211A
    FRANCE 11/28 NX
CORRN 2ND LD FRANCE PARIS 207A 2ND PGH BGNG: DE GAULLE, REVISING FIGURES
    DE GAULLE SAID THAT TWO BRIGADES OF ARMORED TROOPS AND TWO COMMUNICATIONS UNITS WOULD BE WITHDRAWN FROM THE BERLIN GARRISON.
PICKUP 3RD PGH: HE SAID
    CM535PES

SUBS—Revised, rather than corrected, information, the updating of figures or the addition of details, may be handled in an existing dispatch through the use of one or more substitute paragraphs.
219A
    LBJ 11/29 WA
SUB 2ND LD LBJ WASHINGTON 202A 2ND PGH BGNG: HIS PLANE
    JOHNSON'S PLANE TOOK OFF FROM LA GUARDIA AT NOON AND LANDED AT DULLES AIRPORT 45 MINUTES LATER.
PICKUP 3RD PGH: THE PRESIDENT
    JL117PES

KILLS—Inaccuracy or other factors may require that an entire dispatch be eliminated from the news report. Kill orders take bulletin priority. The slugline on the bulletin uses the word "kill." It is followed immediately by an advisory, using the slugword of the dispatch being killed. The order must give reason for the kill action.

220A
    KILL 11/8 NX
BULLETIN KILL
EDITORS
    KILL MOON MOSCOW 205A. NO MOON LANDING CLAIMED.
    UPI NEW YORK
    JR304PES

221A
    MOON 11/8 NX
BULLETIN EDITORS
    MOSCOW—MOON MOSCOW 205A HAS BEEN KILLED. A KILL IS MANDATORY. MAKE SURE THE STORY IS NOT PUBLISHED.
    UPI NEW YORK
    JR306PES
The note to editors must be carried in the next news cycle since some subscribers on a 24-hour basis could miss the initial kill.

When only a portion of a dispatch requires mandatory deletion, the kill note should identify the story by slugline, dateline and number, as well as the location and opening words of the paragraph or paragraph to be deleted. A substitute should be sent separately and promptly, or a note that no sub will be sent.

EDITOR'S NOTES—There are two forms, one for the information of editors, the other for publication if desired.

The former may tell anticipated time of an event, possibilities of a new lead on an existing dispatch, etc., as in the first example given below. The second type, as in the second example, often is used as introduction to a special enterprise dispatch or on a "sidebar," an accompanying story to a main news dispatch.

NEWS CIRCUIT STYLES

100A
   ADVISORY 1/31 NX
EDITORS:
   WE ARE RECEIVING FROM PARIS AN OFFICIAL TRANSCRIPT OF DE GAULLE'S NEWS CONFERENCE REMARKS. A LEAD DE GAULLE PARIS 083A WILL BE CARRIED ON THIS WIRE WITHIN THE HALF HOUR.
   UPI NEW YORK
   JR1019AES

102A
   ROBBERY 1/22 NX
(EDITOR'S NOTE: FRIDAY IS THE MOST POPULAR DAY FOR BANK ROBBERIES. THEY GENERALLY OCCUR BETWEEN THE HOURS OF 10 A.M. AND 2 P.M. BUT A SURPRISING NUMBER OF BANDITS USE TOY GUNS. FBI DIRECTOR J. EDGAR HOOVER DESCRIBES THE PROBLEM OF BANK ROBBERIES IN THE FOLLOWING DISPATCH WRITTEN FOR UPI.)
   BY J. EDGAR HOOVER
   DIRECTOR OF THE FBI
   WRITTEN FOR UPI
   WASHINGTON (UPI)—etc.

HOLD-FOR-RELEASE COPY—Copy moved in advance for future release bears one of the following slugs at the top and at the bottom on monitor copy:

ADV FOR PMS WEDS DEC 1

ADV FOR WIRE RLS ABT 1 PM EST

ADV FOR 630 PM EST TUES NOV 30

On TTY wire copy it would appear:

109A HFR
   COMMENT 11/28 NX
ADV FOR PMS WEDS DEC 1

Adds, inserts or corrections which move before the release time or in the cycle in which an advance has been released must bear explicit directions. Example:

111A HFR
   COMMENT 11/28 NX
CORRN COMMENT UNDATED 109A ADV FOR PMS 12/1 4TH PGH: PRESIDENT ROOSEVELT (FIXING DATES)
   PRESIDENT ROOSEVELT'S ELECTION IN 1932 MARKED THE BEGINNING OF THE LONGEST OCCUPATION BY ANY ONE MAN OF THE OFFICE OF CHIEF EXECUTIVE, 1933-1945.
PICKUP 5TH PGH: ROOSEVELT

008A
   COMMENT 12/1 NX
INSERT COMMENT UNDATED 109A MOVED 11/28 HFR PMS TDY AFTER 6TH PGH XXX MAINTAINED.

SIDEBARS—Information related to an existing news story but not necessarily an integral part of it may be reported in a separate dispatch properly labeled:

225A
   DE GAULLE 11/8 NX
WITH FRANCE 225A

On teletypesetter circuits, bylines and credit lines are boldface and centered, with the name capitalized. The "y" in "By" is lower case.

Examples:

By H. D. QUIGG
United Press International

Identification is up and down for describing special writers:

By MILTON RICHMAN
UPI Sports Writer

NEWS CIRCUIT STYLES

For undateds:

By United Press International

If copyright, below the identification:

Copyright 1967

When a story is written for UPI:

By HANK BAUER
Manager Baltimore Orioles
(Written for UPI)

or it may be:

(As Told to UPI)

A series should be identified:

107A HFR

GUNS 3/15 NX

ADV FOR PMS MON MAR 20

1ST OF THREE

LAST OF THREE

On TTS—only circuits, special numbers are used for UPIN, moved early each Sunday morning (700); for World Horizon features (800); for bulletins and urgents (900).

When material is sent for agate setting, tape bears visible AG after the item number.

UPI NEWSPICTURE CAPTIONS

Cutlines should be short but contain all information pertinent to the photo and the event it covers. Give the bare facts, but all of them. Use short declarative sentences. Never inject personal opinion into cutlines.

Don't stress the obvious. Do not say "photo above shows." If something needs explaining, use the fewest possible words. Use abbreviations, when they are commonly used and understood, to save space.

Correct identifications are essential. Use titles of people when needed, and a simple (L to R) to identify them, or (L), (C) (R) identify them, or (L), (C), (R) when grouping requires. Get your facts right in simple and clear English. The picture caption should be a label and a good one. It should be proofread, by another if possible, to eliminate typos and other errors.

Use a typewriter with elite type if possible. Write with a fresh extra black ribbon on UPI's adhesive backed paper. Do not XXXX out words.

Start cutlines with bureau code, date-time group, and the month, day and picture designation. Example: WAP122309-12/23/66. This indicates it is WAP's ninth picture transmitted Dec. 23, 1966. Next in CAPS put city where photo originates, following newsside style whether to indicate state or country too.

Use capitalized sluglines only to identify competing athletic teams or players. Sluglines are for identification only and not to be used as general headlines for other photos. Follow the body of the caption with the credit line UPI TELEPHOTO. Add the source in the credit line if this is required or adds authenticity to the photo. Example: Dept. of Defense Photo by UPI TELEPHOTO.

Captions to be signed off with the initials of the cutline writer followed by the initials of the staff photographer. Example: grg/fc. If the photo is obtained from a client paper, indicate this with paper's initials in quotes. Example: grg/ "P". Photos from stringers and other outside sources should be indicated this way: grg/st.

A sample caption:

WAP012309-12/23/66-WASHING-TON-President Lyndon Johnson and daughter Lynda join in singing Christmas carols at the annual tree-

NEWS CIRCUIT STYLES

lighting ceremony on the White House lawn. UPI TELEPHOTO grg/fc

Captions should be single spaced. They should be written the long or short way with a safety margin of three-quarters of an inch on each side, then placed on the print so as not to cut into the important photo area. Captions must be placed across the top of a horizontal photo, not the bottom. Whenever possible, all cutlines should be written the long way for all prints. The print should be placed on the transmitter drum with cutlines at the left to insure that the caption precedes the picture as it appears on the fax receivers.

SPORTS

United Press International recognizes only one All-America team in football and basketball annually. That is the team chosen for UPI each season by the vote of newspapermen and radio-TV broadcasters from coast to coast.

UPI's weekly ratings of college football and basketball teams are based on the votes of a Board of Coaches for each sport and for each of the major and small college divisions. (National Collegiate Athletic Association designation of "major" and "small college" governs individual school classification.)

The major college boards in each sport are comprised of 35 coaches, five each from the seven geographic divisions of the country. These are the East, South, Midwest, Midlands, Southwest Rocky Mountains and Pacific Coast.

Each weekend during the sports' season, these coaches send in their top 10 ratings to New York Sports. The ratings are tabulated on a 10-9-8-7-6-5-4-3-2-1 basis for votes from first to 10th place, respectively. The teams are rated according to the number of points they receive under this system.

At the conclusion of each season, both the major and the small college champion, as determined by the UPI Board of Coaches, are honored as national champions.

Index

APPENDIX

I N D E X

GLOSSARY

Angle—Point of view from which a news story is written. Also known as news peg.

AP—Associated Press.

Attribution—Indentification of a person who makes a statement used in a news story.

Beat—Series of news sources assigned to a reporter who calls or visits them on a regular basis.

Body Copy—News story facts that appear after the lead of the story.

Boil Down—To cut or condense news stories.

Bold Face—Type that is darker than the type of the text in which it is used.

Break—Point at which a story can be continued on another page.

Time when story facts become available for publication.

Byline—Line of type, set after headline and before news story, containing name of writer of the story.

CAM—Composition and Makeup terminal.

Captions—News facts accompanying a picture; also called cutline.

Clips—News stories filed in news library.

Copy—Typewritten news stories.

CRT—Cathode Ray Tube.

Cut—To shorten a news story.

Cutline—See Captions.

Date Line—Opening words in a paragraph identifying story origin and sometimes including the day's date.

Direct Quote—Word-for-word presentation of what a person has said. Direct quotes are always enclosed in quotation marks.

Feature—Usually a non-dated story with human-interest angle in which only one side of a story or issue is presented. Also called soft news.

Flag—Name of newspaper printed on page one. Also called logo.

Filler—Material used to fill a news hole on the printed page or air time in a broadcast.

Folo Stories—Follow-up or second-day story about a news event that contains the latest information in the story.

Graf—One paragraph of a news story.

Handouts—News releases sent to news media from outside sources such as clubs, organizations, business and industry.

Headline—Type above a news story that gives a preview of story contents.

Hold—News story that cannot be used upon receipt because release date or permission is needed for publication.

Italics—Type that slants to right.

Jump—To continue a news story begun on one page over to another page.

Kill—To stop publication of a story or to discard a portion of a news story already set in type.

Lead—First sentence or two of a news story in which are contained most important and latest facts of a story.

Logo—Printed design of newspaper or magazine name.

Made News—Non-news items that reporters make into news stories.

Masthead—Statement, usually on editorial page, containing publication's name, location, officers, subscription rates, publishing schedule and sometimes circulation as well as other descriptive information.

Morgue—Name given to a news medium's library. Contains copies of stories and pictures used in the publication.

Must—Dated material necessitates immediate publication of story.

News Peg—See Angle.

Obituary (Obit)—Death notice containing funeral data and biographical sketch of person as well as listing survivors.

OCR—Optical Character Recognition.

Off-the-Record Comments—Data given news media for their information but not for publication.

Pad—Filler used in a story to extend its inch count or running time. To stretch a story.

Pix—Slang for picture.

Play—Emphasis given a news story, particularly in the location of story in publication or in a newscast.

Paraphrase—Restate a direct quote by putting it in third-person context.

Proof—Copy set in type and shown to editors before publication for correction purposes.

Punch—To give a story some emphasis. Usually refers to lead.

Rewrite—To write a story over or revise it. To take a story by telephone from a reporter in the field.

Sidebar—Secondary story that supports or expands a major story.

Slant—Selection and presentation of facts made in such a way as to sway audience interpretation.

Slug or Slugline—On reporter's typewritten copy, one or two words identifying story. Usually placed near upper left of page.

Stet—Copy reader's mark for "follow original copy—ignore any editing corrections or changes."

Straight News—Clear, concise recitation of facts without an indepth attempt to interpret, explain or background them in the news story. Also called hard news.

Stringer—Part-time reporter or correspondent for a news medium who is paid by the number and length of stories and pictures submitted.

Style Book—Contains rules and examples of usage, punctuation and typography used in preparation of copy for publication.

Take—One page of double-spaced, typewritten copy.

Trim—To condense copy. See Boil Down.

Typo—Short for typographical error.

UPI—United Press International.

VDT—Video Display Terminal.

Whammy—Fact which makes an incident unique from all other similar incidents.

SUGGESTED BIBLIOGRAPHY

The following are suggestions of readings and workbooks that a beginning reporting student might find useful. It is divided into sections and the books might be considered as supplements to this text, especially the use of one of the workbooks. This bibliography does not contain a complete listing of books available in each category but presents only the personal preferences of the author.

Workbooks

Fedler, Fred. *Reporting for the Print Media.* New York: Harcourt Brace Jovanovich, Inc., 1973.

Julian, James L. *Practical News Assignments for Student Reporters.* 4th ed. Dubuque, Iowa: Wm. C. Brown Company Publishers, 1976.

Both workbooks contain grammar and style exercises and fact sheets for writing practice in leads, body of the news story, obituaries, speeches and meetings, features, government and crime reporting. Both have city directory and wire service style books. Fedler also has a brief summary of newswriting techniques to be applied in the exercises preceding each section in the book.

Interviewing

Sherwood, Hugh C. *The Journalistic Interview.* New York: Harper & Row, Publishers.

Excellent comprehensive text on interviewing. Deals with techniques of getting, preparing, recording and conducting the interview.

Terkel, Studs. *Working.* New York: Avon Books, 1975 (Paperback).

Excellent example of journalistic research using a tape recorder. Through skillful editing of the tapes, Terkel gives the reader insight into the character and fabric of the lives of the people talking about their jobs and working conditions.

Writing

Fontaine, Andre. *The Art of Writing Non Fiction.* New York: Thomas Y. Crowell Co., 1974.

The author, a free-lance writer, looks at the new journalism reporting techniques as he practices them. While other books on new journalism have shown the results of the techniques (the stories as published), this book discusses and shows via examples how the stories are researched and written.

BIBLIOGRAPHY

News Reporting

Bernstein, Carl, and Woodward, Bob. *All The President's Men.* New York: Simon & Schuster, 1974.

A documentary on investigative reporting as performed by the two *Washington Post* reporters who won a Pulitzer Prize for their writing.

News Stories

Morris, Richard B. and Snyder, Louis L. *A Treasury of Great Reporting.* New York: Simon & Schuster, 1949.

Journalistic masterpieces written under the pressure of daily deadlines and, many times, perilous conditions. Reporters represented among the 175 stories are Daniel DeFoe, Charles Dickens, Ernest Hemingway, Rebecca West, Edward R. Murrow, Ernie Pyle, Meyer Berger and Lowell Thomas.

News Media

Alder, Ruth. *A Day in the Life of the New York Times.* Philadelphia: J. B. Lippincott Co. 1971.

A look at the worldwide operation of the *New York Times* through the eyes of the reporters and editors who kept detailed memoirs for the 24 hours of February 28, 1969. Reporters, editors, copy clerks and pressmen kept notes on their jobs for the day starting at 3 A.M., with the foreign correspondents getting and filing their stories from stations around the world, and ending as the last paper rolls off the presses at 3 A.M.

News Reporters

Alder, Ruth. *The Working Press.* New York: Bantam Books, 1970 (Paperback).

Often the effort a reporter puts in to get a story is as interesting (sometimes more so) than the story that is printed. Ruth Alder, editor of the *New York Times* house magazine *Times Talk,* asked *Times* reporters for their story behind the story and printed the replies in *Times Talk.* A reprint of the best is found in this book.

Grammar

Callihan, E. L. *Grammar for Journalists.* Revised Edition. Philadelphia: Chilton Book Co., 1969.

An English grammar designed and written for the journalist.

Strunk, William Jr., and White, E. B. *The Elements of Style.* Second Edition. New York: The Macmillan Co., 1972 (Paperback).

A 78-page book that "cuts the vast tangle of English rhetoric down to size."

Law

Gora, Joel M. *The Rights of Reporters.* New York: Discus Books, 1974 (Paperback).

An American Civil Liberties Union handbook that uses a question-and-answer format to explain a reporter's rights under present law and offers suggestions on how these rights can be protected.

Research

Rivers, William L. *Finding Facts.* Englewood Cliffs, N.J.: Prentice-Hall, Inc., 1975.

Research plays a major role in a journalist's job. This book is designed to make the job easier. It contains a very useful chapter on resource references for the fields of government, newspapers, magazines, television, religion, music and theater arts, sciences, business and economics, education, history and many, many more. Other chapters include information on pursuing, interpreting and evaluating facts and of interviewing and observing.

Thesaurus

Roget, Peter M. *Roget's International Thesaurus.* New York: Thomas Y. Crowell Co., 1962.

Miscellaneous

A current *World Almanac*

A good, comprehensive dictionary.

INDEX